The Handbook of Showing

The Handbook of Showing

REVISED EDITION

Glenda Spooner

J. A. Allen
LONDON

First published in 1968, second edition 1977
Reprinted 1979
This third edition published by
J. A. Allen & Company Limited,
1, Lower Grosvenor Place, Buckingham Palace Road,
London SW1W 0EL
1990

British Library Cataloguing in Publication Data
Spooner, Glenda, *1897–1981*
   The handbook of showing – 3rd ed
   1. Livestock: Horses. Showing
   I. Title
   636.1'0888

   ISBN 0–85131–485–6

Designed by *Nancy R. Lawrence*
Phototypeset by Input Typesetting Ltd, London
Printed and bound in Hong Kong

Contents

Glenda Spooner

and the Ponies of Britain Club

Glenda Spooner was born in Poona, India, in 1897, the only daughter of Sir Frederick Graham Bt and his wife Irene, but spent most of her childhood in Scotland. Her passion for animals was manifest at a very early age. As a child her first 'horse' was a polo pony of her father's which had broken down. This Arab stallion, bought in India, was nursed back to soundness by her, and during all the years she rode and drove him he never went lame again. From her devotion to him, grew her love and intense concern for all horses and ponies.

In the 1920s Glenda came to London to work and live independently. After a short venture into theatrical life, an opportunity arose for her to enter Fleet Street, where she enjoyed a most successful career for fourteen years and during which time she wrote her first novel.

Her supremely happy marriage to Captain Hugh (Tony) Spooner, then chief pilot of Misr Airwork, Cairo, and brother of the famous pioneer airwoman, Winifred Spooner, ended tragically after just two years when he was killed in a flying accident. This prompted Glenda to move to the country. At her cottage in Sussex she soon acquired a motley collection of dogs, cats, goats, hens, ducks, pigs and, inevitably a couple of ponies; the latter led her into the world of dealing and breeding.

During the Second World War, whilst living in the New Forest, she became acutely aware of the plight of Britain's native ponies and the need to protect their future. It is largely due to her single-minded efforts that they are now flourishing, protected by their own breed societies.

In 1952 she founded the Ponies of Britain Club, formed from a nucleus of people who cared about ponies and their welfare. The Club was created at the request of Sir John Crocker Bulteel to run a pony show in the Royal Paddock at Ascot in coronation year, with the profits going to equine charities. This one-off venture was so successful that a generous sponsor, Miss Gladys Yule, came forward to ensure that the Club would be able to continue with its good work.

The show became an annual event, and, with Miss Yule's backing, the Club went from strength to strength. Gradually more events were added to the calendar, with funds being raised for the protection and benefit of ponies, especially the nine native breeds of the British Isles.

In 1957 Gladys Yule died suddenly, and for a while the future of the Club was in doubt. However, because of its great value to the pony world and the unique qualities of its founder, Glenda Spooner, support was forthcoming from many loyal friends. Donations and subscriptions poured in, enabling the Club to continue its work in encouraging the production of *good* ponies (providing at its shows a 'shop window' for breeders), and with its important welfare activities on behalf of *all* ponies, whatever their status.

An important innovation was the Club's Trekking and Riding Holiday Centre Approval Scheme, set up to provide protection for the animals employed in trekking and riding holiday establishments. Centres were inspected annually. To assist the public in their choice, a list of those having reached the required standard was issued annually.

The Ponies of Britain became a recognised authority on the welfare of equines and was represented on the working committee which drafted the Riding Establishments Act (1964). This has since been amended as the Riding Establishments Act (1970).

Glenda Spooner played a large part in helping to prepare the Ponies Act, 1970. Under its provisions, minimum values, individual inspection and other safeguards protect ponies, mules and asses exported from this country.

In addition to its shows, the Ponies of Britain ran young judges' training schemes, courses and seminars; it also offered awards for broodmares, stallion progeny and yearlings.

Glenda Spooner succeeded Miss Yule as chairman, an office which she considered an honour to hold, and which she retained until her death in 1981. When finally she became too ill to run the organisation, Joan Lee-Smith was asked to take over the shows. This she did with admirable efficiency and financial success until the Club was dissolved at the end of 1988.

Glenda Spooner invested the Ponies of Britain with her own high standards and principles; incapable of deviousness or double-dealing, she never ceased to be surprised at finding it in others. Glenda did not suffer fools gladly and had no time for pretentiousness. No one was ever left in any doubt about where they stood with her. Her dedication to the cause of equine (and indeed all animal welfare) was complete. Outspoken and forthright, inevitably she made enemies,

8

but even they could not fail to respect her.

In 1970 the British Horse Society presented her with their Medal of Honour, in recognition of her unsparing and indefatigable work for the benefit of all horses and ponies.

A prolific writer, Glenda produced not only novels and amusing verse, but also articles and instructional books concerning horses and ponies, which have been of immense value to several generations. Her thorough and practical knowledge of her subject – acquired, as she would say, 'the hard way' – is amply demonstrated by this *Handbook of Showing*.

As a fair and universally respected judge, with a great natural 'eye' for a horse, she was much in demand at major shows.

The strong influence on pony breeding in this country exerted by her famous small Thoroughbred stallion Ardencaple, and the successful careers of his progeny in many fields, were a source of pride and pleasure to her.

Glenda Spooner was a unique personality, who will be remembered not only for all that she did for the equines she loved so much, but also for her splendid sense of humour, her wit and wisdom, and as an unswervingly loyal friend.

The Glenda Spooner Trust was founded in 1987 as a tribute to her many achievements in the field of equine welfare; it aims to continue her vital work on behalf of all ill-treated and exploited horses and ponies. The Trust's Patron is Her Grace, the Duchess of Devonshire.

For further information about the Trust and its activities, write to: The Glenda Spooner Trust, Emmetts Hill, Whichford, Warwickshire, CV36 5PG.

Author's Preface
to First Edition

Before World War II, horse shows were a rarity. There were the big occasions, such as the International, established in 1907, the Royal, Richmond Royal (now amalgamated with the South of England) and the Royal Highland, which were firmly established, as were many of the older county shows. Otherwise show dates were comparatively few.

Today there are many shows a week throughout the spring and summer, often several on one day. That shows are with us and will remain with us, so long as there are exhibitors eager to enter and people willing to stage them, I have no doubt, though personally I think there are a great deal too many. But competition is all the rage today and exhibitors delight to show their wares. I honestly believe they would enter and show even if the showground were completely devoid of spectators.

It takes extremely good organisation, however, and realistic schedules and not a little business acumen, to make these affairs pay their way. The large agricultural and county shows get their gate by a wide variety of exhibits and trade stands. Small local shows, with a minimum of overheads and voluntary labour, can also be made to pay their way, even possibly to make a small profit, especially if held for charity. To make breed shows pay is virtually impossible, but these are, after all, specialist shows.

Too many shows are run more by good luck than good guidance, while at horse and pony shows there is not the knowledge of basic conformation today which was absorbed by former generations. There is therefore less interest among the general public. In past generations, everybody at one time or another had something to do with horses. There are, however, so many different types of shows that one can only generalise.

The big three, namely, the International, the Royal Windsor, and the Horse of the Year, are all purely equine events.

The big agricultural shows such as the Royal, Great Yorkshire, East of England, Royal Highland, Bath and West, South of England, Royal Norfolk – to mention but a few – and the county shows such as Kent, Sussex, Berkshire, Devon, etc., all include equine classes and events. Most now stage classes for riding pony brood mares, youngstock and for native ponies.

Then there are the purely breed shows such as the National Hunter Show, the Arab Horse Society, the National Pony Society, the British Palomino Society, and all the individual native breed societies which hold their own shows. All these shows include both ridden and in-hand classes in their schedules.

As well, there are innumerable smaller local shows, jumping shows, and gymkhanas; some run for the benefit of a charity, some for the benefit of the organisation, and all run by amateurs – sometimes with more enthusiasm than efficiency! The outcrop of small gymkhanas has evolved inevitably through the owning of ponies by many children whose equivalent in past generations could not have afforded them. I am all for these events, provided the organisers have the moral courage to stand firm on any abuses such as the working of immature unfit ponies, ill-fitting tack, severe bits and over-use of the whip, riding of ponies which are three years old or under, and the use of ponies as 'grandstands' between events. Show organisers should be careful to insert a clause in their rules which enables them to deal with such matters. Every exhibitor should sign a form stating that he will abide by the rules, and the rules should contain a clause whereby any exhibitor can be asked to leave the ground without being given a reason, or whereby an entry can be refused.

All the above are outdoor events dependent on the weather, which greatly affects the gate. There are, as well, shows mainly confined to show jumping; there are combined training events, one- and three-day events, hunter trials, point to points, dressage competitions, and now long-distance rides, team chases and carriage driving trials. These, thank goodness, are outside the scope of this book.

This book has not been an easy one to write. It has been done with interruptions, due to my job, and I am fully aware of its errors and omissions. I hope, however, that it will be of some benefit to future judges, breeders, exhibitors, spectators and the ringside critics without whom showing would be a dull affair; and ensure the best care for the horses and ponies, to whom the book is dedicated.

Glenda Spooner

List of Illustrations

13

Acknowledgements

Author's Acknowledgements to First Edition
I owe my grateful thanks to Count Robert Orrsich, Mr Harry
Bonner, Mrs I. M. Yeomans, Mrs N. Pennell, and Mr E. G. E.
Griffith, for their help and advice on the chapters on basic confor-
mation, judging and showing in hand; to Mr R. W. Bird for reading
and advising on show administration and to Mr J. Martyn Gliddon
for advising on the duties of an honorary treasurer; to Mr John
Oliver (former editor of *The Sphere* and *The Tatler*), the late Lieut.-
Colonel C. E. G. Hope (Editor of *Pony* and *Light Horse*), to Miss
Margaret Mole and Miss Rosemary Hare for reading the drafts and
advising on various cuts and improvements; to all the Societies who
obliged by sending us the particulars of their activities and of the
various breeds; to the late Mr David Rook for his diagrams for basic
conformation, etc.

I also have to acknowledge with gratitude the co-operation of
those who supplied me with photographs of their animals.

It was, however, Mr Brian Young, director and chief instructor of
Crabbet Park Equitation Limited, who first suggested I should write
this book, and, whilst acknowledging that the idea was his, I do not
know whether to thank him or not.

Publisher's Acknowledgements to Third Edition
The publishers would like to thank Vivien McIrvine, the author's
niece and Director of the Glenda Spooner Trust, for her sterling
efforts in helping to revise the text. They are also grateful to the many
people who kindly supplied information or advice in connection with
the revision of this new edition. In particular, thanks must go to the
officials of the various horse organisations and breed societies who
provided up-to-date details of their activities and rules, to the pho-
tographers who supplied the illustrations, to the late Anne Muir for
her patient assistance and advice, and to Dianne Breeze for redrawing
David Rook's original diagrams.

nd Defects

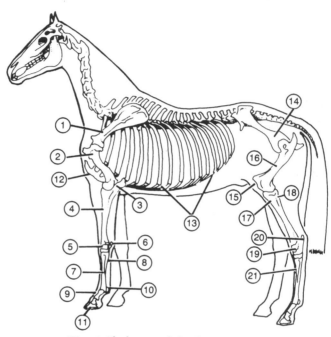

Fig. 1 Skeleton of the horse

FRONT END
1 Scapula
2 Humerus
3 Elbow or ulna
4 Radius
5 Carpus
6 Trapezium
7 Metacarpal bones
8 Splint bones
9 Pastern
10 Sesamoid bones
11 Coffin bones in foot

MIDDLE
12 Sternum
13 True and false ribs

BACK END
14 Pelvis
15 Patella
16 Femur
17 Tibia
18 Fibula
19 Tarsus
20 Os calcis
21 Metatarsal bone

1 Basic Conformation

Let us start off with the end product, namely horses and ponies, for they are what shows are about.

I will try to describe as far as possible on paper the structure which makes for a good-quality animal for whatever size or purpose. Because it is easier to learn through the eye than through the ear, I have included a number of illustrations and diagrams. I hope that they will help readers to see what I am driving at and that when they meet good and bad conformation in the flesh they will gradually come to recognise them, although ability to do so really only comes through experience.

Effects on Balance, Temperament, Quality and Movement

Basic conformation applies equally to a 16.2 hh hunter and a 12.2 hh pony. They should differ only in type, characteristics, way of going, or performance. Upon conformation depends the balance, temperament and the quality of the animal. What is more difficult are the things you cannot see, that is, the bone structure beneath the flesh, and especially if the animal carries a lot of flesh.

What, then, is conformation? It is the foundation, framework or structure, call it what you will, upon which the finished article is built, just as the foundations, wall, beams and rafters, are the framework upon which a house is built.

It also, to a large degree, determines the quality of that horse or of that house. A horse with bad conformation can never really be a quality one in the way that I mean, any more than a bungalow, however well furnished, can be a quality house. On the other hand, a horse with correct conformation will automatically have the sort of quality one attributes to a well-built period house. Proverbially a house should be built upon rock and not upon shifting sands. So too a horse, to endure, must stand on four good legs and feet. A house must have sound, well-seasoned beams and rafters correctly placed, if it is to stand up to the stresses and strain of wind, rain and

19

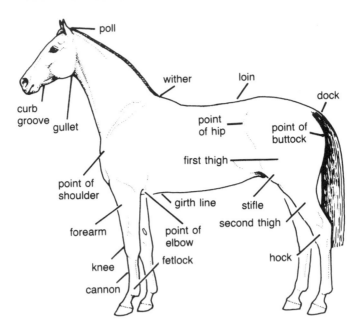

Fig. 2 Points of the horse.

snow. It not only must stand up but also must look right when bricks and mortar, doors and windows are added. What would be the use of adding these if the house were not basically sound? And although you can of course live in a house that is sound but ugly, it is much pleasanter to do so in one that is both sound and attractive. No one wants a jerry-built house.

It is much the same with horses. If the finished article is to stand up to the strains and stresses of work and everyday use, its foundations, namely its legs and feet, must be sound and good. The bones, which are the framework, must be of good material and correctly placed if the muscles, tendons and ligaments attached to – or passing over – them are not to suffer. That is why knowledgeable people prefer buying animals 'in the rough'. Fat and muscle can hide a multitude of sins. The better the framework, the better the finished article will be. A jerry-built house is like a horse with indifferent conformation.

The business of learning about conformation is complicated by the fact that people so often disagree – yes, even on fundamentals. Judges can be heard arguing whether or not a hock is good or bad, whether in fact an animal has 'quality', while even veterinary surgeons disagree on soundness. I freely admit that it is difficult, and

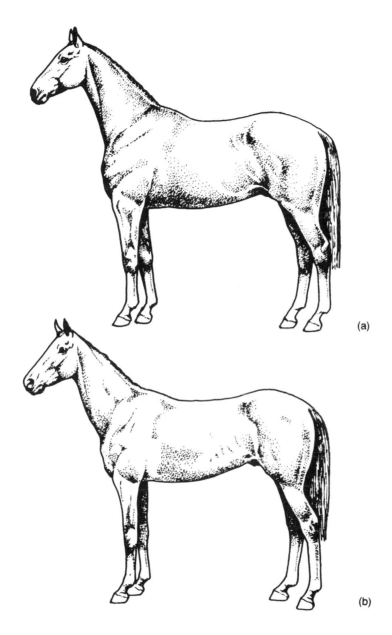

(a)

(b)

Fig. 3 Good and bad conformation. (a) Good sloping shoulder; defined withers; short back; strong loin; well ribbed-up; good girth line and elbow room; length from point of hip to point of buttock. (b) Straight, loaded shoulder; round ribs under the saddle; sternum bone running up under tied-in elbow; slack loin; gap between last rib and hip; cut in above the hock; hocks in the air; short from point of hip to point of buttock.

21

that one sometimes despairs of ever emerging from the maze. But it can be done, and experience is the only way from darkness into light.

Few are born with an eye for a horse. I have, however, noticed that good judges of other animals, especially cattle or dogs, have a pretty shrewd idea of the finer points of a horse or pony. This particularly applies to those subtle assets, quality and balance. A good beast and a good dog must have both.

Head

Horse: In a well-bred animal this should be fine, clear-cut with good bone structure, of a size that fits the animal, and above all well set on to the neck. A show horse, be it hack or hunter, should by rights have an attractive chiselled head, although those with Roman noses have won, and many a horse with a large common head has led the field out hunting.

It is, however, of the utmost importance that the jawbone should not be large, for if to this most undesirable conformation are added large parotid glands (glands which lie between the jawbone and the neck and appear as hard lumps when the horse flexes at the poll), this will make it difficult, if not impossible, for the animal to flex at the poll without acute discomfort, even pain. That it should flex at the poll is essential if it is to be a balanced ride. If it flexes only from the lower third of its neck it will overbend and be out of balance.

How often one sees these unsightly lumps causing horses and ponies to reach for the reins, toss their heads, stiffen their neck muscles, cross their jaw, all of which are evasions due to the discomfort of these glands being nipped.

Sometimes, when these glands are not very obtrusive, it is quite possible for an animal with large jawbones to flex, provided its head is well set on to its neck, and the parotid gland is not pronounced enough to come into conflict.

If, however, you find yourself with a horse or pony with both over-large jawbones and protruding glands, do not force the animal to flex, or you will run into trouble. Be patient. Massaging the glands with olive oil for half an hour every day and putting a small hood over that part of the head will help to soften the glands and then, if flexion is introduced gradually, the glands will gradually find somewhere else to go.

Pony: Obviously, a pony must have a small, neat head, although

22

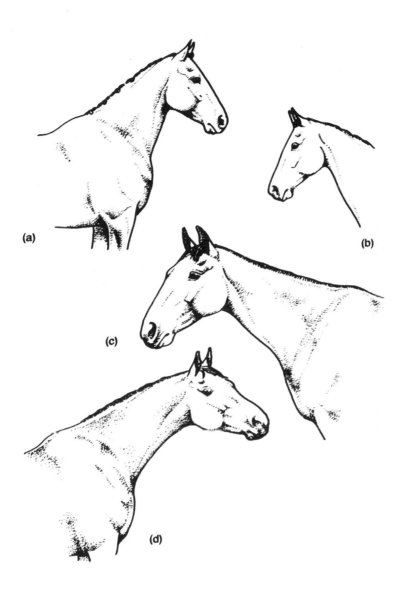

Fig. 4 Heads. (a) Good hunter head, short neck, but running into a good shoulder and so still giving a good front. (b) Pony head lacking quality. (c) Common head, piggy eyes, thick nostrils, large jawbones, pronounced parotid gland, neck upside down; straight, loaded shoulders. (d) Long, well-set-on neck running into perpendicular shoulder, giving impression of a good front, but actually not so. Beautiful quality chiselled head, clean gullet, good eye, fine nostrils.

23

some length of muzzle is permissible provided it is fine and lean. Thick, coarse lumpy heads, however small, are not desirable, while horsey heads and very large ears are frowned on in pony classes.

Ears

Horse: Personally I rather like horses with large ears, but for a show horse these should preferably be in keeping with the size of its head. They should be fine and readily pricked. Lop ears can be seen on many a good performer, but are not acceptable in the show ring.

Pony: Small ears are essential on a pony, whether on riding ponies or on the heads of our native breeds. The ears of Arabs are very fine, pointed, even sometimes slightly curly, and add greatly to the beauty of the head.

Nostrils

These are important, if only because they are part of the breathing apparatus. Narrow, coarse nostrils, especially in a hunter, are to be deprecated. The nostril itself should be fine, sensitive, of velvet texture, as free of hair as possible, and, above all, full.

Eyes

Large bold eyes are a great asset and usually go with a good temperament. Small, mean, piggy eyes are as unattractive in the equine race as in the human. They also frequently go with a bad temperament.

Eyes should not normally show the whites, but if they do it is a natural pigmentation and does not denote an excitable temperament, as some people think.

A lump between the eyes on the forehead is unsightly and frequently goes with a headstrong tendency.

Neck

It is important that this should be longer on the top side than on the lower, making for a pretty arch from wither to poll when the animal flexes, when it should bend from the poll and not from the lower third of the neck. The whole should be well arched without being crested.

It should be well muscled. A number of people tend to describe an animal as fit whose neck, instead of being muscled and hard, is hard simply because it carries neither flesh nor muscle and what one feels is simply bone and gristle. In other words, it is literally poor, whereas a fit animal's neck should be well muscled up. Show animals are shown fat – often too fat – and one is therefore unlikely to meet a poor horse in the ring, anyway at major shows. But it is important that you should be able to distinguish between a horse or pony that is big and hard and therefore fit, one that is fat and soft, and one that is simply poor. In the last instance, the ribs will be showing, hip bones protruding, and there may well be 'poverty lines' running down the back of the quarters from dock to second thigh.

A neck should be of a length which makes the animal look 'in balance'; it should not be too long or narrow, nor yet short and thick.

One can easily be deluded into thinking that an animal has a good front, when in fact all it has is a long neck. Likewise, an animal with a short neck can have a good front. This is because a good front is not dependent on the neck alone but on the neck and shoulders together. Therefore, an animal with a straight, upright shoulder and a long neck cannot be said to have a good front, whereas one with a very good sloping shoulder, and possibly a little short in the neck, *can* have a good front.

The ideal is a neck in proportion added to a very good sloping shoulder and well-defined wither.

It will make for better balance if the neck does not come out of the chest too low, but at an angle which helps balance and improved head carriage. It is always very difficult to balance an animal whose neck comes out low down on its chest as then it will always tend to be on its forehand.

Short, thick necks make it hard for the animal to flex, and therefore to be a balanced ride. They are often found in horses and ponies that take a strong hold.

It is important that the neck should be fine through the throat, while the gullet itself should be clearly defined, loose, flexible, and clear-cut. The space between the jawbones and the first neck bone below the skull should not be too narrow – there should be plenty of width between these near the gullet. In short, the line at the throat should be clear cut, permitting free passage of air. The animal should not be 'thick through the gullet'. All this applies equally to a horse or pony.

Withers

This is the highest part of the vertebrae (between the neck and the back), and should be pronounced and fine, higher than the majority of the dorsal ridge but level at maturity with the croup or top of the quarters. They should not be ill-defined and, above all, not lower than the croup, as this gives a downhill ride.

Flat withers not only tend towards a downhill ride, but also allow the saddle to move forward and so in front of the centre of balance. Flat withers also very often accompany straight upright loaded shoulders.

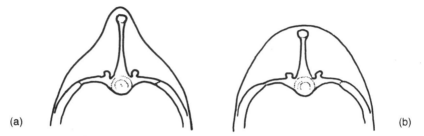

Fig. 5 Withers. (a) Cross-section through good wither. (b) Cross-section through under-developed wither and loaded shoulder.

Shoulders

These should be long, narrow on top, and well sloped back. The blades (scapulas) should themselves not be narrow, as this will allow the saddle to move forward. They should be as flat as possible, vanishing into the withers. They should be near together on top and sloping backwards.

If they are wide apart they make for a lumpy shoulder with breadth on top of the wither, which is both unattractive and detracts from performance. This is called a 'loaded' shoulder.

Upright shoulder blades also cause the saddle to move forward, while broad, lumpy shoulders are not comfortable and interfere with movement. Upright scapulas make for an abrupt meeting of shoulder and neck, therefore lacking 'front'.

Behind the shoulder blades lie the triceps muscles. These run down to the point of the elbow on each side and should form a cushion behind which the saddle, and thereby the rider's thighs and knees, should remain.

Chest

This should be neither too narrow nor too broad when viewed from the front. A chest that is too narrow gives the impression that the forelegs come out of the same hole, whereas one that is too broad gives a bosomy look, and its owner has a tendency to roll in the canter and gallop.

A narrow chest may cause an animal to 'go close'. Or he may 'plait' in his paces (see page 54). This may occur in young animals and improve, even disappear, when they broaden out, strengthen and become balanced.

If the point of the shoulder is too high – in other words if the humerus bone reaching from the point of shoulder to the elbow is too long – this raises the point of the shoulder and gives a thick, bosomy look, suitable for carrying a collar, but not conducive to comfort and speed when ridden. Sometimes it can cause the forelegs to be too much *under* the animal instead of standing four square.

The Body: Natural Girth Line

It is essential that this should be deep through the heart, which in turn gives a *natural girth line* and plenty of room for the lungs, which lie under the eight pairs of ribs. These are attached to the vertebrae above and the sternum below, whereas the ten pairs of false ribs are attached only to the vertebrae (see under 'Ribs').

It is also essential that the sternum bone should be deeper behind the elbow than further back. If, on the contrary, the breast bone runs upwards under the elbow, as it often does in a harness type of animal, then the girth will always ride up behind the elbow and the saddle move forward. This is a most important point in conformation. It is what makes for a *natural girth line*. In short, the sternum bone of a horse should resemble that of a greyhound rather than that of a bulldog.

The body should, as I have said, be as deep as possible, making the animal appear short-legged. If he is shallow through the heart, he will automatically 'show a lot of daylight'. While this is forgivable in a young animal, it is unlikely that, even with maturity, a 'leggy' young pony that lacks depth through his heart, while he may deepen to a degree, will ever be anything but 'on the leg'.

Ribs

There are eight pairs of true or sternal ribs attached to both vertebrae and sternum bone, and ten pairs of false or asternal ribs, attached only to the vertebrae. The length of the ribs is important. If the true ribs are short, the animal will lack depth and tend to be 'leggy', whereas it is desirable that the lowest point of the girth should be as nearly equidistant between the top of the withers and the ground as possible.

Under the true ribs there must be plenty of room for lung expansion. They should be deep, long, and flatter than the false ribs. Harness animals have rounder ribs and are lacking in depth through the girth. A saddle horse should be deeper and flatter under the saddle flaps, enabling the rider to settle his thighs and knees well in behind the triceps muscles.

Under the false ribs lie vital organs such as the kidneys. The depth of the back ribs should also be considered because an animal that runs up 'light' is not only unsightly but objectionable for the reason that, with a 'herring-gutted' animal, not only is there difficulty in keeping the saddle in its place, but it will be hard to keep the animal in condition. It may be necessary to girth tightly, while in extreme cases a breast strap may be necessary. Tight girthing is also the only way to keep the saddle in place on an animal with narrow shoulder blades, or with no natural girth line. Not only does tight girthing add to the horse's discomfort but it will cause him to tire quickly, and may even spoil his temperament, and is therefore an undesirable, if sometimes necessary, evil.

It is also important that the distance between the last rib and the hip bone should not be more than a hand's breadth. It is often longer in mares, when it is excusable. A horse or pony that is slack in this region is difficult to build up, and to keep in condition.

Summing up, the judge should look for depth through the girth, flat ribs under the saddle, and well-sprung ones behind it. Ribs should be long, and there should be as short a gap as possible behind the last rib and the point of hip (that is, a hand span).

Back

A back that is hollow, although it makes for comfort for the rider, is definitely a weakness. Conversely, a hog or roach back, which is the opposite, makes for strength, but is unyielding and makes a horse uncomfortable to ride because it causes harsh and rough movements.

28

But you must remember that a hollow back can be simply due to the age of the horse, for a back tends to become hollow as the animal ages, and the ligaments connecting the vertebrae stretch.

The muscles along each side of the back of a healthy, fit horse *should be higher than the bones of the spine*, which should look as if it formed a groove between them.

While a short back is a strength, and is much favoured, it tends to throw one up and out of the saddle. Long backs, while permissible in a mare, may give a comfortable ride but are a weakness.

Looking at a naked horse or pony, be it young or old, the shoulders and back should look as if a saddle would sit in position, and *stay in position*, almost without a girth. The set of the saddle should be such that the shoulder muscles of the animal can work freely in front of the rider's knees. The seat of the saddle should not tilt either forwards or backwards.

The line of the back, while rising *slightly* towards the croup (highest part of the quarters) should be almost straight.

Loins

The loins lie directly behind the saddle. They are made up of muscles and tendons, chief of which is the main dorsi muscle extending from the neck bones to the sacrum. This muscle is the longest and strongest in the body. It helps to raise the head and neck, and working against the muscles beneath the spine which form this roof of the stomach, supports the spine and protects it from undue strain. Strong loins are essential. Weak loins can cause a fracture of the spine. 'Slack' loins are unsightly.

From the loin, and indeed the whole of the animal behind the saddle, comes all the motivating power, and that is why strength and symmetry are essential in this area. A loin should also be broad and not narrow, as again, under it lie vital organs such as the kidneys.

The Top Line

In judging a horse, you should stand back from it and survey dispassionately what is called its 'top line', that is the outline of the neck, withers, back, loins, and dock, which should be a series of beautiful curves from the poll to the end of the dock. Any deviation from this, such as a mean neck, low withers, slack loins, ragged hips and a low-set tail, detracts from this most desirable line.

Pelvis and Quarters

Hips should be broad and rounded, and not ragged and bony.

The tail should be well set on, as described under 'The Top Line', above. Animals with a landslide from the top of the pelvis to the dock are most unattractive, although I have seen remarkable achievements in building up the muscles in this area to hide this defect.

There is a slight difference between what is called a 'goose rump' or 'jumping bump' and this landslide effect seen on some animals. With the latter there is usually a lack of length between the hip and the dock, whereas a goose-rumped horse often has plenty of length, and often outstanding jumping ability.

Viewed from behind, the quarters of a quality animal should appear almost 'pear-shaped', widening very slightly towards the second thighs, which in turn should give an impression of squareness. The expression 'a good one to follow' means that, when viewed from behind, the impression is of squareness and of power, with well-developed second thighs below rounded quarters and above strong, clean hocks.

What we call the hips are really the ends of the femur bones. These should be broad over the top and hidden from view. They should not be protruding and ragged. They should be level; if one is lower than the other the horse is said to have a 'dropped pin', which is almost always due to an accident, such as a sideways fall or hitting the point of the hip on the doorway of a stable.

It is the muscles of the quarters rather than of the loins that operate the hind legs, while the muscles of the quarters and of the second thigh propel the animal and lift it over obstacles.

Forelegs

These should be well placed. If the humerus bone (see page 18) is over-long it will tend to make the animal look bosomy and/or his forelegs will be too far underneath his body. To be correct he should stand four-square.

Forearm

It is impossible to overrate the importance of correct conformation in the lower extremities. This is the region of the most frequent seats of unsoundness. Faulty conformation here predisposes the animal to a number of unsoundnesses to which he is heir.

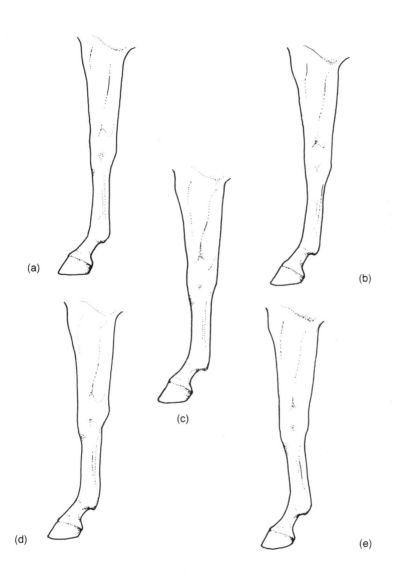

Fig. 6 Forelegs. (a) Light of bone, long cannons, small knees, tied in below the knee. (b) Small knee, back of the knee. (c) Good foreleg, with good flat bone, large knees, fluted tendons, average pasterns, well-developed forearm. (d) Good foreleg, with well-developed trapezium bone. (e) Over at the knee (no fault).

31

Viewing the horse from the side, let us first take a look at the line from the forearm to the ground. If this is straight and true and parallel from knee to fetlock, with tendons and ligaments standing out tense, fluted and distinct between good flat, flinty bone, then the odds are in your favour. If they are not straight, if the knees are small, fetlocks round, tendons and ligaments undefined and thick, then there will be trouble. The forearm should be well developed with plenty of muscle when the animal is fit.

Elbows (or Ulnar Bones)

Whether these are placed well forward or carried under the body depends, as already said, largely upon the length of the humerus bone (see page 18).

Elbows should stand well away from the ribs. If they are tucked in against the ribs the horse or pony will obviously be unable to use its shoulder, and therefore really to move. With a tucked-in elbow it can only move from the elbow.

A *free* elbow is therefore all-important. This enables the animal to move its whole shoulder, to raise its knee upwards, and at the same time forwards, and so to cover a lot of ground, whether at the walk, trot, canter, or gallop, but especially at the faster paces (page 50).

An animal that moves only from its elbow is known as a 'scrambler'. It is almost invariably 'tied in at the elbow' (page 51).

Knees

These, too, should be large. A well-developed trapezium bone is an asset, for the simple reason that it widens the points of attachment of tendons and ligaments, and so increases leverage. But here is a trap for the unwary, because a well-developed trapezium bone can make the bone below look lighter than it really is, and you should watch for this (pages 18 and 31).

Cannon Bones

Whether below the knee or the hock, these should be the same width all the way down from knee to fetlock and from hock to fetlock.

In the foreleg, if the leg is narrower just below the knee, this is called 'tied in below the knee', which is not a good thing (page 31).

If the whole leg bends slightly back from the knee this is called 'calf-kneed', which so aptly describes it, or 'back of the knee'. This conformation is often found in carthorses and the commoner breeds, and therefore has come to be associated with low breeding. If excessive, it can be unsightly, when it is frowned upon in the show ring (page 31).

Being 'over at the knee' is the reverse of this conformation. While it may not be regarded as an asset in the show ring, it is not – if not exaggerated or due to strain – a fault in a hunter or a racehorse, as horses with this sort of conformation are less liable to strained tendons. But in the show ring, a horse that is very much 'over at the knee' cannot really be regarded as a top-class specimen (page 31).

If the bone just below the hock is of less circumference than that lower down the leg, it is called being 'light of bone below the hock'.

Thick, round, lumpy lymphatic limbs and joints, if not caused by overwork, under-nourishment or injury, not only denote low breeding but predispose to unsoundness. Limbs composed of broad, flat, hard bone, short cannons, well-defined tendons, and flat, clean fetlocks, determine whether or not a horse or pony has quality.

Stifles or Patellas

Together with the hock joints, stifles work harder than any other joints in the anatomy. The two joints work in unison. The stifle joint joins the femur and fibula bone on either flank. The joints should work in line with the body and should not be thrown outwards each time they flex. The way to determine this is to stand in front when the horse is trotted towards you. Sometimes the stifle joint can be seen turning outwards as it is brought forward. When this happens, ten to one the animal is also cow-hocked.

Thighs

These must be well developed and muscled up, whether they be the thighs (or 'trousers') which lie on either side of the quarters, or the muscles of the second thigh or 'gaskin', which is the area between the thighs and the hocks. The gaskin should be broad. The length of the bone in the hock, or point of hock – known as the 'os calcis' – is responsible for the breadth of the gaskin, and leverage depends on the length of this bone, which is why it is so important for a horse to have strong, clearly defined thighs and hocks. If the gaskin is 'tied in' above the hock, then the animal is said to be 'cut in above the hocks' (page 37).

The angle at which the hind legs are put on is all-important. If they are hung on to the hips in such a manner that they stand away behind a vertical line drawn from the point of the buttocks to the ground, they are called either 'hocks that are away from the animal' or sometimes 'out in the country'. This conformation obviously makes it very difficult for a horse or pony to get its hocks underneath

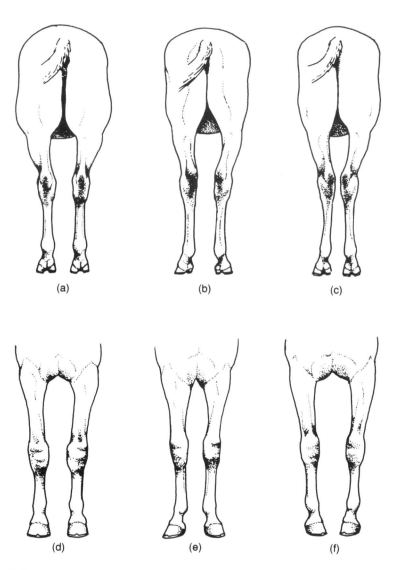

Fig. 7 Legs. FROM BEHIND: *(a) Good. (b) Split up and poor – poverty line; hocks up in the air. (c) Cow-hocked, no second thighs.* FROM THE FRONT: *(d) Good; short cannon bones. (e) Forelegs 'coming out of one hole'; turned-out feet; light of bone. (f) Bosomy and pigeon-toed.*

its body, thus making for loss of balance and impulsion. It also makes it difficult to raise an animal's forehand and tends to make for a downhill ride.

Hocks

The point of hock should form the middle of a straight line between the point of the buttock and the ground when the horse is standing naturally.

If the inward bend of the hock is excessive it causes a conformation known as 'sickle hocks'. This conformation predisposes its owner to curbs, which are caused by strain. While hocks with a tendency to curbs may be hereditary, the actual curb itself is almost invariably caused by a strain. Naturally, bad hocks strain more easily than good.

Cow hocks are a conformation which is not acceptable in the show ring, although they do not interfere with performance. The points of the hocks nearly touch when the animal is standing, while the lower part of the limbs turn outwards. Bowed hocks are the opposite. 'Split up behind' is when the inside thigh muscles are poorly developed, leaving a gap under the dock. 'Going wide behind' is another fault, frequently described as 'you can drive a bus between his hind legs'. This is often caused by over-trotting and is most unsightly and frowned on in the ring.

Lumpy, untidy hocks are also a weakness, prone to such bursal enlargements as thoroughpin and bog spavins, to curbs, and to bony formations such as spavins.

Very straight hocks, especially if they are without a compensating over-long pastern to absorb the shock, are liable to bursal enlargement over and through the hock and/or to bog spavin. In other words, hocks should not be straight like that of a chow dog any more than they should be 'sickle' like those of the German Shepherd. It is not always easy to recognise the happy medium as a lot depends on how the animal is stood out.

Hocks, then, should be placed directly under the centre of gravity, and in order to give plenty of leverage to the thigh muscles, the tibia bone should run well down into the hock, which in turn should have the appearance of being close to the fetlock. This is called being 'well let down' (page 37).

To recognise good from bad – a sound from an unsound hock – requires a lot of experience and is the cause of considerable controversy. I have often heard two good judges disagreeing on this point,

35

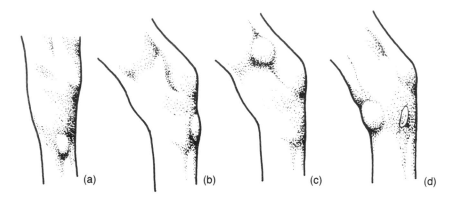

Fig. 8 Unsoundnesses. (a) Splint. (b) Curb. (c) Thoroughpin. (d) Bone spavin.

and, as I say, while it is easy to describe a good hock it is not so easy to recognise it in flesh and bone.

Taking it by and large, the outline of a hock should be clean and flat and, in an adult animal, well-defined. Bone should be large and prominent. Size is essential for strength, and prominence is necessary to allow due leverage and attachment to tendons and ligaments. Large bones are usually accompanied by large, well-developed tendons and ligaments.

A hock, when viewed from the side, should appear wide both above and below. There should be no signs of puffiness; they should not be untidy.

Pasterns

These should be neither too long nor too short and upright. If too long, while they may make for a comfortable ride, they are not altogether desirable and can be a weakness. If too short this conformation causes jar and not only tends to cause unsoundness but gives an uncomfortable ride. If a show animal has slightly long pasterns behind, calkins fitted to the hind shoes will make this much less noticeable.

Ponies, cobs and half-breds have a tendency to short, upright pasterns. Nearly all common animals have this fault. On the other hand, Thoroughbreds tend to be the opposite.

Long pasterns are frequently found in an over-straight hind leg. This is nature's way of counteracting concussion and strains which can accompany over-straight hocks.

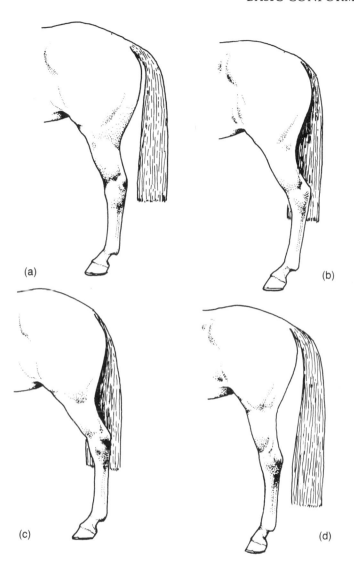

Fig. 9 Hind legs (side view). (a) Good hind leg, length from hip to point of buttock and from hip to hock; good gaskkin (second thigh); clean well-let-down hocks. (b) Sickle hock, light of bone, no second thigh; cut in above hock. (c) Hocks up in the air; short from hip to point of buttock and from hip to point of hock; cut in above hock. (d) Overstraight hocks.

Fetlocks

Here again there should be an impression of flatness rather than roundness, with clearly defined tendons and ligaments – in fact so

37

well-defined that you can run your fingers down the grooves on either side. This is not possible on limbs that are thick and lymphatic, or poor-quality bone, like pumice stone. A horse or pony with limbs like this is said to be 'round of his joints', or he may have done a lot of work, when he will most likely shuffle at the trot.

Fetlocks do, of course, thicken, and even become callous, with wear and tear. The first sign of this is when there is a projection or swelling in the front of the fetlock, or round the sesamoid joint at the back of the fetlock.

An animal that is stiff because its tendons have thickened or calloused, or because it has a spavin or is tied in at the elbow, often clears the ground by resorting to flexion only at the fetlock. This produces a stilted manner of going, sometimes described in the trade as 'knuckly'. It can be demonstrated by throwing out alternate wrists in front of one's hands.

Feet

Feet can also be a factor deciding whether an animal has true quality. These should be of good sound horn, open and of normal size. In front they should be round, and behind slightly oval.

Boxy feet are always suspect and unacceptable in a show animal, whether in hand or under saddle, although you frequently see them in harness classes, especially amongst hackneys, where abnormally long feet, shod with heavy shoes are encouraged. They are undesirable in any horse and are often a symptom of navicular disease.

Over-large feet, especially if they are shallow or 'shelly', are a menace. Not only will the animal go tender at the slightest provocation but they make for clumsiness and stumbling.

Small feet are a disadvantage even if well shaped, especially in deep going. In other words, extremes are to be avoided.

It is important that both fore feet should be a pair. Hind feet are usually smaller. Any shrinking or shrivelled frogs or contracted heels should be suspect.

Flat feet, which often have thin soles, are a nuisance as they cause the animal to move like a cat on hot bricks over rough or stony ground; they also bruise easily and contract corns.

Soles which appear concave instead of convex (that is, dropped soles) are almost invariably the result of the animal having at some time suffered from laminitis, or foot fever. The whole foot will have the appearance of being down at the heel and tipped up in front.

The foot of a animal suffering from, or having at one time had,

38

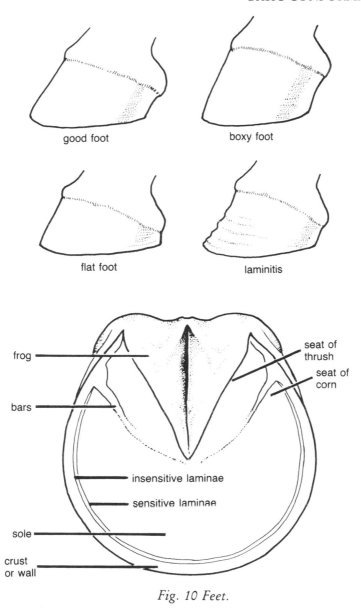

good foot

boxy foot

flat foot

laminitis

frog

seat of thrush

seat of corn

bars

insensitive laminae

sensitive laminae

sole

crust or wall

Fig. 10 Feet.

laminitis may have rings round the outer side horn. It is important to be able to differentiate between rings on the hoof which are the result of laminitis, and grass rings, which often appear on the hooves of horses, and especially of ponies, after a period at grass. Generally speaking, laminitis rings appear on either side of the hoof emanating

39

from the heels, whereas grass rings appear round the front of normally shaped feet with good concave soles and healthy, well-developed frogs.

The pear-shaped pad in the centre of every foot, known as the 'frog', plays an extremely important part. It is the shock-absorber. It should therefore be well-developed and soft. Any sign of shrinking or hardness is suspicious. A strong, nauseous smell indicates that 'thrush' may be present.

Scope

Both a young horse or pony and a matured one should 'stand over a lot of ground', as it is termed. This is difficult to put into words, and again is something which can be recognised only with experience. The best explanation I can give is by saying that if a horse or pony has a long, flat, sloping shoulder, and a long, horizontal croup (the space between point of hip to point of buttock), and provided these are combined with good limbs, the animal's back will then appear short compared with the distance between the fore and hind feet when standing normally.

2   Temperament

Temperament is of foremost importance, for whatever purpose a horse or pony is used. An animal with a perfect temperament is worth its weight in gold, whatever it looks like, but a true show horse, as well as having the temperament, must also have the conformation, balance, movement, presence and quality to justify this title.

But no horse or pony is likely to have this temperament if its conformation is such that it is difficult, if not impossible, for it to do as the rider asks, or to perform in the manner expected of it. For then it is uncomfortable – even in pain. Or it may be unsound, immature or weak through one cause or another. All these things naturally irritate it through causing pain or discomfort.

Nor can it be expected to carry itself in a position which its conformation makes difficult, uncomfortable, or patently impossible. Persisting in cases like this can eventually destroy its temperament.

That is why conformation plays such an important part, not only because of looks.

On the other hand, good conformation avoids those irritations which often ruin the temperament of good honest animals without it, turning them into sour, even vicious ones. It also makes unsoundness less likely and prevents ailments, both of which, to say the least of it, are a nuisance.

One can only generalise, however. There have been, and will be again, horses and ponies in certain spheres with every sort of physical drawback, which have proved themselves good performers and whose temperaments, even under provocation, have remained unspoilt.

I have, time and again, speaking purely of ponies, seen those with perfectly good temperaments literally forced into doing wrong. I remember one in particular that was sold to me as one of the wickedest ponies that had ever looked through a bridle. She was said never to be off her hind legs. Actually, that pony had a sweet temperament, and was most generous. Generous, and therefore full of courage. All she wanted was to get on with the job, whereas she had constantly been 'disappointed' by having her very light mouth hung on to. She therefore reared up because there was nothing else to do.

Another thing to remember is that horses have not the power of connecting up incidents. That is why it infuriates me to see show jumpers that have refused in the ring, being beaten up outside it. It is equally futile, when a dog or lost hound has been away hunting, and eventually returns, to beat him. If he is wise, next time he won't come back at all.

Finally, it is obviously as senseless to place an inexperienced rider on a keen highly bred high-powered horse as it is to hand the wheel of a sports car to an 'L' driver.

I always take it with a grain of salt when someone says to me that he has a really bad or vicious horse. I deeply distrust advertisements in which offers are made to take 'bad 'uns' and put them right. I maintain that in nine cases out of ten anything a horse or pony does wrong, while his reactions may depend on his temperament, is attributable to his handling and treatment by humans at some period in his life – just as I blame parents for some of the youthful delinquency today.

No two horses are alike. There is the slug, the cunning one, the one that sulks, and the one which abounds in courage. Give me the one with courage every time. He may be more difficult in some ways. You may have to wait longer to get what you want out of him, but no show animal, and certainly no hunter or racehorse, is much use without this asset.

Courage has, however, to be directed into the right channels. A horse or pony that is full of courage is not for a novice to ride, and certainly not to school. Given a horse with courage – and provided you handle him the right way – you will at least get free forward movement which, with balance, are two prime factors. If you fail, the animal will probably set up evasions such as rearing or refusing to go where you want him to go. To hit and hold a horse with courage is fatal. You have to be able to ride well enough to let him have the free forward movement that is inherent in him; in other words, you must not disappoint him by hanging on his mouth. If you have occasion to hit him, you must be efficient enough to do so without at the same time checking him, which, by disappointing him, is simply asking him to rear, just because there is nowhere else to go.

It is very much less rewarding, and certainly harder work, dealing with a slug. But to be fair, animals are often regarded as slugs when in fact they are suffering either from malnutrition, overwork, or, as I have already emphasised, faults in conformation. The cure of the first two is obvious. To cope with the latter requires sympathetic understanding and time.

Cunning animals have almost invariably been made so either by being asked the impossible or by bad handling. Horses and ponies are like children, they are quick to take advantage of weak or inexpert handling, and get up to all sorts of tricks and evasions. The majority can be cured by expert or sympathetic firm handling but they will invariably go back to their old ways in the hands of novices.

I personally do not believe that horses are born vicious. I have only known one that, while being perfectly healthy, was a real delinquent. Any vice they have is man-made at some time in their career, unless of course they have some physical defect such as a tumour on the brain.

A typical example of this erroneous outlook is the stallion who earns the reputation of being a 'man-eater'. In almost every case his attitude is attributable to the fact that he has been shut up, looking at four blank walls, either over- or under-fed and under-exercised. He has probably been taken out and lunged in the same old circle day after day, or he may be left in for the whole autumn and winter. In the spring he may receive some more exercise and some more food to fit him for his job, but again he is only taken out of his stable either to be lunged or introduced to a mare. In the latter instance he may often suffer from frustration and be returned to his box with his natural instincts unfulfilled. When he shows signs of resentment he may then be knocked about, which is fatal to chances of improvement. All stallions and young colts should be reasonably, firmly, but kindly treated. They should have periods of freedom out in a paddock or they should be ridden out. Shutting them up and perpetual lungeing is enough to spoil the best temperament.

Success or failure in establishing a good relationship between a man and his horse – a person's ability to recognise a horse's limitations or his potential and then to produce the maximum performance without setting up evasions and resistance – this is good horsemanship. The ability to keep him in bodily health, fitness, condition and happy – this is horsemastership. Both are equally important and are complementary to each other.

Alas, horsemastership, or if you prefer to call it so, stable management, is fast becoming a lost art. The change in this during the last fifty years is depressing. The reasons are many – labour shortage, the attraction of higher wages in other trades, above all in industry, the high cost of feeding, the spread of TT herds, the need to produce more food, resulting in lack of grazing, the passing of money into different hands. Gone are the stud groom and the family coachman whose pride and joy were the horses in his care. They were professionals, whereas today the large majority of horses and ponies are looked after by amateurs. Good feeders are like gardeners, born with green fingers. The lack of this gift is very apparent today. You only have to look inside our riding schools.

Can you, for instance, imagine our forebears entrusting racehorses, hunters, polo ponies, etc., valued at thousands of pounds to a teenage girl groom with a few months' training in a dubious riding school, or with no training at all? Yet this is what happens today.

Here we have to acknowledge the service and value of *good* girl grooms. What we should do without these, as dedicated as their male predecessors, I do not know. The good ones are worth their weight in gold, just as were the old stud grooms and the top racing lads. They are cheerful, willing workers, frequently underpaid, and while of course they cannot be as physically strong as their male counterparts they have a much greater sympathy and understanding of horses. If this is not carried too far – in other words, if they don't become 'soppy' over their charges – this soothing influence works wonders. It also contributes to the very necessary peaceful atmosphere in any stable.

While on the subject of girl grooms, although there are any number of good ones, there are many more who take on the job without having any qualifications. Parents should realise that if their sons and daughters are going to make horses their career, then they should serve an apprenticeship as for any other trade. Employers should be prepared to pay as good a wage to a good girl groom as they would have to pay to her male equivalent.

These remarks may appear to be irrelevant in a chapter dealing with temperament, but because of the good influence that so many of the really good girl grooms have in a stable, not only through the dedicated care they give their charges, but because they handle them with equine tact, I feel this is the chapter in which this tribute to the good girls should appear.

While I do not agree that all horses are fools – some are and some are not – this does not mean that I think they have the intelligence of, for instance, dogs. Feline and canine intelligence is of a different kind. It would be unfair to expect canine intelligence from horses. Naturally, the more human contacts and the more education an animal has, the greater will be the development. The intelligence of dogs kept in kennels is not nearly as high as that of dogs that are constantly in the company of humans. Compared with dogs the equine race has to a very much lesser degree a sense of right and wrong. Horses know what they like doing and what they do not like doing; what they can and cannot get away with. What a good thing it is, however, that they do not realise their strength!

Some, especially our native ponies, have a sense of mischief, even of humour; all have an uncanny instinct which enables them, at least when mature, to sum up the ability and character of their rider or handler. Like children and dogs, they are quick to take advantage of any sign of weakness. They have prodigious memories. Time and again I have seen a naughty little pony or a nappy horse being straightened out by a good rider. I know perfectly well, and so does he, that that horse or pony will revert to his bad habits when returned to the person he originally played up, even if some time after. They will also revert in the hands of other novices. I have also noticed how ponies, for instance, which have been stabled and, therefore, taught manners, when turned out to grass again quickly revert to natural conditions. The herd instinct very easily reasserts itself.

All the equine race are gregarious. This can be used to great advantage. Equally it can be a perfect nuisance. When a young horse or pony first hesitates to leave his companions, or refuses to come out of line at a show, this is the first indication of trouble and should be vigorously and tactfully opposed. Gregariousness can, however, be an advantage. For example, racing lads could not remain on board if two-year-olds at exercise did not go out in a string. Trekking ponies follow each other so closely that I would never be surprised to see them pick up each others' tails like elephants, but unless they proceeded in this crocodile the beginners that bestride them would have no control whatsoever. Take also the hunter which, unwilling to perform in cold blood, is brilliant when hounds are running, or the racehorse that dislodges his jockey and yet continues to accompany the other runners, even over a steeplechase course.

Many horses are highly strung and, therefore, highly nervous. These, too, may be rendered nappy and unmanageable by harsh, unfair and unsympathetic treatment, or again, by being asked to perform in a manner which their conformation makes difficult or uncomfortable, if not frankly impossible. All the equine race appreciate kindness and all are improved by it. But by kindness I do not mean over-petting, feeding of tit-bits, or soppiness of any kind. As with children, respect is the key to the door. Always remember that you, not your horse or pony, must be the boss, but do not, having obtained this satisfactory situation, then exploit it. Lucky are those persons born with, or who have managed to learn, equine tact.

3 Quality

Quality, like mercy, 'droppeth as the gentle rain from heaven'. It is extremely difficult to define and only by experience can you hope to recognise a truly quality horse or pony.

Again, opinions differ, for there are not only degrees of this elusive asset, but also types of quality. Primarily, it depends on bone structure (and therefore on limbs and conformation), and also upon an intangible refinement which I personally define as good breeding. But while being well-bred is regarded as an asset in the animal world, it no longer seems to apply to humans. Increasingly, horses, ponies, dogs, cattle, even cats, are registered in their respective breed stud books, when their value increases. But to be in *Debrett's*, or even *Who's Who*, is now a crime against democracy!

There are, however, degrees of quality in the horse world. Let us therefore try classifying quality into groups, namely:

(1) True quality
(2) Hunter quality
(3) Arab quality
(4) Some quality

(1) A truly quality object has *correct proportions*. If it is a horse or pony he has a finely chiselled head with *good bone structure*, large full eyes, fine alert ears, fine sensitive nostrils, lips and dock, and fine silky hair with no coarse whiskers on either head or heels. Limbs, too, are a deciding factor. Bone – and plenty of it – must be flat, tendons defined with good, open, well-shaped feet made of plenty of good sound horn. Action should be straight, free-flowing, although there are quality animals which are anything but classic movers. You only have to watch racehorses going down to the post to see this fact illustrated.

Both humans and animals, more often than not, derive quality from being well-bred. They can, however, be too well-bred, even in-bred, and this leads to degeneracy, when the introduction of fresh blood is very necessary.

Top-class quality ponies are small replicas of top-class quality hacks, but with pony character.

(2) Next we come to hunter quality, where all the above qualifications are there but with just that little less refinement for which is substituted that much more substance, and a general workmanlike appearance. You also have hunter-type ponies, and good luck to them. Personally I prefer a really quality hunter-type pony with limbs – provided he is a pony and not a 'little horse' – to what is described as a 'real pony' but which, alas, has long spindly shanks and hocks up in the air, or rather sickle – a type we see rather too often today.

(3) Take next Arab quality. Unquestionably most Arabs exude quality but as a breed they are something quite different, and the same surely applies to their type of quality. They can have the loveliest heads, lustrous eyes, fine nostrils and silky hair, which are amongst their chief characteristics, but so many fail on conformation. The best have good bone yet none, in my opinion, has quite the same degree of quality as the best in category (1).

(4) We now come to the fourth category, namely horses and ponies of which it can be truly said that they have *some* quality. For instance, they may have a beautiful silky coat and hair with plenty of bloom and good limbs, but their head, while sensible, may be over-large and their quarters sloping. Or they may have a beautiful head, but, alas, wrongly put on, a fine coat and fine silky mane and tail, but their limbs are lacking in bone and their joints round.

Lastly, we have that snare and delusion, the 'blood weed', oozing quality but really a 'useless tool,' to borrow one of the late Count Orssich's favourite expressions. But then, you can also have this effete type in the human race.

One further point: it must be rather confusing to the inexperienced to name quality as something to look for and to be found in carthorses and in our native ponies, but undoubtedly some have more quality than others and some have a lot. Just as dogs, cattle, even rabbits, have or have not got quality, so do carthorses and our native ponies, some of course more than others.

I admit it is harder to decide 'Yes' or 'No' in these types of animals but again, I think, proportion, limbs, texture of coat and general refinement all come into it.

Racehorses and hunters are bred for speed and performance over varying distances and/or fences. Without Thoroughbred blood they are unlikely to be fast or brilliant enough to be in the top flight, and certainly not to carry any appreciable weight at a fast pace. A hunter or event horse which is fast and can at the same time carry weight is clearly valuable, because rare. A carthorse, on the other hand, is only required to move slowly and to use brute force. Yet he can have quality even if incapable of moving faster than a stately trot or a lumbering canter, paces which are fortunately not asked of him.

Given that all the other attributes are equal, a quality horse or pony not only has refinement but is generally a very much better performer in all fields than his commoner counterpart. Horses with hot (southern) blood also have more staying power, more courage and more speed than those with cold (northern) blood.

There is no doubt, in my opinion, that it is good breeding which more often than not produces quality. 'Hairy heels' is an expression commonly used to denote ill breeding. Actually, in equines it is nature's protection against the weather, but it is true that in the equine world, coarse wiry hair, especially hair that curls, is an indication of low breeding, while fine silky hair is a sign of good breeding.

In animals the coat also helps in deciding whether or not they have quality; but beware. Fine feathers do not always make fine birds; in other words, beware of the silky-haired, fine-skinned 'flat-catcher'.

Good coats in good health carry 'bloom', like the bloom on a grape. Greys and duns, colours which show little or no bloom, have to make up in other ways for this lack of bloom, without which they tend to look common. That many greys have quality, even without bloom, is proved by the number that win in all classifications.

There is something arresting, even exciting, about a top-class well-bred animal. Only by experience can you come to recognise and to respect the real article.

Quality is the refinement that comes from breeding from generations of *proved* stock. This is why one can see quality in anything from a Shetland pony to a Shire horse provided they are the result of breeding from the best available stock and not that haphazard breeding from any old stallion available put to an indifferent mare. There are exceptions to this rule, but they are rare.

Quality gives to those who possess it just that extra something which, for lack of a better word, I have to call 'class'. Until someone invents a better, and despite the fact that it is not a popular word today, it is the only one I can honestly use.

4   Action

A good mover, whether in hand or under saddle, moves its whole shoulder, has slight elevation of the knee, and full extension of the whole foreleg, and touches down toe first, with slight suspension in the air before the foot is brought to the ground.

In order to get this extension and elevation the elbows must be placed well away from the ribs, and not tucked in against them. Only if there is plenty of room between the elbow and the ribs can a horse or pony really move.

If an animal is tucked in at the elbow he will then move only from the elbow and this is called 'scrambling'. Many people, even judges, are misled by the fact that because he has low action, or what is called 'daisy cuts', he appears to move well, but if they look again they will be able to see quite clearly that all he is doing is flipping a toe, but only from the elbow.

High knee action should not of course be confused with the degree of elevation that enables an animal to get its knee *up and out*, and so throw its toe out in the graceful floating action of the truly good mover. High-stepping harness animals, of course, have a very much higher knee elevation, but the best of them also have extension. High knee action that is simply an up-and-down action is no more desirable in harness animals than it is in the riding type. High knee action is frowned on in a saddle horse, yet here again we meet with a contradiction, for undoubtedly many animals that have this, such as some Welsh Cobs, can and do give you a wonderful ride.

High knee action can be, and of course is, encouraged and intensified by shoeing with very heavy shoes. What cannot be done is to turn an animal that naturally uses its knee a great deal into a really good mover under saddle. Very high knee action usually goes with a straight shoulder and a straight shoulder will never produce classic movement in a riding animal. Some horses, notably Arabs, that have straight shoulders do move them, and do flip a toe, but this is done mostly with a practically straight knee, and therefore without really classic movement, which to be so has to have a certain amount of elevation and suspension.

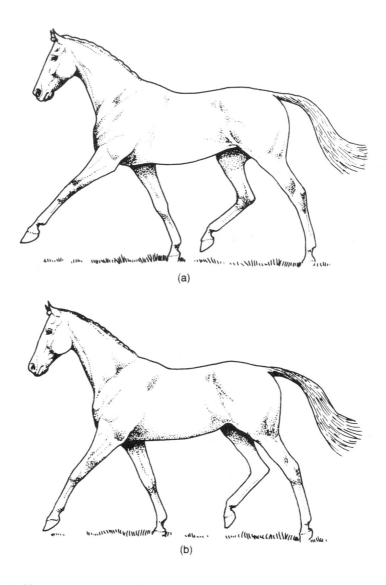

(a)

(b)

Fig. 11 Trotting. (a) Extended trot, using shoulders and hocks, with slight elevation. (b) Ordinary (or working) trot, from which further extension can be developed.

But no horse or pony can be said to be a good mover if it does not also move behind. It is quite useless to get a toe out in front if at the same time the hocks are not flexed and the hind legs trail behind. This defect is perhaps more noticeable when the animal is shown in hand than under saddle, yet any number of judges forget

50

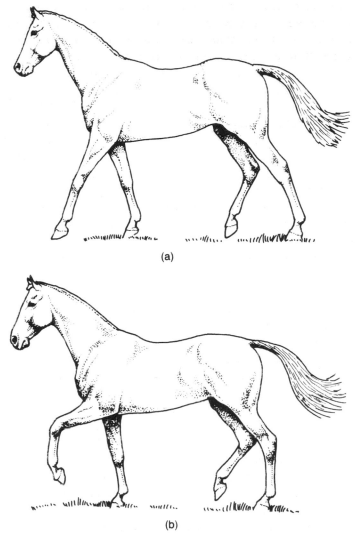

Fig. 12 Trotting. (a) A straight shoulder, tied-in elbow and indifferent hock action; higher behind the saddle than in front, resulting in movement from the elbow only. (b) High knee action due to a tied-in elbow, a straight shoulder, indifferent hock action and therefore no extension.

to look behind and appear to be mesmerised by a flipping toe in front.

The rear end is all-important, for there lies the engine that produces the very necessary impulsion, which in turn produces free forward movement. Without the latter you get nowhere. A strong loin, well-

51

developed quarters and thighs, and above all, strong active hocks, are the parts that supply this essential motive power. The hocks should be well underneath the body. If when standing still they are behind a line drawn from the point of the buttocks to the ground (in other words, 'hocks away from him/her') then it will be difficult to achieve this and the animal will automatically be thrown on to his forehand. If an animal is on his forehand, it obviously makes it more difficult for him to move correctly, and lightly in front.

Slightly different movement is looked for according to the type of animal. For example, an exaggeratedly extended trot is not wanted or even desirable in a hunter. All that is wanted of him in his trot is a balanced and cadenced movement from the shoulder, whereas a hack must be able to give a more exaggerated and elegant performance. Hunters and cobs are naturally expected to gallop on. They must use their hocks and get on with the job. A hunter that goes up and down in the same place is obviously useless. He must have scope. A hack, on the other hand, is rarely asked to gallop, though, in my opinion, he should be able to do so without bucking his rider off. His best pace is a collected canter, when again it is important that he should use his hocks and be a pleasant and, above all, balanced ride.

It is both unsightly and a fault if a horse or pony puts its heel down before its toe in front. This is frequently seen in animals which were not born naturally good movers and which have been artificially produced. It is caused by forcing so that they have to reach for extension instead of either having it naturally or having it produced *gradually*. It can also happen as an animal gets on in years and loses his elasticity and it can happen temporarily in young animals that are out of balance.

Animals that nod their head as they put their forefeet to the ground, giving an impression of plodding, are yet other examples of over-schooling and forcing.

Another example is an animal that goes wide behind. Some are born this way, but the majority have been forced into this ungainly gait by being over-trotted both in hand when they were young, and later under saddle, in an endeavour to get front extension without engaging the hocks.

You only have to watch top-class hackneys to see an example of hocks that are well and truly engaged. Note the punch and vigour of these which, although of course exaggerated, show what powerful hock action can produce in balanced, free forward movement, and a light airy front action.

Ponies are naturally inclined to have quick darting action,

especially the native breeds. While there is nothing to object to in this for the ordinary utility pony, a show pony should move like its larger counterpart in the hack classes.

We have now established that a really good mover uses its shoulder, knee and fetlock. If it moves from the elbow only then it is not a truly good mover, but only a scrambler. If it has a lot of knee action it is said to 'step'. It is essential that its hocks are engaged.

Action to avoid is of course any unsoundness, any stilted cramped action resulting from sore shins, upright pasterns, worn joints, calloused limbs, loss of elasticity through any cause, old age, rheumatism, or simply from lack of free forward movement which may in turn be due to immaturity, weakness, greenness, lack of hock movement due either to wrong conformation or indifferent schooling.

All these possibilities will pass through your mind whether you be buying or judging. You have only seconds in which to decide what matters and what does not. If you are buying you have to decide whether indifferent action is due to something that is incurable or to something which can be overcome, either by building up muscles or by good schooling and patience. If you are judging, you are judging on the day and have to judge what is placed before you, and you must not be tempted into putting up an animal that is not really moving on the day because you personally can see its potential.

Straight and Defective Action

A horse should move dead straight both fore and aft. There should be no deflection from a straight line. Due allowance should, however, be made for young immature animals as one of the hardest things for a horse to do is walk in an absolutely straight line. His hind feet should follow in the track of his forefeet. It is obviously easier for him to do this under saddle when he has the rider's legs to help to keep him straight than it is when out in hand. *A good mover at the walk oversteps with his hind hooves the imprint made by his forefeet.* He is then likely to be a good mover at all paces. His forelegs should be dead straight; often they can be straight down to the knee and crooked thereafter. Many fetlock joints turn either out or in, possibly owing to neglected feet when the animal was young.

Behind he can have either cow hocks, namely those that turn in, or hocks that bend outwards; both are unsightly but not necessarily a weakness. They should not be accepted in a show animal unless there is simply nothing better in the ring.

Curby hocks are not conducive to impulsion but they are usually

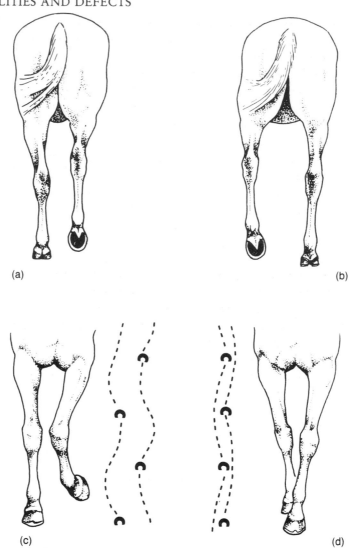

Fig. 13 Hind legs: (a) moving straight; (b) moving wide, slightly bow-legged. Forelegs: (c) dishing; (d) plaiting.

caused by strain. They are not acceptable in a show animal. But make quite certain it is a curb and not simply a large bone (see page 36).

If a horse or pony throws its feet out sideways, at whatever pace, either from the knee or from the fetlock, then it is said to 'dish'.

If a horse or pony places a forefoot in front of the other at the walk and trot, he is said to 'plait'. This may be very slight – he may even only do it with one foot; and if he is young he may cease to do it; as he strengthens and broadens he will go straight. As a judge

54

you should also be careful, first, that you do not falsely accuse an animal of this defect, especially when shown in hand because his attendant has not run him straight but held his head inclined towards her, or because he is not yet fully muscled up. On the other hand you should make sure that you are not being hoodwinked by a clever presentation into believing that a horse or pony is moving straight when in fact he is not.

A judge should certainly look for any signs of brushing or knocking as obviously this is a defect, since in time a joint is bound to suffer ill effects. It is, after all, not a judge's business to say whether or not this is due to faulty shoeing, faulty schooling, bad riding, or what have you. Again, he has to judge on the day, and, by the way, if a horse does knock himself in the ring, the exhibitor will of course tell you either that he did it in the box on the way to the show or that he has never done it before. It is up to you to decide how important this is.

The same thing applies to movement behind. As I have said before, it is a defect if, as the saying goes, you can 'drive a bus' between a horse's or pony's hind legs. In my opinion this is a worse fault than if he goes slightly near, but nothing could be worse than when a horse really brushes behind.

Brushing, Cutting or Interfering

These are different names given to an injury of the fetlock, either fore or aft, through being struck by the opposite foot.

This can be caused by the horse or pony being narrow in front, by movement that is not true, by a badly shaped foot or leg that is not straight, and by bad shoeing, especially if the clenches are not properly hammered down.

A judge should watch for this very carefully and, while some slight excuse can be made for young horses because of immaturity or weakness, it is a bad fault in a mature animal.

Clicking and Forging

This noise is produced by the toe of the hind shoe striking against the under inner or posterior edge of the toe of the fore shoe when in action. Primarily, it arises from a quicker action of the hindquarters than that of the corresponding motion of the forequarters. The remedy as regards shoeing is to shorten the toes of the hind feet. Good riding, collecting the horse, and making him step out quickly and lively are, however, truer remedies.

Speedy-cutting

This is more serious than brushing, but very much less common. It is an injury caused by collision of one or other foot with the opposite leg immediately below the knee. It is due to peculiar action and is generally incurable. It is most common in impetus with exaggerated action, or in animals which have high head carriage. The pain caused by the knock is often so severe that the horse can come down, especially if it hits a nerve.

5   Balance

Fortunate indeed is the owner who acquires a naturally balanced horse or pony, for this is a gift from God. It is particularly so in the case of a child's pony, as naturally no child can balance a pony, just as no novice is capable of doing so.

No animal can be a really good ride unless it is balanced. It takes an expert or at least a very good rider to do this artificially.

It is possible to produce balance except when, at maturity, a horse or pony is lower in front than behind (a young animal is nearly always higher either in front or behind at various ages up to three or four years old, as this is the way it grows, but we are not speaking here of immature horses and ponies but of fully grown and mature ones).

It is difficult to balance an animal whose neck comes out of his chest at the wrong angle or whose hocks, when standing still, are *behind* a vertical line drawn from the point of his buttocks to the ground. Both these faults in conformation tend to force the animal on to his forehand and what is called 'send him into the ground'.

Nor can balance be achieved without free forward movement. A horse must go freely into the bit and carry not only itself but its rider without loss of balance.

A balanced animal carries its own head and tail. The rider sits in the middle of it and remains there at all paces. It does not lean on the rider's hands, so pulling him in front of the centre of balance, nor does it, by having its head on upside down, that is, the lower line of its neck longer than the upper, become 'light in front' and so again out of balance.

Good, knowledgeable schooling can most certainly improve, if not completely achieve, balance in an animal not born with it. This is done by getting the hocks underneath the body, motivating them, encouraging free forward movement and so gradually lightening the forehand. Or, if the animal is too light in front balance can again be achieved by impulsion and by dropping the forehand.

But, as I have said, natural balance is a tremendous asset and you can tell at once whenever you get on a horse or pony whether in fact it has this, whether it can be produced, or whether in fact it will always be on its forehand whatever you do.

Presence
This is another essential in a showman or show horse. Obviously they will attract more attention if they are not just 'flashy' but have personality. When a horse or pony with presence enters the ring you are immediately aware of it. Because of this great asset it can defeat those that are less assertive even if possibly better built. But take care you are not looking at a 'flashy' nothing – a flat-catcher. Presence derives from a controlled vitality, usually coupled with intelligence. If the animal also has conformation, balance, quality, and movement, it is a world beater, but like Arkle, they are not born every day. The French call it *élan*.

Horses may substitute 'presence' with that 'varminty' look which can be so attractive. If they have it, they are generally good ones and with intelligence.

6 Bone

The texture of bone varies. It can be of ivory-like density or of the substance of a pumice stone. The first is found *par excellence* in top-class Thoroughbreds, or good Arabs bred and reared in the desert and fed on hard, dry rations; the latter in horses bred and reared on land unsuitable for horses, that is, acid soils.

Modern breeding methods in this country seem to be producing a lot of dubious bone which is liable, therefore, to exostosis, such as splints, spavins, ringbone, and ossification of the lateral cartilages (that is, sidebones). This, I think, applies more especially to large animals. I am all for those not bigger than 16 hh and even in favour of those not exceeding 15.3hh!

While the capacity for standing up and remaining sound in hard work largely depends upon the amount of bone, its texture is even more important. (For measuring bone see page 90.) A Thorough-bred with 8 inches (20 cm) of good, flinty, hard bone is likely to be more durable and efficient than a horse with 9 inches (23 cm) of bone but descended from a common-bred sire or dam. A 16.2-3 hh hunter which also has any amount of good bone is, of course, most valuable.

There is a lot of bone disease about, especially in Thoroughbred racehorses, but this is too vast a subject to go into here. I would, however, venture the remark that the breaking-in at a year and racing at two years must be detrimental, and I view with apprehension the tendency for owners of other animals, notably ponies, to do the same thing, which is even more disastrous, as at least Thoroughbreds are born very early in the year and therefore mature earlier than other types, are not subjected to schooling in a circle, and are ridden by light lads on straight, level surfaces.

In my humble opinion, far too many animals today – both horses and ponies – are being bred light of bone, with long spindly shanks and hocks up in the air, which makes it even more imperative that no young riding animal should be more than just handled – and certainly not broken in or ridden – before the latter part of its third year. Before that, its bone is not set and its muscles are not formed.

59

The incidence of bone disease is fortunately less in colder-blooded animals such as hunters, showjumpers and, of course, ponies. But then these types certainly in the past were given more time to develop, are less subject to forced feeding, and are given more time, when bone has a chance to stand up to speed, shock and weight.

My advice is to breed from sound mares with good bone, the mare being the most important. I also advise owners and breeders not to force the growth of their youngstock, particularly just after being weaned, which is the most important stage in their life.

In the last ten years, the type of owner has changed considerably. These new owners are very impatient; they push trainers into sending young horses and ponies out to compete far too soon, with the result that they are ridden as over-fed babies, and therefore start training in an immature condition. This leads inevitably to 'napping' and other evasions, and can ruin an otherwise good temperament. Hurrying production is not only disastrous but also just plain stupid.

Good experienced trainers in all spheres hate to be hurried, but are at the mercy of the owner, who is anxious to see a return for his capital. Or in the case of ponies it may be fear that it grows overheight or the child that is to ride it grows over-age. Nevertheless, I deplore the showing of three-year-old ponies under saddle – to say nothing of those even younger – except for two or three minor shows in the late summer of their third year, and then mostly to gain ring experience.

To get a young pony to the stage when they can win at three years, in nine cases out of ten means that they have been forced. There are exceptions when you are fortunate enough to find yourself with a 'natural'. But even they are liable to throw splints, contract ring or sidebone, or even arthritis of the fetlock joints, and sesamoiditis. Even worse, it may start up navicular disease.

It is even more horrifying to know that young ponies, even yearlings, are being used in riding schools and trekking centres, where the work is infinitely harder. If only the public could be taught to recognise very young animals and have the courage to refuse to ride them, this malpractice would automatically cease.

To sum up, the more naturally a young animal can be brought up, the better – and the same applies to children!

7 Muscles, Tendons, Ligaments, and Leverage

Briefly, muscles are attached to bone by tendons and have powers of contraction with elasticity. They can contract but can then resume their original form. But they can only pull, not push.

All movement is a contraction of the muscles and it should be understood that every muscle, to compensate, must have a fellow muscle pulling the opposite way. In other words, if one muscle bends a limb there must be another to straighten it.

The fibres of the muscles merge into tendons which in some instances are in the form of cords. Wherever they meet bones these open out in a fan-like shape so that the actual attachment is spread over an area.

Tendons should not be confused with ligaments. Tendons are elastic whereas ligaments reach from bone to bone, have no muscular portions or attachments and contribute nothing to movement. On the contrary, their function is sometimes to check movement and generally to support and maintain the bony framework. Those which hold joints together have a certain amount of free play, but the suspensory ligaments of the forelegs for instance, are not elastic. Perhaps that is why this ligament in particular so often breaks down. I have seen an unfit horse with both its fetlocks almost level with the ground at the end of a point-to-point in heavy going and carrying a very much too heavy man, resulting in a breakdown of this important ligament in both forelegs.

The most important ligaments are in fact in the forelegs. The aforementioned 'suspensory' ligament supports the column of bones in the leg and is tense when the foot is on the ground, whether standing still or in motion. A horse bears the most weight on its forelegs. There is therefore more strain on ligaments here than in the hind legs, of which the hocks and joints above the hock make a sort of spring.

You may have noticed that a horse can sleep supported by his foreleg ligaments while resting the muscles of his hind legs, generally alternately.

Leverage, too, plays a most important role and is one of the main factors in ability to carry weight. The more generous the proportions of a joint, the greater the leverage and therefore the greater staying power and ability to cope with weight. Poor leverage, on the other hand, leads to early fatigue. Perhaps the most important leverage in the whole frame of a horse is the hock joints, hence the need for strong, clean ones.

8   Skin and Hair

The hairs of the mane and tail, while always growing, are permanent, unlike the coat, which is shed and renewed twice yearly. This usually occurs in spring and autumn, though some horses, especially the common-bred ones, do not finish casting their winter coats until quite late in the summer. I knew a pony which never cast his coat at all, but when he died a post-mortem revealed innumerable internal tumours.

A tight skin is a sure sign of ill health. Hence the horseman who invariably picks up a fold, whether it be of a horse or a cow, does so in order to test its looseness. If tight, it often means the animal has worms or is out of condition from one cause or another.

Fine, silky hair and skin is one of the signs of quality, though many a horse and pony has this and yet has not got *real* quality.

The dock of a quality horse is fine and thin and the hair soft and silky. A thick, coarse dock denotes lack of breeding.

No hair should curl; this is also a sign of ill-breeding.

Thoroughbreds and Arabs and well-bred animals carry little or no hair on their heels, whereas carthorses have an abundance. Native ponies also carry some hair, but because of this they should not be dubbed common – unless this is excessive – for this is nature's protection against the weather. If heels get wet they are liable to crack. The hair carries the moisture straight down on to the ground.

It is an essential for any show animal that it carries its tail well – not too high, but certainly not tucked into its dock. Very high tail carriage is characteristic of Arabs, and for some strange reason some of them also carry it to one side.

Not only does a drooping tail, or one actually tucked into the dock, deprive its owner of all 'presence', but also it can mean the animal has a poor constitution or is suffering from some vitamin deficiency. Before a horse kicks it invariably tucks its tail in, and to have one permanently in this position gives an impression of meanness, which is both unfair and depressing. But do not be entirely discouraged. The animal, be it horse or pony, may carry its tail thus because it is either out of condition or tense. When its condition improves, or it relaxes, it may well surprise you by carrying its tail as it should. But if the dock, when you handle it, feels flaccid, then there is little hope, and it is bound to count against the horse in the show ring.

Undoubtedly, a tail also acts as a balancing pole, especially when jumping, and it therefore has a value over and above being an adornment and a fly-switch.

Fortunately, docking and nicking is now illegal in this country, which is the reason why bolster-like cruppers are now used to raise tails of harness animals, and these in my opinion are very ugly.

9 Teeth

A horse or pony at maturity has twenty-four molars (or grinders), six at the top each side and six at the bottom each side – and twelve incisors (or front teeth) – six at the top and six at the bottom. Males have four canines (or tushes), which rarely develop in females, and which begin to appear at about four years old.

Foals are born with no molars; at two to four weeks old, temporary molars (one, two, and three) appear.

At one and a half years old, these three temporaries are still there, and two permanents (four and five) join them.

At two and a half to three and a half years old the temporaries are replaced by permanents.

At four years old the last permanent (six) erupts.

The temporary incisors (that is, the milk teeth) are all shed and replaced by permanent teeth by the fifth year. A five-year-old horse has all its permanent teeth. Horses' teeth never stop growing but when all these permanent teeth are through a horse is said to have a 'full mouth' and can be likened to a man of twenty-one years. This is a good reason to deprecate the racing of two- and three-year-olds, and the riding of one-, two-, and three-year-old horses and ponies at all; it is the same thing as working children of six to nine years of age, for to compare the age of a horse with a human you only have to multiply the horse's age by three.

Sucking or milk teeth are rounder, squarer, more hollow and whiter than permanent ones and have a 'neck' at the gum line which gives a rounded appearance where the tooth inserts into the gum, unlike the square appearance of a permanent incisor. They are also upright, whereas permanent incisor teeth start to slope forwards with age until at great age they literally 'jut'. All incisors are upright when viewed from the side until seven years old.

All permanent incisors have a black mark in their centres, which gradually wears out with age.

As well, male animals will have grown a tusk or 'tush', which is a small single tooth on the bars of the lower jaw between the last incisor and the first molar on each side. Mares, except on rare occasions, do not grow tushes.

At six years, the mouth contains six complete incisors in each jaw and the corner teeth are fully developed and in wear, with a well-defined 'mark' in the centre of each. The tush in male horses and ponies is also well developed and the incisor teeth will be seen to meet evenly and almost upright if you lift the upper lip and look.

At seven years old, changes begin to take place which may only be discernible to the practised eye. These are that the teeth viewed from the side, are beginning, as I have said, to jut forwards ever so slightly. The mark in the centre of each is beginning to fade and their whole shape is getting broader rather than rounder, and often there is a 'seven-year-old hook' in the upper corner incisors.

At eight years these changes in the middle incisors are more accentuated and are beginning to show also in the next teeth on either side. There is also a 'hook' appearing at seven years on the back edge of the corner incisors and the animal is now said to be past mark of age, or simply 'aged'.

Thereafter, it is mostly guesswork, but a knowledgeable horse-master can tell the approximate age, again by the slope of the front teeth, the angle at which they meet, and the gradual disappearance of the 'mark'. The centre 'mark' of the incisors disappears at five years, the laterals at nine, the corner incisors at nine years. Other signs of age are a deepening of the hollow above the eye, and a falling-in above the nostrils. Grey horses become white and grey hairs tend to appear on heads and noses and other parts of the body. Backs begin to dip.

A horse is said to be 'three off' when he has turned three but is nearer three than four years. If he is nearer four than three, he would be described as 'rising four'. If anyone tells you that a horse is 'five off', this means he will be five years old the following spring. Thoroughbreds are usually dated from 1st January, though actual dates of birth are also recorded.

Teeth need rasping to keep them even and to remove sharp edges, which are often the reason for bit evasion and other bad habits, even rearing. This particularly applies to aged animals when, as a result of the top jaw being slightly wider than the bottom, the outer edge of the upper and the inner edge of the lower molars or grinders become sharper.

Caries (decay) in teeth or uneven teeth can cause 'quidding', namely the collection of food in the cavity, which forms a ball either in the tooth or in the cheek, goes bad, and causes an evil smell. This has to be removed regularly, or a vet should remove the infected molar under general anaesthetic.

Some horses grow what are called 'wolf' teeth, which develop at about two years old. These are very small extra teeth on the bars, usually in front of the first molar. Again, they can cause irritation, even pain, when the bit is in the mouth, causing evasions and reluctance to accept the bit. These wolf teeth, being superfluous, are best removed, but only if they are the cause of bit evasion. If properly done by a veterinary surgeon this need not upset the animal.

The bars of the mouth are the areas void of teeth between the incisors and the molars and – in males – behind the 'tushes', on both the upper and lower jaws, where the bit should rest. They are part of the fulcrum in the ridden pony or horse, hence 'good hands' are low, supple, and flexed from the wrist. The low position and good hands ensure that the bit rests on the bar and not on the cheek, as when hands are kept up high.

It is essential not to over-bit, for the simple reason that severe bits damage the mucous lining covering the bars, which eventually become enscarred and loses its sensitivity. The horse, when the bars have reached this stage, becomes a 'puller'. The normal bar is smooth to the touch and is very sensitive. Bars which have been damaged by rough hands or over-bitting are scarred and bony enlargements due to damage to the jawbone can be felt.

Scarification of the inside of a cheek is quite common when horses' and ponies' teeth have not been rasped. The damage here is caused by the cheek being caught between the sharp edges of the first molar and the bit. This is exaggerated by a rider with heavy hands. It is essential in both ponies and horses to have the teeth done regularly – in some cases every three months. The younger the animal, the more often he requires dental treatment.

It is now possible to have your horse or pony's teeth attended to by a specialist 'horse dentist'. Inspection at least once a year is strongly advised. If an animal cannot chew its food properly, its digestion suffers and it will not thrive. Moreover, it will not accept the bit if its teeth are causing it pain or discomfort.

10 Height

This is another controversial subject about which there are differing views, often vehemently expressed.

Ridden Classes

Hunters Mercifully these have no height limit. Owners of *Small Hunters* must either produce a certificate from the Joint Measurement Board (see page 81) or submit to having their horses measured on the showground.

Hacks, cobs, and riding horses These have either to hold a certificate from the Joint Measurement Board or to submit to measurement on the showground (page 81).

Riding ponies These must have a certificate from the Joint Measurement Board (see page 81). Not all shows, however, accept this, and some insist on measurement on the ground.

Ridden mountain and moorland ponies Unless otherwise stated, these must be registered with their respective breed society, which (except for Welsh section Ds) automatically limits their height (see pages 110–30).

In-hand Classes

Broodmares As many of these may at one time have been in ridden classes, they will already hold certificates under the Joint Measurement Board. The majority are mature animals and height certificates are therefore easily obtainable (see page 81). Show executives are well advised, however, to reserve the right to measure at any time, or if and when the judge requests this.

Youngstock This is where opinion differs so greatly. These animals are not old enough to come under the Joint Measurement Board, so some people consider that they should be measured on the showground; others realise that (1) this can never be a true measurement, especially when dealing with youngstock; and (2) this is not possible when dealing with large numbers and a tight schedule. Others advocate measuring in the ring, which in my opinion is a farce, and I know some veterinary surgeons who refuse to undertake this. When it is done, and a pony is measured out of its class, it may then be permitted to enter the next classification; that is, if a pony in a 12.2 hh class is deemed to be 12.2½ hh when measured on the day in the ring, and should the timetable be so arranged as to permit this, it then competes in the 13.2 hh class. Likewise, a 13.2 hh pony measured out, competes in the 14.2 hh class, while a 14.2 hh pony measured out either has no class into which to go or has to compete in the 15.2 hh class (if one is staged), when it will be dubbed a 'little horse' for the rest of its life.

The objections to this are that it creates chaos, since the numbers of these exhibits are then not entered in the class in the programme, so that the stewards, the commentator and the public – let alone the Press – are completely confused. Secondly, public notice is drawn to a measurement which, in the circumstances, cannot be a true one. Not only is the stand upon which it is measured not often a properly levelled one, but the animal may naturally become excited by the surroundings etc., and therefore be so much on its toes as not to give a true measurement. The decision can therefore only be the opinion of the veterinary officer concerned, and what difference is there between his opinion and the judge's? A lot of people feel that the judge should be the one to decide, because he/she not only decides on height, but also upon two other important factors, namely type and character, both of which are right outside the vet's sphere of operation. Further, if the decision is left to the judge, it is then only an 'opinion' and the animal is not branded as over-height for life.

I fully realise that there are exhibitors who will try to get away with anything; there are, however, many genuine borderline cases. For those who enter mature animals, or youngstock that are obviously over-height when entered, there is no excuse, but allowance should, I feel, be made for owners with young, immature animals. They can stop growing at any time and never move again, just as they can also suddenly shoot up. I have known two- and three-year-olds remain within the height right up until they are six years, and then shoot up.

Height, as long as I can remember, has been one of the main topics of conversation and argument, and always will be. I believe that the majority of owners today are honest and that those who cheat will be found out sooner or later. Those owning borderline cases have my sympathy, as I have owned some myself. They can measure one day and in certain circumstances, and not measure another, even in similar circumstances. One vet may measure them in; another outs them.

I do think, however, that it is an excellent thing that some of the big shows with the proper facilities do in fact insist on measuring mature, ridden animals. This acts as a double check if the job is done properly, when it can be regarded as pretty accurate, provided it is done in a quiet corner of the showground and the animal is given time to settle.

I also think that it is a good thing for show organisers to reserve the right to measure any animal at any time, as this at least makes the owners of the obviously over-height animals think again.

Another ruling which some shows adopt is to measure all 14.2 hh pony exhibits in classes where the classification is 'not to exceed 14.2 hh at maturity'. This at least ensures that no pony is over the accepted height of a pony on the show day.

To demand a height certificate signed by a veterinary surgeon to be sent in with the entry is useless and costly. An animal can easily grow between the date of entry and date of show.

It is for all these reasons that I personally consider it best to leave this knotty problem to the judge, who has the matter of type and pony character to help him in coming to a decision. I also emphasise that if he puts the animal down it is only an *opinion*, whereas if a vet does so the animal is dubbed for life. It may well be that when measured at home he is within the height limit. If he is spun by the vet when one, two, or three years old he is virtually grounded until he can be measured under the Joint Measurement Board as a four-year-old, when he may well conform.

In other words, while unfairness does exist where young ponies are *not* measured, it can equally well happen when they are.

Height is measured in hands: a hand equals 4 inches (10.1 cm). Measurement is taken at the highest point of the withers with a special stick fitted with a spirit-level for accuracy. The site chosen on which to measure should be level and smooth. The animal should stand firmly on all four feet with forelegs together and should be measured without shoes. Further details on measurement are given under the heading 'Joint Measurement Board,' page 81.

PART 2

Societies

11 Horse and Pony Societies

This chapter contains a list of horse and pony societies with a brief description of the functions they fulfil.

From time to time letters appear in the equestrian press suggesting that there are too many equine societies and advising amalgamations, and even that they should all be put under one 'umbrella'. I do not subscribe to this view. I believe that, within limits, competition is essential and stimulating. Without it, people, institutions, societies, parliaments, or what have you, tend to sit back and become lethargic and complacent. Besides, each society has, and indeed must have, individuality, much of which would inevitably be lost under an umbrella. Each breed, for instance, has its characteristics, its environment, and its individual members with special characteristics – which often resemble the characteristics of the breed in which they are interested! These dedicated people would inevitably lose interest were they subjected to dictation by people who, they could rightly assert, were without local knowledge and, most important, centuries of tradition.

Let us within limits do our best to maintain our individual breed societies, and at the same time support and maintain a friendly liaison with other societies who may have influence in other spheres.

'In reviewing British breeds we come to the final satisfactory conclusion that, whatever the system upon which British breeders work, British horse and pony stock of all kinds, taken as a whole, is the best in the world.' – the late Baroness Wentworth.

The British Horse Society

This is the leading horse society. In 1947 the National Horse Association of Great Britain and the Institute of the Horse and Pony Club Ltd amalgamated to become the British Horse Society.

Though originally based in London, in 1967 it set up the National Equestrian Centre (now re-named the British Equestrian Centre) on the same site as the Royal Agricultural Society showground at

Stoneleigh, near Kenilworth, Warwickshire, which has become the Society's headquarters.

The Society's Council, which consists of approximately fifty Council Members, meets four times a year. All the day-to-day decisions are taken and the work done by the General Purposes and Finance Committee of about ten members. This body receives recommendations from the Executive and Policy Committees, which are as follows:

Riding and Road Safety Policy
Access and Rights of Way Policy
Training and Examinations
Dressage
Horse Trials
Riding Clubs
Pony Club
Horse Driving Trials
Riding Establishments Policy
Long Distance Riding
National Committee
Scottish, Welsh, and Northern Ireland Committees
Horse and Pony Breeding
Welfare Policy
British Equestrian Centre
Royal International Horse Show Sub-committee

Dressage The BHS Dressage Group is responsible for the rules of dressage in the UK, and stages dressages competitions, conferences, courses and judge training. In 1988 membership stood at around 6000. There are some 400 days of dressage competitions annually, and two international meetings at Goodwood, plus national championships.

Horse trials The Horse Trials Group oversees the annual three-day events at Badminton and Burghley and innumerable one-, two- and three-day trials held throughout the country. Membership is currently running at around 6,600. The Badminton Three-Day Event, first staged in 1949, is the most famous horse trials competition, as well as the oldest.

Horse driving trials The Horse Driving Trials committee administers three-phase events – presentation and dressage, marathon, and obstacle driving – for teams of four horses or ponies, singles, pairs and tandems. It is responsible for the selection and training of teams

74

to compete in international competitions at home and abroad. It also promotes scurry driving and heavy horse obstacle driving competitions.

Long-distance riding Long-distance riding is the youngest of the Society's competitive disciplines and boasts almost 800 members.

Riding Clubs Since 1953 the Society has run an affiliation scheme for riding clubs. Nearly 400 clubs are affiliated and make a contribution to a central fund, while retaining autonomy in the conduct of their affairs and programmes. In 1988 there were 38,000 individual members.

The Riding Clubs Committee maintains panels of lecturers, instructors, examiners and judges. The improvement of riding horse care is encouraged by graded tests and stable management phases, instructors' conferences, and national championships in horse trials, dressage, Prix Caprilli, show jumping, and equitation jumping.

Instructor training With the financial assistance of the Sports Council, the Society sponsors a National Coach whose duty it is to organise courses for instructors in riding, both professional and amateur.

There are four grades of professional examinations:

(1) The BHS Assistance Instructor's examination, known as the BHSAI.
(2) The BHS Intermediate examination, known as the BHSII.
(3) The BHS Instructor's examination, known as the BHSI.
(4) The BHS Fellowship examination, known as the FBHS.

There are also Horse Knowledge and Riding certificates for amateurs and Progressive Riding Tests 1–12.

Riding Establishment Approval Scheme Following the lead of the Association of British Riding Schools and the Ponies of Britain, it was decided in 1962 to run a scheme for the approval of riding schools. Establishments which offer sound instruction in riding and horsemanship and whose premises, facilities and animals are properly looked after, are given the BHS 'seal of approval'. At this time approximately 580 riding schools hold BHS certificates out of an approximate number of 2,500.

Horse and Pony Breeds Committee This provides a forum where matters affecting horse and pony breeding can be discussed.

Parliamentary representation Bills presented before Parliament, likely to concern horse and pony owners, are looked into by the

Society's Parliamentary representative.

Welfare Committee The BHS sees its prime duty as working for the well-being of the horse. To keep a watch on welfare its voluntary County Welfare representatives are co-ordinated by a National Equine Welfare Officer. The Society's aim is to try to prevent neglect and cruelty before it ever takes place, i.e. by educating and advising owners on correct management practices.

Riding and road safety The BHS organises riding and road safety tests throughout the country and a wealth of information is given on equipment and clothing, particularly hats. Some seventy-five BHS Road Safety representatives train riders in roadcraft and examine candidates.

Access and Rights of Way Committee Intensive farming methods and the spread of urbanisation have resulted in the ploughing up of ancient rights of way and the rural rider is faced with fewer and fewer safe places to ride. Over one hundred Bridleways Officers, co-ordinated by the National Access and Rights of Way Officer, are in continuous consultation with county councils and a variety of other organisations on all matters concerning provision for recreational riding.

Publications The *BHS Members' Yearbook*, published every spring, and three issues of *Horseshoe*, the BHS magazine, are mailed direct to all members. *Horse and Hound* publishes a weekly newsletter. The Society also publishes a wide range of books and booklets, obtainable from the BHS Bookshop at Stoneleigh.

The British Equestrian Federation

The British Equestrian Federation represents the interests of the British Horse Society and the British Show Jumping Association in all matters concerned with the Federation Equestre Internationale (FEI). The BEF is responsible for all international events held in this country under FEI rules, and for all arrangements in connection with the British equestrian team's participation in the Olympic Games.

Questions of competitors' amateur or professional status and the interpretation of the FEI and International Olympic Committee rules on this subject are dealt with by the BEF. All contracts and agreements entered into by non-professional competitors for sponsorship and advertising have to be authorised by and administered through the BEF.

For further information contact the BEF, British Equestrian Centre, Stoneleigh, Kenilworth, Warwickshire, CV8 2LR (Tel: 0203 696697).

Association of British Riding Schools

This Association was the first organisation to undertake voluntary inspections of riding schools. Membership is given only to licensed riding school proprietors and the Association's aims are: (1) to raise the standard of stable management and to train potential staff; (2) to improve the welfare of the animals therein; (3) to carry out inspections of all establishments which apply; (4) to look after the rights of riding school proprietors and offer to the general public a minimum standard of service.

Secretary: Old Brewery Yard, Penzance, Cornwall, TR18 2SL (Tel: 0736 69440).

The British Show Jumping Association

This large and prosperous Association deals with everything to do with show jumping both at home and overseas, whether adult or junior. All horses and ponies jumping under its rules at any show must be registered with the Association. There is no height limit for horses but that for ponies is 14.2 hh.

Shows staging jumping under its rules must affiliate and are recommended to do so. The Association arranges coursebuilders, loan of jumps, timing equipment, etc. It issues a list of area representatives, a judges' panel, commentators, and rules and regulations which show organisers are urged to enforce, with a view to discouraging abuses which undoubtedly exist.

Apply to the Secretary, BSJA, The British Equestrian Centre, Stoneleigh, Kenilworth, Warwickshire, CV8 2LR (Tel: 0203 552511).

The Pony Club

This organisation (founded in 1928), while housed under the same roof as the BHS, conducts its own affairs and is very active, with its own Committee (half the members elected nationally and half nominated by the Society), and its own Secretary.

The Pony Club is a recognised national voluntary youth organisation and a member of the Standing Conference of National Voluntary Youth Organisations. The National Committee publishes an impressive list of textbooks, widely used in the horse and pony world, including *The Manual of Horsemanship, The Instructors' Handbook*, etc.

Currently the Pony Club has a membership of over a million with over 370 branches in the British Isles and many others overseas. Branches in this country are attached to a local hunt. It is designed for children up to the age of seventeen, whether they own a pony or not. Over seventeen years and under twenty-one, Pony Club members can become associate members.

Each branch has a district commissioner, local committee and secretary. Members join the Club through their local branch and are expected to take part in its programme of activities. These include local working rallies, instruction in riding and ponymastership, Pony Club camps, talks, film shows, visits to places of interest, and competitive events; also examinations for a series of graded tests.

There are six annual inter-branch team championships: horse trials, mounted games, dressage, tetrathlon, show jumping and polo.

Membership is effected through the local branch secretary, whose name can be obtained from headquarters. A club badge and tie are available to members.

While ownership of a pony is desirable, it is not essential. Some members hire from local riding schools, in which case parents are advised to see that the ponies hired are in good condition and fit to compete in activities which can be quite strenuous.

Many parents do a dedicated job of work, looking after their children's ponies during the school term. I ask them all to remember to remove the shoes of ponies turned out during term-time and to have them freshly shod at the start of the holidays. I have seen so many instances of feet in a deplorable condition as a result of failing to do this.

I also beg parents to feed the ponies during holidays, and of course in winter. Ponies have to stand up to a lot, as, having been idle for weeks, they are suddenly caught up at Christmas and Easter and expected to do a day's hunting or long hours at jumping and gymkhana events, without having been either fed or exercised adequately, and therefore are unfit. It says a lot for ponies that they are able to cope where few horses could.

Membership Applications should be made to your local branch. If not known, apply to the Secretary, The Pony Club, The British Equestrian Centre, Stoneleigh, Kenilworth, Warwickshire, CV8 2LR (Tel: 0203 696697).

The British Show Pony Society

This Society was formed in 1949. Its prime concern is to look after the interests of owners of ponies under saddle and to administer the wide range of classes that are open to children showing their ponies; to implement the rules regarding height, registrations, and rider's age; to compile a judges' panel and to regulate the qualification status for the leading shows.

The Society runs two major annual championship shows and has over 500 affiliated shows. The classes it caters for include: show pony, working hunter pony and show hunter pony, in which riders aged three to eighteen may compete; in addition, there are associate classes for riders aged between sixteen and twenty-one.

All ponies must be registered with the Society and, depending on their age, will require either a veterinary surgeon's certificate of age or a Joint Measurement Board height certificate.

Further details can be obtained from: Mrs J. Toynton, 124 Green End Road, Sawtry, Huntingdon, Cambridgeshire, PE17 5XA (Tel: 0487 831376).

The National Pony Society

Founded in 1893, the Society exists to encourage the breeding, registration and improvement of riding ponies and mountain and moorland ponies, and to foster the welfare of ponies in general.

The Stud Book This contains the breeding and registered numbers of riding ponies where the pedigree is known and approved for at least three generations. It also contains a Register and an Appendix. In earlier years the Stud Book contained the stud books of the English Connemara, Dales, Dartmoor, Exmoor and Fell breed societies. All these societies, as well as the Highland, New Forest, Shetland, and the Welsh, now issue their own stud books. Application for entry in the Stud Book, Register or the Appendix, should be made to the Secretary together with all available information.

Horserace Betting Levy Board For many years this Society has received a substantial grant from the Horserace Betting Levy Board.

79

This is paid to the National Pony Society for the improvement and encouragement of British mountain and moorland ponies. The Society sub-allocates the grant to the native breed societies, the NPS Show and the NPS Scottish Show.

Judging panel The Society publishes a list of judges on each of its four panels. Each year this list of judges is reviewed by the Society. Included in the judges' list are the judges' panel approved and supplied by the British native pony breed societies.

The Society operates a probationer judges' scheme. Candidates normally appear before an assessment panel before they are accepted. Probationer judges then spend a period of probation during which they are reported upon by experienced judges. Final acceptance on to the 'B' panel is at the discretion of the Judges' Selection Committee. After two years on the 'B' panel judges are eligible for elevation to the 'A' panel.

Shows The annual two-day show takes place on the Three Counties Showground at Malvern during the first week in August. It includes in-hand and ridden classes for riding ponies, all the British native breeds of ponies as well as part-bred classes for the mountain and moorland breeds and Arabs. There are also dressage classes and driving classes. A show is also held in Scotland each year.

Diplomas The Society conducts a system for training young people at approved training studs which embraces the training agency's Youth Training Scheme. The Society conducts examinations for its Stud Assistant's Examination and the NPS Diploma.

Championships Four championships are run each year by the Society: the Mountain and Moorland Ridden Championship; the Mountain and Moorland Working Hunter Pony Championship; the Mountain and Moorland Driving Championship; and the Riding Pony In-hand Championship.

Membership and registration Apply to Col. A. R. Whent, Brook House, 25 High Street, Alton, Hants, EU34 1AW (Tel: 0420 88333).

Ponies Association (UK)

This organisation was founded in 1988. Its shows provide exhibitors with an exceptionally wide range of classes, both ridden and in hand. Spring shows are held at Stafford and the East of England Showground, as well as in the south. The summer four-day show, for which there are many qualifiers all round the country, is also held at the East of England Showground.

The Ponies Association (UK) now operates an inspection, approval and affiliation scheme for riding holiday and trekking centres, which was originated by the Ponies of Britain. It also runs a series of instructional courses and seminars.

Further details can be obtained from Mrs M. Mills, Chesham House, Green End Road, Sawtry, Huntingdon, Cambridgeshire (Tel: 0487 830278).

The Joint Measurement Board

The Joint Measurement Board (formerly known as the Joint Measurement Scheme) was established in 1934 to run a national scheme for the measurement of the height of horses and ponies for the purpose of description and classification of such horses and ponies for competition. It applies particularly to hacks, cobs, riding horses, small hunters, children's riding ponies, and show-jumping ponies. The height of mountain and moorland ponies (except Welsh section D) is automatically limited by their registration.

The minimum age for an animal to be measured under the Rules of the scheme is four years. From the ages of four to six years, the animal will be issued with the *annual certificate, which expires on the following December 31st. Every animal regardless of its age has to have one annual certificate before it can have a life certificate.* Life certificates are issued to animals aged seven years and above, who have held an annual certificate.

All measurements must be carried out on a registered measuring pad, and must be taken by a veterinary surgeon whose name appears on the current panel of official measurers. A list of official measurers appears in the JMB rule book. Requests for measurement should be made direct to the official measurer chosen. All official measurers keep a supply of the necessary forms.

It is the owner's responsibility to ensure that the animal is correctly prepared for measurement, accustomed to the application of a measuring stick, etc. The animal must have all four shoes removed and feet prepared as for shoeing. The official measurer has the right to postpone the measurement if the conditions are unsuitable, the animal is unfit, or shows signs of improper preparation.

The animal should be positioned for measurement with the front legs parallel and perpendicular; the toes of the front feet should be in line, allowing not more than 1.5 cm (½ in.) difference. Both hind feet must be taking weight and as near perpendicular as possible; the toes of the hind feet should be not more than 15 cm (6 in.) out of line with each other.

The animal's head must be in its natural position in relation to its neck, positioned so that the eye is not lower than, nor more than 8 cm (3 in.) above the highest point of the withers.

The measurement must be taken at the highest point of the withers (i.e. immediately above the spinous process of the fifth thoracic vertabra), which should be identified, by palpation if necessary, and marked before any measurements are made.

The veterinary surgeon carrying out the measurement has the responsibility that the stick he uses is an accurate one; it must have been passed by a Weights and Measures Officer. The stick must be fitted with a spirit level and must be shod with metal.

The measurement should be the true height of the relaxed animal.

The completed measurement forms together with the fee will then be sent to the Joint Measurement Board for processing and a certificate will be issued and forwarded to the owner of the animal.

The rules of the scheme provide for an arbitration procedure in cases where doubt is thought to exist concerning the height of an animal. This procedure is in the form of a re-measurement performed by two referees. Details of this procedure can be found in the rule book.

Copies of the current Joint Measurement Board rule book may be obtained by sending a large stamped, addressed envelope to the Secretary, Joint Measurement Board, British Equestrian Centre, Stoneleigh, Warwickshire, CV8 2LR (Tel 0203 696620).

The British Driving Society

To quote from *Driving and Harness*, written by my friend Colonel R. S. Timmis of Toronto, 'It is far more enjoyable to drive a good horse or horses than to drive any motor car, and far better for your health.'

I wonder how many people today would concede him this? A small minority would agree wholeheartedly, for alas, the pleasure of driving has largely been ruined by modern traffic conditions and road surfaces.

Retracing our steps sixty years, driving a horse was, of course, the usual way of life. Everyone drove everywhere, until the internal combustion engine gradually swept horse traffic off the roads and the farms. Two World Wars, the increased momentum of life and the craze for speed all but exterminated this form of transport, and very nearly killed it as a recreation. Fortunately there remained a large number of enthusiasts with an inherited love of driving as a recreation, who were keen not only to indulge themselves but also to infect others. This they have certainly achieved.

Led by the late Mr Sanders Watney, these enthusiasts formed themselves into a society in 1957 and have since gone from strength to strength. You only have to see the huge number and variety of vehicles meet up in the ring of the Royal Windsor Horse Show to realise what enthusiasm can do when directed aright.

The Society encourages and assists all those interested in driving in the choice of horse, cob or pony, vehicle, equipment, and the art of driving. The choice of vehicle is vitally important; for example, a cob could look thoroughly out of place in a phaeton just as a quality harness horse would look all wrong in a pickering float.

Activities include lectures and area rallies where members and their friends meet under pleasant surroundings and circumstances. There are no monetary awards attached, which is an object lesson to the pot-hunters.

In addition to non-competitive driving activities, some 300 shows affiliate to the Society and organise private driving and concours d'elegance classes. The BHS Driving Trials Group govern national horse driving trials and driving scurry classes at shows. Lists of all driving classes and competitions are sent to BDS members annually.

Panel of judges A list is available from the Secretary, and all shows are asked to use this panel.

Membership Application for membership of any persons interested in the driving of horses and ponies should be made to Mrs J. Dillon 27 Dugard Place, Barford, Warwickshire CV35 8DX (Tel: 0926 624420).

London Harness Horse Parade

This title resulted from the amalgamation of the London Cart Horse Parade and the London Van Horse Parade Society in 1966.

The London Cart Horse Parade was founded in 1885. The first parade took place in 1886 when 150 turn-outs met in Regent's Park. The following year the entry was 383 and thereafter, right up to 1914, these entries were limited because the streets became so blocked. In

1965 the figure was reduced to 26 by the increased number of motor cars and the effect of two World Wars.

The London Van Horse Parade was started in 1904 and was held every Easter Monday except during the wars. The largest parade was in 1914 when 1,259 animals were presented. In 1926, 864 vehicles turned up but, when, after the Second World War, a parade was again held, the entry was reduced to 204. After 1950, however, there was a gradual decline until in 1962, when the entries again began to increase with the happy result that in 1965 there were 125 exhibits.

At a meeting of the combined Committees of these two parades, it was agreed that, from 1966, the two parades should join together to stage the London Harness Horse Parade and that the event should again take place in Regent's Park on Easter Monday. In the first amalgamated parade 137 vehicles took part; twenty years later the parade has more than doubled in size.

The standard set was the same as before, based upon the condition and presentation of the animal, the harness, and the vehicle, which must, however, be suitable to the type of horse or pony. As conformation does not count, all exhibitors have an equal chance of success. Every animal receives a bunch of carrots.

The parade is divided into:

(1) Single commercial light horses and ponies.
(2) Private turnouts (singles).
(3) Mules and donkeys.
(4) Commercial light horses and ponies (pairs).
(5) Private turnouts (pairs).
(6) Commercial light horses and ponies (teams).
(7) Commercial heavy horses (single).
(8) Commercial heavy horses (pairs).
(9) Commercial heavy horses (teams of four).

Certificates of merit are also awarded to the farriers of well-shod animals in good working condition.

This excellent event is enjoyed not only by exhibitors, but by a large and enthusiastic crowd of spectators. Its aims are to improve the general condition, treatment and management of horses and ponies and to encourage and assist all those using horse-drawn transport to achieve a high standard of care and cleanliness.

For further details contact the Secretary, Miss B. E. Mills, Young & Co. Brewery, The Ram Brewery, Wandsworth, London, SW18 4JD (Tel: 01 870 0141).

The General Stud Book – Thoroughbreds

The word 'Thoroughbred' originated from the Arab *'Kehilan'*, of which Thoroughbred is the literal translation and which is the generic term for the Arabian breed, meaning 'pure all through'.

The term Thoroughbred today, abbreviated as it often is simply to TB, is conceded by many, especially sportsmen, to apply only to horses registered in the English General Stud Book or in the affiliated stud books of other countries, such as France, USA, Australia, New Zealand, South Africa, etc.

It should not, however, be confused with the term 'pure-bred' for, while every Thoroughbred is pure-bred, not every pure-bred horse is Thoroughbred. Nor are all Thoroughbreds registered in the stud books of other countries also eligible for the English General Stud Book.

One thing is certain – the modern race and riding horse owes its origin and excellence to Eastern (southern) blood.

Compared to other breeds, the Thoroughbred is comparatively young, dating back only about 300 years, whereas other breeds go back into antiquity. But in that short space of time, the best Thoroughbreds are universally acknowledged to represent the acme of perfection in the horse world.

It is not always easy to appreciate the full significance of classic Thoroughbred conformation. Many of the horses we see on race-courses have anything but perfect conformation. In addition they are in hard training, while a great number are immature and therefore high on the leg.

Many look very poor specimens, but, as the saying goes, 'they go in all shapes'.

A mature Thoroughbred should have all the best points of a technically good horse, but with these added distinctions – quality and class.

There are unfortunately large numbers of non-classically bred horses bred annually which are, to put it badly, useless tools. I look more in sorrow than in anger at people who, mostly through sheer ignorance, go on happily breeding from 'blood weeds', the ultimate destination of whose progeny is the bad riding schools (where they are kept on low rations to enable inexperienced riders to ride them) or the dog-meat tins. I beg people to think twice before they start breeding.

Temperament Thoroughbreds are highly sensitive and many are highly strung. Rough, unintelligent usage ruins their temperaments, as does asking them to perform tasks for which they are not ready or which are beyond them. By nature they are friendly and co-operative; any vice is attributable to man or to some physical or mental defect. In nine and threequarters out of ten a horse that becomes what people love to call a 'man-eater' has at one time or another been given this depraved appetite by a human being. So long as owners in all fields are in a hurry and out to make money, abuses will continue, and so, therefore, will wastage.

The uses of Thoroughbreds are manifold. Primarily, of course, their field of operation is the racecourse, under Jockey Club Rules of racing. They also dominate the point-to-point season, excel in the hunting field, the show ring, at show jumping, polo, and eventing. The presence of Thoroughbred blood in the children's riding pony classes ensures the quality you can obtain from no other source. I freely admit that I love Thoroughbreds: 'How beautiful they are, the lordly ones.' Yet how often does one go into a stable to be shown a 'toast-rack' and be told proudly, 'Of course, he's Thoroughbred. I suppose that's why we can't get any flesh on him – he's the worrying sort.' No wonder he's worried – so should I be, not knowing where my next meal was coming from! As for the theory held by some people that some horses are naturally thin, I do not believe it. If you cannot get flesh on a horse then there must be something basically wrong with him, either physically or mentally.

Given sensible handling by someone who can ride, who has a sense of anticipation, and who acknowledges that to be a good horseman you have to get to know and therefore treat each horse as an individual; provided he is fed sensibly but well and given work to do for which he is both capable and fit, there is no equine in the world like a good Thoroughbred.

Thoroughbred stallions These stand at stud all over the world; most of them come out of training and many of the really top-class ones are syndicated. Stud fees vary according to breeding and performance.

A number go into private ownership and stand at stud in various parts of the country, and compete for the premiums given by the Horserace Betting Levy Board through the Premium Stallion Scheme of the National Light Horse Breeding Society (HIS) (see page 88).

Small Thoroughbreds – that is those not more than 15.2 hh, and especially if their pedigree contains small blood lines – are most popular and valuable for breeding quality ponies. They stand at various private studs throughout the country and serve large numbers not only of riding pony brood mares (that is, mares of mixed breeding), but also of registered mares of the nine famous native breeds.

No one should expect the 'no foal, no fee' clause as a matter of course; it should be regarded as a concession to be gratefully received.

Some stallion owners have a lower fee for mares of any of the native breeds, which is a good thing as breeding from this stock is the basis of all our ponies and many of our horses.

The first General Stud Book was published in 1791. Previous to this most important date in equine history, horse breeding had been pretty haphazard and experimental, and information had been difficult to obtain. The GSB is kept up to date and published every few years, with annual supplements. Horses entered in this book are not allotted numbers, only the volume in which their name appears, and the page. All foalings must be recorded before the animal reaches four years old.

For conditions of entry and registration procedure contact: Weatherbys, Sanders Road, Wellingborough, Northants, NN8 4BX (Tel: 0933 440077).

The Non-Thoroughbred Register

This Register, also compiled by Weatherbys, replaced Prior's Half-bred Stud Book which was published from 1914 to 1972 and recorded the histories, pedigrees and racing performances of all the best-known half-bred families of racehorses. Up to 1987 the Non-Thoroughbred Register was for produce by Thoroughbred stallions out of non-Thoroughbred mares who had been registered by Weatherbys. Entry has now been widened to include the produce of certain non-Thoroughbred stallions registered with Weatherbys.

For fuller conditions of entry and registration contact Weatherbys at the address above.

The Thoroughbred Breeders' Association

Formed in 1917, the main objective of this Association is to encourage the science of producing and improving the Thoroughbred horse in this country. To this end the Association maintains a library and information service for breeders, government departments, members, etc., liaises with other bodies sharing common interests, and attempts to ensure co-operative effort in matters pertaining to the breeding of Thoroughbreds.

Membership is open to all. Apply to Mr S. G. Sheppard, Stanstead House, The Avenue, Suffolk, CB8 9AA (Tel: 0638 661321).

The National Light Horse Breeding Society (HIS)

This Society has a large membership, maintains its own Register and implements the Thoroughbred Premium Stallion Scheme, whereby selected Thoroughbred stallions stand at stud in various districts. These districts are not necessarily precisely the same each year; the list is revised each autumn.

This scheme provides a valuable service to owners of half-bred and Thoroughbred mares, by providing first-class, easily accessible, sound Thoroughbred stallions at a moderate fee. Most of these stallions are bought out of racing; the majority are good winners and are well, if not classically, bred. They are chosen for their conformation, bone, substance, movement and quality, and are bought by various interested persons. Every stallion provides an annual certificate of freedom from listed diseases and defects.

No stallion may be under four years or over eighteen years. Stallions up to twenty years are considered, provided they have previously been awarded premiums and have satisfactory foaling records. All are registered in or eligible for the General Stud Book at Weatherbys.

Registration in the Stud Book This Stud Book as a publication ceased in 1975, although the Society maintains a Stud Book Register which is continually being updated to include all new registrations of hunter stock. For further information regarding the registration of stock, application should be made to the Secretary of the Society.

How the stallion premium scheme operates The Society holds an annual stallion show at the Park Paddocks, Newmarket, in March, through the courtesy of Messrs Tattersalls.

The stallions are paraded in classified order before two judges, who select those stallions which will stand at stud in, or travel, the counties as premium stallions. These premiums are provided through a donation made by the Horserace Betting Levy Board every season. Each premium amounts to £1400. The total number of premiums awarded in 1989 was 51.

There are fourteen additional 'super premiums' ranging in value from £1000–£1500.

The Society also stages a class for stallions new to the scheme, with £2000 in prize money.

The fee for a non-Thoroughbred mare owned by a member is between £100 and £150, depending on the stallion selected. The stud fee for Thoroughbred mares is by arrangement with the stallion owner.

The season commences on 1st April and ends on 31st July, but mares may be served before 1st April provided a record of the service is entered in the service book supplied to the stallion owner by the Society.

The fact that a good stallion is readily available at a reasonable fee saves transport costs and encourages the breeding of good types of animals.

Shows The annual stallion show at Newmarket – see above.

The National Hunter Show, which changes its venue every two or three years, is held in August. It offers classes for broodmares and foals, youngstock, ridden and working hunters, and competition horses. At the Hunter show, produce premiums are also awarded for groups of three young horses under four years of age by the same Thoroughbred or registered hunter sire.

Affiliation Affiliation, for an annual fee, is open to all shows providing classification for hunters. The Secretary will furnish all necessary details on application, and advise on classification and judges. Broodmare premiums of £50 are offered at certain selected affiliated shows throughout the country, subject to certain conditions.

Judges A panel of judges recommended by the Society to officiate at both ridden and in-hand classes is available on application to the Secretary.

Veterinary surgeons The Society also publishes a list of recommended veterinary surgeons.

Membership On application to Mr G. W. Evans, 96 High Street, Edenbridge, Kent, TN8 5AR (Tel: 0732 866277).

Hunters

The National Light Horse Breeding Society (HIS) official classification for hunters is as follows:
    Lightweights to be capable of carrying up to 12 stone 7lb.
    Middleweights to be capable of carrying over 12 stone 7lb up to 14 stone.
    Heavyweights to be capable of carrying 14 stone and over.

Should a show give only two classes for hunters, the classification should read:

Hunters capable of carrying up to 13 stone.
Hunters capable of carrying over 13 stone.

A Novice is one that has never been awarded a first prize value more than £25 or a total of £75 in prize money in ridden hunter classes (the amount can vary).

For ladies' hunters there is no weight classification. They simply have to be suitable to carry a lady. The term 'ladies' hunter' usually means that the exhibit should be ridden side-saddle, but show schedules will state whether this is the case or whether entrants may ride astride.

Small hunters, which must not exceed 15.2 hh, have no weight-carrying limitation.

The first question a novice will ask is 'But how am I possibly to know into which category I should put my horse, especially if he is a borderline case?' Here, indeed, is the rub, for really experienced judges and dealers do not always agree about a hunter's classifications.

The advice and accumulated wisdom of an experienced hunter judge or dealer should be sought. Failing this, here are a few generalisations upon which to base an assessment.

To begin with, when judging what weight any horse is up to, the assessment should be made when it is undertaking its normal, not abnormal duties, and when fit and in condition. Obviously, a horse below par, or straight off grass, is not at that moment up to the weight it is built to carry, or the work it is able to do when it is corn-fed and fit. At the same time, an experienced person can tell what a horse or pony is potentially capable of carrying without stress or strain when fit, even when it is standing out in a field, half starved. This is because weight-carrying capacity is largely judged on the amount of bone, and the quality of that bone.

Measuring bone Bone is measured round the cannon bone, just below the knee. While an experienced person can judge this more or less by eye, if you want a yardstick these are the approximate bone measurements applicable for horses (ponies vary but the larger native breeds can have up to 8 inches):

Lightweights: not less than 8 inches (20.3 cm)
Middleweights: 8½ inches or so (21.5 cm)
Heavyweights: 9 inches or more (22.8 cm)

A short back, a strong loin and depth through the heart (or girth) are also weight-carrying potentials.

Height does not determine capacity to carry weight, but the approximate height of a lightweight hunter should be 16 hh or thereabouts, a middleweight 16 – 16.2 hh, and a heavyweight 16.2 hh or over.

If a hunter entered in a lightweight class is, in the opinion of the judges, up to more than that stipulated in the schedule, the horse is usually allowed to go forward to the middleweight class. Or if a middleweight, he can go up into the heavyweight class.

Hunter type If I were setting out to buy a show hunter, I should want him to conform to all the points I have made in the previous chapters on conformation etc. But he would definitely have to be *hunter* type. This is difficult to define but easily recognisable to anyone with experience. The best way to describe it to a novice seems to be that a hunter must above all be workmanlike, with good conformation, good limbs, balance, and performance. A show specimen must have plenty of quality. Working hunters can have varying degrees of this.

If, on the other hand, I wanted a good hunter, not necessarily to show, but on which to go across a country like the Shires, the first essentials I should want would be balance, good limbs, and performance, in that order. If he had the first two it would be reasonable to suppose that he could acquire the latter.

I emphasise balance because, if a horse has this, and especially if he is *naturally* balanced, he will automatically be a good ride, while it will undoubtedly be an aid to his performance over country.

No one, I hope, would select a Thoroughbred weed unless he himself is a lightweight with an overdraft at the bank! Even so, he will probably rue the day unless all the animal is required to do is hack about. This type costs more to keep than a 'good sort', which may be less well bred but which at least has four sound limbs upon which to stand, and a good constitution.

Naturally, one prefers a chiselled, quality head, but many a first-class hunter has a large one – even a Roman nose. This, although it is often a sign of intelligence, is also a sign of common blood somewhere. Neither do I like a very small head in a hunter, any more than I like an over-large one at the end of a very long neck. The first is too pretty-pretty for a hunter and the second will tend to make the animal heavy in the hand.

Length in front of the saddle is both essential and pleasant, like sitting in a Rolls-Royce. This should be obtained by means of a good sloping shoulder and not simply by having a long neck. A sloping

91

shoulder is a great asset when riding up and down dale and over fences.

Depth through the heart not only ensures plenty of heart room, and therefore staying power, but also a good girth line, which in turn keeps the saddle in the proper place.

Well-sprung ribs behind the saddle not only give the lungs very necessary space, but prevent the saddle slipping back. Horses that have short ribs tend to run up light, especially on a long day's hunting. The distance from the brisket to the ground should be the same as from the brisket to the top of the withers. A horse with these dimensions is called 'low to the ground' or 'well let down'. The opposite is called 'leggy' or 'on the leg' (or 'showing a lot of daylight'), which is never a good thing.

A herring-gutted hunter is a perfect nuisance as he runs up light after a day's hunting and is therefore difficult and expensive to keep in condition.

Again, a horse with a large space between his last rib and his hip bone, or with a slack loin, will also be difficult to build up and maintain in condition. A hollow, or sway back, while making for a comfortable ride, is a weakness. A roach back is both unsightly and uncomfortable.

There should be plenty of length between the hip and the buttocks, and it is no detriment to a hunter to have a goose rump, that is, sloping quarters. Indeed, it can be an asset as many horses with this conformation are good jumpers.

All limbs should be as described in Chapter 1 on basic conformation. Although many good hunters have had round joints – even lymphatic limbs – they are not the sort to buy if you can afford better. The importance of the limbs cannot be over-emphasised, for from the knees and hocks to the ground are found most of the ills to which hunters are subject.

The all-round impression should be of a good 'top line'. Prominent withers are good provided they are not too knife-like and are especially necessary if the horse is to carry a side-saddle. I should discard a horse with a very low wither if I rode side-saddle. You should feel, as you look at the animal, that the saddle would almost stay in position without girths.

The chest, viewed from in front, should be neither too narrow – when he will tend to knock his front joints and fail to stay – nor too broad, when he will tend to roll in his paces and be slow, neither of which is desirable in a hunter. All the same, many a slow animal will carry you well, offsetting his tortoise-like paces by jumping like a stag. It is, after all, better to arrive later than not to arrive at all.

A free elbow is essential. A horse with a tied-in elbow will never be a really first-class performer.

'Scope' is most important, especially in a young animal, and this I have tried to describe on page 40.

Temperament is less likely to arise in the hunting field than anywhere else. Proverbially all equines love hunting and a season with hounds is the best possible cure for a nappy, bored, or lethargic horse or pony.

'A good sort' This brings me to a type of horse or pony which in both human and equine worlds is called 'a good sort'. Whereas the term when applied to humans can be slightly derogatory, the very opposite is the case when applied to a horse or pony. Again it is difficult to describe this inestimable type in words. I can but try.

Take, for example, a hunter. He may be plain of his head; may have a Roman nose; he may use his knee more than you really care for, but there is something about him that you instinctively like. For instance, no one can deny that although a bit plain and lacking in quality, he stands four square on first-class limbs, his bone is flat and there is no impression of roundness or lymphatic tendencies. True, he is slightly back at the knee, but what depth through the heart, what a good loin, and just look at those hocks! Stand behind him and see what a good one he is to follow; those good thighs for instance. Oh yes, his tail is set a bit too low but then so are his hocks, and he has the look of a real workman.

A good sort is an invaluable animal. He may not win you prizes in the show ring, although there are many occasions when preference can justifiably be given him over an eye-catching but inferior type. He may lack quality but he will be capable of giving you infinite pleasure over a maximum number of years. He will be easier to keep in condition, and nine times out of ten will be an extremely good ride and a good all-round performer. Above all, he frequently is that rarity, a no-trouble horse.

This is one of the many contradictions constantly met with in the world of horses, to which the inexperienced must gradually become accustomed if they are ever to be all-round horse judges.

The Arab Horse Society

The term 'Arab' means a horse in whose pedigree there is none other than pure Arab blood.

The term 'Anglo-Arab' means the progeny of breeding between

Arab stallions and Thoroughbred mares, or vice versa, or inter-breeding of their progeny; so that there is no strain of blood other than Arab and Thoroughbred in the pedigree. For this purpose Thoroughbred refers to a horse entered in the Thoroughbred General Stud Book maintained by Weatherbys or in the Thoroughbred stud book of any foreign country whose records are acceptable to the Stud Book Committee of the Society.

The term 'Part-bred Arab' means a horse or pony other than an Arab or Anglo-Arab whose pedigree contains not less than 25% (12½% for animals born before 1st January, 1974) of Arab blood deriving from a parent or parents registered with the Society or such foreign authority as shall be acceptable to the Council of the Society.

Arabs

Pure-bred Arabs are registered in the main body of the Arab Horse Society Stud Book. There are also an Anglo-Arab Stud Book and a Part-bred Arab Register.

The greatest debt we owe to Arab blood is that, as I have said before, it is the root source of all our Thoroughbreds. Arabs stand next to their improved descendants, the Thoroughbred racehorse. The Arab blood undeniably gives just that something which others have not got.

While none can approach the Thoroughbred for speed and per-formance, no one can doubt the stamina of the Arab. This blood is also extremely prepotent.

The characteristics of a pure-bred Arab horse are a small, chiselled head with concave profile, tapering to a small muzzle with full, sensitive, fine nostrils; large lustrous eyes placed slightly lower on the skull than in other breeds; broad forehead, small pricked, alert ears, slightly curled; deep, wide jowl; proud arched neck; well-set-on head; clean windpipe; withers not always well defined, but run-ning into a short, strong, level back; deep chest; well-ribbed-up body, with a tendency to round ribs; strong loin; well-set-on and gaily carried tail.

The best Arabs have good, hard, flat bone of excellent quality. Thighs are usually well developed but sometimes with a tendency to less well-developed second thighs; excellent hard, well-shaped feet.

Movement is low, with good shoulder movement but little, if any, raising of the knee, which is typical. The canter is their natural gait.

Nearly all have presence and nearly all have 'Arab' quality.

At the same time, there are a lot of 'flat-catchers' about (especially amongst the part-breds), lacking in bone and of indifferent conformation. They get away with it because they present an attractive picture to the unwary.

Arabs are now bred all over the world. Everywhere it goes this blood has tremendous influence on other breeds. I can never understand why so many Arab adherents get so hot under the collar over any criticism. Instead, they should surely have a superiority complex because we undoubtedly have to thank Arab blood for so much. Fanatical breeders are apt to resent the fact that Arabs sometimes have to stand down to the very thing they themselves have created. To me it is like a beautiful mother being jealous of an even more beautiful daughter. There can be no disputing the fact that Thoroughbreds dominate all fields, but this is no reason to decry the source from which they sprang. I am certainly the first to acknowledge this debt, while preferring the best upgraded from the original source: *upgraded* is the operative word.

Pure-bred Arabs may not be able to compete equally with Thoroughbreds on the racecourse, in the show ring, the jumping arena, the polo ground or in three-day events, but they shine in endurance and long-distance tests demanding stamina, while their influence and value as foundation stock is immense.

Anglo-Arabs

The mixing of the best Thoroughbred and Arab blood produces extremely good results. The Anglo-Arab in the UK is the result of crossing Arab horses and Thoroughbred horses registered in the main body of the GSB, and the consequent crossing and re-crossing of these animals and their progeny, allowing any percentages of Arab and Thoroughbred blood in the produce.

For a time too much emphasis was placed on Thoroughbred blood which resulted in a loss of Arab attributes of hardness and endurance.

Anglo-Arabs make first-class riding horses. Though they do not beat the Thoroughbreds in show classes, they have done so in long-distances riding, and show jumping, horse trials and dressage.

Part-bred Arabs

Many and varied are the horses and ponies in this Register, and to qualify for entry a minimum of 25 per cent Arab blood is necessary. While many top show animals are included, there are many more which leave much to be desired, especially in conformation. To me, a *bad* part-bred Arab is an abomination.

Having said this, I freely admit that a large proportion of our leading children's show ponies are part-bred Arab. The operative word here, however, is *part*. Too much of this blood is a mistake – a little is immensely valuable.

Shows Two annual summer shows are held by the Arab Horse Society, one in the north at Haydock Park, and the other adjacent to London. Classifications include pure-bred Anglo- and part-bred Arabs, both in hand and ridden. In addition eighteen regional organisations of the AHS have been formed and run their own local shows.

Classes for Arabs are usually included at other major shows, while part-bred Arab ponies are catered for in-hand all over the British Isles, and are eligible for any open class under saddle, especially children's classes. Also, Arab horseracing, under regulations approved by the Jockey Club, is growing in popularity.

Membership and registration Apply to the AHS Administrative Centre, Windsor House, The Square, nr Marlborough, Wilts.

The British Show Hack, Cob and Riding Horse Association

This Association's objects are:

(1) To improve the conditions under which hacks, cobs and riding horses are shown.
(2) To encourage shows to use the Association's recommendations, especially in selection of judges from the Association's panel and with regard to its classification of classes and height.
(3) To safeguard the interests of members in every possible way.

The Association also emphasises the importance and necessity of appointing lady judges who ride side-saddle to officiate when a class for ladies' side-saddle is in the schedule. It also hopes to obtain more classes for novices with a view to encouraging new owners.

Membership and panel of judges list are available on application to Mrs R. Smith, Rookwood, Packington Park, Meriden, Warwickshire, CV7 7HF (Tel: 0676 23535).

Hacks
The various classification for hacks are as follows:

    (a) Hacks – mares or geldings exceeding 14.2 hh but not exceeding 15 hh.
    (b) Hacks – mares or geldings exceeding 15 hh but not exceeding 15.3 hh.
    (c) Ladies' side-saddle – mares or geldings exceeding 14.2 hh but

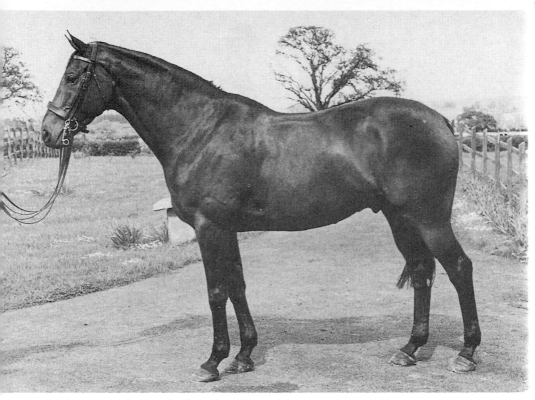

Lightweight hunter – Swanborne.

Middleweight hunter – Elite.

Heavyweight hunter – Seabrook.

Small hunter – Swindon Wood.

Hack – Tenterk.

Small hack – Vitality.

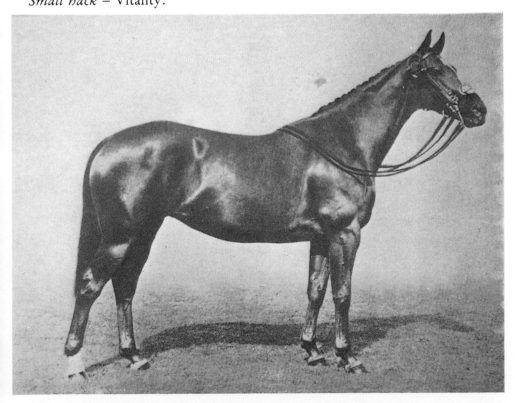

Cob – Sport.

Working hunter – Classic Tales.

15 hh working hunter pony – Sunnydale.

13 hh working hunter pony – Sefton Tony of Alderbourne.

Thoroughbred pony stallion – Ardencaple.

Thoroughbred pony stallion – Celtic Ballad.

Riding pony broodmare – Comberton Dance of the Eagles.

Riding pony broodmare – Arden Tittle-Tattle.

Riding pony stallion – Twylands Troubadour.

Riding pony yearling – Rosevean Sea Pigeon.

not exceeding 15.3 hh, suitable to carry and be ridden by a lady side-saddle.

(d) Novice hacks – mares or geldings which have not won £25 or more in hack classes (ladies' and pairs classes excepted), at shows affiliated to the Association, prior to the 1st January of each season.

The word 'hack' dates from the days before the internal combustion engine changed the face of the world. Hacks in those days were the horses upon which foxhunters, doctors, clergy, notaries, etc., rode to the meets or on their various duties.

The show hacks of today should be quality animals. Hacks cannot be bred – they happen. The best are undoubtedly Thoroughbred. Many have been bought off the racecourse, but only those with exceptional temperaments ever settle down enough to behave as a show hack should, and temperament is all-important. The hack must have manners and be a comfortable ride. There may be disagreement about what constitutes a hack, but the basic principles are the same: namely, correct proportions, 'scope', good limbs with plenty of bone, balance enabling the animal to give a smooth performance, a steady head carriage, acceptance of the bit resulting in free forward movement with no evasions, a flowing, graceful movement using the whole shoulder, with slight knee elevation, a little suspension, and – to use common parlance – a pointing of the toe. He must have presence but not a peacocky outlook.

As in the theatre or film business, the producer is all important. His task is made easier if the animal he has to produce has natural balance and natural movement and is of an equable temperament. But expert production can and often does hide a multitude of sins: as on the stage or film set, so in the showring; many a star has been produced from unpromising material. How often have I sat and smiled when I have seen what I have known to be a thoroughly indifferent animal mesmerising the judges by virtue of clever production and presentation, while the owner of by far the best horse sat disconsolately in the background. Change the producer and the result would have been very quickly reversed.

Temperament is all-important in a hack. He must have manners, and yet these are the very classes where we can usually anticipate a rodeo! You have only to sit at the ringside at Wembley and, if it hasn't happened before, wait till the awards are presented and the clapping breaks out, to see how a hack should *not* behave! There must surely be something wrong with production that this almost invariably happens.

97

I am probably again committing the sin of thinking that things are not what they used to be, but I am not the only one who considers that hack classes have deteriorated of recent years. Is it because they cannot be found or because people do not recognise them when they see them, or because, having recognised them, they fail in production? I suspect that it is a bit of all three.

As stated, the best are undoubtedly Thoroughbred. Many have been bought off the racecourse and many that could have been hacks were spoilt before they got a chance to prove it. Breaking and schooling, if any, in the racing world, leaves much to be desired.

Watching some novice hack classes today, I cannot help wondering how their owners could ever have imagined they could win with them. However, it is better to have competed and lost than never to have competed at all.

Small hacks have always been hard to find. Today, these classes seem to be headed by out-grown ponies. Just as one often sees a hack in a pony class, so one sees ponies in hack classes. They may have excellent conformation and quality but some lack bone, or they may have bone and conformation but lack quality. Small hacks today lack that essential substance and *élan*, or they interpret the latter by exuberance, which is not at all the same thing.

I am not going to try to describe here how to produce a hack. All I will say is that it is very much better to do a little well than to be too ambitious and try to do a lot only to do it badly.

Do not overdo it in your enthusiasm. I once saw an exhibitor so anxious to impress that, having at the end of his show dropped his reins to prove the manners of his mount, he then took out his handkerchief with a flourish and blew his nose; whereupon his horse took off!

In my opinion, a hack should be rideable with the reins in one hand. Well-trained polo ponies are infinitely better rides than many so-called hacks.

Cobs

A cob is a cross-bred animal, or he can be simply a mongrel. In any case he is another example of chance breeding. You can also have a cob-type pony.

The show classification is: not exceeding 15.1 hh, lightweights capable of carrying up to 14 stone, heavyweight over 14 stone.

As well as cobs of riding type, there are harness cobs.

Breeding cobs – like hacks and ponies (other than native breeds) - is pure fluke breeding. Many good ones have happened, however, through crossing Thoroughbreds with miscellaneous mares of substance.

A riding cob if he is to qualify for the title of a real show animal, must be up to weight but must also have quality. You only have to look at an Aldin print to see his make and shape; the sensible head, sometimes Roman-nosed, full, generous eye, readily cocked ears on a shapely neck, crested on the top side and running into well-developed withers.

In the better types there is no suspicion of a loaded, straight shoulder, which is laid back like a Thoroughbred's, with depth through the heart. The round-barrelled, harnessy types were and still are correct in the cart, but not to ride.

He must be short-coupled, with a good front and powerful quarters. His limbs can be common and lymphatic with rounded joints, but a show cob must have all the attributes of a good hunter, with short cannon bones, plenty of good flat bone, and clean, strong hocks.

Because of suspected common ancestry at least on one side, many cobs are *slightly* back of the knee which may be forgiven, but not at top shows.

He may also use his knee a little, but even if he does gallop a bit high he will be a good ride provided he is balanced, which so many of this type are.

He is economical because cobs are nearly always good doers; because he is short-coupled he is easy to keep in condition, and carrying weight is nothing to him. He is usually mannerly and very lovable. The quality cob is capable of being up with hounds all day and can win hunter trials. The coarser-bred, phlegmatic type is the old gentleman's patent safety.

Docking cobs' tails was once all the fashion. But no one would wish to continue this indignity, which also deprives the animal of his chief defence against flies. It was therefore a good thing when docking became illegal.

Riding Horses

Riding horses are one of the most popular show classes, staging two sections: up to 15.2 hh, and 15.2 hh and over. The true riding horse is an animal with quality, that could be described as being between a hack and a lightweight hunter. There are now qualifying classes at county shows for both the Royal International and the Horse of the Year Show.

99

The British Warmblood Society

This Society was formed in 1978 to develop a British-bred competition horse using proven European warmblood competition lines and their crosses. It holds two shows per year: a stallion grading show in February, and a two-day breed show in mid-August. The prime purpose of both shows is to assess all breeding stock.

Stallions are shown in hand and loose; mares and youngstock are shown in hand only. Exhibits are expected to be forward-going and should extend well at the trot.

For membership and registration contact Mrs Debbie Wallin, Moorlands Farm, New Yatt, Witney, Oxon (Tel: 0993 86673).

The Cleveland Bay Horse Society

One of the oldest British breeds, fixed in type for many years and closely allied to the foundation stock of Thoroughbreds. Today Cleveland Bays and their crosses are valuable as show jumpers, hunters, eventers, and show, dressage and police horses. Used extensively in the past as carriage horses, and still used in the Royal carriages, the Duke of Edinburgh has had considerable success with his team of part-bred Clevelands in international driving competitions.

In 1983 a Stallion Premium Scheme was set up, with the help of the Horserace Betting Levy Board. Horses are inspected during the autumn and premiums awarded for the following year.

Many shows now include Cleveland Bay classes.

Membership For registration and information apply to Mr J. F. Stephenson, York Livestock Centre, Murton, York, YO1 3UF (Tel: York 489731).

The Clydesdale Horse Society of Great Britain and Ireland

This is the only draught horse of Scotland. Early in the nineteenth century, farmers in Clydesdale – now known as Lanarkshire – were doing their best by selective breeding to perfect a type of draught horse which later became known everywhere as the Clydesdale. Since then, the north of England has been associated with the breed, which has continued to travel southwards until today representatives are to be found in almost every part of England, Wales and Ireland.

A good Clydesdale should give an impression of strength and activity. The idea is not grossness and bulk, but quality and weight. The ideal colour is dark brown with a defined white stripe, dark-coloured forelegs and white hind shanks. They have exceptionally good temperaments and have long proved ideal draught horses for all haulage purposes.

Clydesdale stallions have been used to cross with other heavy breeds of weight and substance, with the added attraction of beautiful legs and feet. No other heavy breed has quite the true and perfect movement of this one. This blood has also been used for producing heavyweight hunters.

The Society was founded in 1887 and the first volume of the Stud Book, which is kept up to date, was published in 1878.

Membership particulars from Mr Robert Gilmour, 24 Beresford Terrace, Ayr (Tel: 0292 281650).

The British Percheron Horse Society

This breed originated in the small district of France of about sixty square miles called La Perche. French farmers had been breeding horses for a hundred years or more, distinctive in both type and colour. In the earliest days they aimed to breed a horse with enough weight, spirit and action to pull heavy vehicles – whether coaches or military equipment – at a fast trot.

During the 1914–18 War, thousands of pure-bred and half-bred Percherons were bought by Canada, Argentine, and USA, where Percherons already outnumbered any other heavy breeds. They used them for Army transport work with the British Expeditionary Force. Thus breeders in this country got to hear of this type of horse and were so impressed with its performance that in 1918 the British Percheron Horse Society was founded, and 36 stallions and 321 mares were imported into England in the years 1918–1922.

With the decline in the use of heavy horses, fewer Percherons are to be seen in this country today, but numbers are still used on farms all over the Fenlands and in County Durham. Percheron mares have also been successfully crossed with Thoroughbred blood to produce useful heavy and middleweight hunters.

Stallions should stand not less than 16.3 hh and mares not less than 16.1 hh. They should have a strong, not too short neck, fully crested in stallions; wide chest, deep laid-back shoulders; back strong and short ribs well sprung; and deep throughout; exceptionally wide

101

quarters with length from hip to tail, avoiding any suggestion of a goose rump. Strong forearms; full second thighs, big knees, broad hocks; heavy, flat bone, short cannons, pasterns of medium length and feet of medium size; heels free from hair. Straight, bold action with a long, free stride; hocks well flexed. Colour grey, or black with a minimum of white. Fine-coated. The whole picture should be of balanced power.

Membership and registrations on application to Mrs A. Neaves, ℅ Neaves and Neat, 52A Broad Street, Ely, Cambridgeshire (Tel: 0353 667005).

The Shire Horse Society

It is claimed for the Shire horse that he is the purest survivor of the early type of the Great Horse, which carried the knights in full armour. Undoubtedly, the Shire breed was originally developed for military purposes, and then as a faster, more thorough method of cultivation than man or ox. In addition the need for transport horses capable of moving great weights caused breeders to turn their attention to the development of horses capable of filling these requirements.

In height, a Shire stands between 16.2 hh and 17.2 hh, the average being about 17 hh. Girth varies from 6–8 feet (1.8–2.4 m); in stallions, 11 inches (27.9 cm) of bone is ample, and in mares from 9–11 inches (22.8–27.9 cm). This must be flat, flinty, and never spongy.

Stallions weigh up to 22 cwt (1110 kg).

Basic conformation is the same as for any other breed of horse or pony, but the true ribs should be well sprung as well as the false. The most important essential is good feet. Action, of course, must be straight and true all round.

Thirty years ago the Shire horse stood on the brink of extinction. But the Shire was held back from the abyss and has recovered to such an extent that it is now preparing a future in the twenty-first century.

In a remarkable and unique act of co-operation the four British heavy horse societies – the Shire Horse Society, the Suffolk Horse Society, the Clydesdale Society and the British Percheron Society – joined together in a three-year research project.

This in-depth appraisal of the possibilities for harnessing heavy horses power beyond the year 2000 has now been completed, with a 75,000 word report published with the support of the Royal Agricultural Society of England.

Despite mechanisation, there are over 3,500 members of the Shire Horse Society, which issues its own Stud Book and holds its annual show on the East of England Agricultural Society's showground at Peterborough. Silver spoons are also offered at 163 national, county and affiliated shows, while specials and rosettes for the best Shire exhibits are given at the London Harness Horse Parade, in London on Easter Monday annually, and at other parades and events.

The Dubonnet Red Shire Horse of the Year Championship is held annually at Wembley's Horse of the Year event in October. Qualifiers for this award are chosen at fourteen of the major agricultural show events during the year.

Membership and registrations on application to Mr R. W. Bird East of England Showground, Peterborough, PE2 0XE (Tel: 0733 234451).

The Suffolk Horse Society

This is an East-Anglian breed. Its genealogy can be traced back to the eighteenth century, but there is mention in Camden's *Britannia* that it dates back to 1506. A curious feature is the fact that every animal of the breed now in existence traces descent in direct male line in an unbroken chain to a horse foaled in 1760. The form of this animal tallies with specimens of today, with slight modifications which judicious introduction of more elegant elements would be likely to effect.

This breed's two chief characteristics I think are compactness and hardy constitution. They are often called Suffolk Punches. The dictionary describes this as 'a variety of English horse, short-legged and barrel bodied – a short fat fellow'.

As a horse for agricultural work, the Suffolk has no superior. On the soil at any work he can hold his own against all comers. He is renowned for his indomitable pluck, his 'never say die' at a dead pull, and his iron constitution.

The ideal Suffolk Punch must be chestnut; a star, a little white on the face, and a few silver hairs, are no detriment. Head – big with a broad forehead, well set on to a strong, well-shaped neck running into long, muscular, well-thrown-back shoulders. Deep, round ribs from shoulder to flank, with a strong back, loin and hindquarters; wide in front and behind, the tail well set up with powerful second thighs. Legs should be straight, with fair sloping pasterns, big knees,

103

clean hocks on short cannon bones, free from coarse hair. Being tied-in at the elbow is a serious defect. Good, large, sound feet. He should walk smartly and truly and be capable of producing a well-balanced trot. They seldom, if ever, contract greasy heels.

Membership particulars from Mr P. Ryder-Davies, 6 Church Street, Woodbridge, Suffolk, IP12 1DH (Tel: 0728 746534).

The Hackney Horse and Pony Society

Established in 1883, the aims and objects of this Society are to improve the breed and to promote the breeding of harness horses and ponies and hackney horses and ponies.

This is one of the oldest and purest breeds. Its origin is almost exclusively British. A good hackney, be it horse or pony, is a lovely and inspiring sight. As well as having good conformation, a top-class hackney should ooze quality, and action is, of course, all-important. They must not only 'go' in front but must use, and therefore flex, their hocks. Shoulder action is free, with high ground-covering knee action, the forelegs thrown well forward and not just per-pendicularly. There should be a slight suspension of the foot at each stride, which lends grace of movement. Action behind should be the same, but to a lesser degree. Action should be straight and true, with no dishing.

Standing still, the hackney stands four square, forelegs straight but with the hind legs extended so that it covers a lot of ground. This stance is peculiar to this breed and should *not* be copied by other breeds. The general impression should be of extreme alertness, even of being 'on springs'.

Hackney blood can also produce good riding ponies without knee action and with quality, for originally the hackney pony was used largely for riding, and has only been driven for the last seventy or eighty years.

There is controversy about registered hackneys and hackney-type horses and ponies competing in open private driving classes. There are two points of view. Obviously, as there are hardly ever enough of the former, except at the larger shows, to justify staging a separate class, show organisers have no alternative but to allow them to compete with non-hackneys or exclude them altogether. On the other hand, if they are permitted to compete, the ordinary harness horse or pony, however good, has little chance against them. My own view is that however much one wishes to have hackneys at a show – especially from the spectator angle – and however hard it may be on exhibitors, a show organiser either has to put on a class for 'hackneys and hackney-type' (and then who is to be the arbiter as to whether the latter are or are not?), in which case the entries rarely if ever justify the prize money, which has to be considerable or the hackney owners will not enter, and the hackney-type owners will not enter because they are up against pure-bred hackneys; or he lumps them in with the ordinary harness horses, when he loses the entries of those who refuse to compete against hackneys. It is a problem which has so far not been solved.

Stud Book First published in 1755, it lists stallions and mares and gives other useful information.

Shows The Society holds its annual show in conjunction with the South of England Agricultural Show at Ardingly, Sussex, in June. Classes are also scheduled at other shows all over the country; particulars are obtainable from the Secretary.

Panel of judges Selected by the Society.

Registration and membership is effected through Miss S. Oliver, Clump Cottage, Chitterne, Warminster, Wiltshire BA12 0LL (Tel: 0985 50906).

The British Palomino Society

The Palomino is not a breed, but a colour, and a very lovely colour too. Known as the 'Golden Horse', Palominos are most attractive and extremely popular. They have been bred in America for very many years. Breeders in this country tended at first to put the accent on colour, but, while this is most important, conformation is equally so. Recently, improvement in the latter is evident and is to be applauded.

The British Palomino Society encourages breeders to improve colour, conformation and quality, maintains a Register of both horses and ponies, lays down a standard by which they shall be accepted for this Register, and offers advice and information. It provides inspectors in an endeavour to ensure that all animals which are registered conform to the required standard.

Classes for Palominos, both ridden and in hand, are staged at several shows, and the Society lays down a standard for their judging. Its own National Championship Show is held annually in June. The plaiting of manes and tails is not permitted.

105

Colour requirements

Body The colour of newly minted gold, or three shades lighter or darker. White non-facial markings and other discolorations should not extend above a line passing approximately through stifle and lower chest and printed on the identification form.

Mane and tail White, with not more than 15 per cent dark or chestnut hairs in either.

Eyes Dark brown, hazel, or black iris, both the same colour.

Skin Basically dark; round the eyes and nose mouse-coloured, brown, or black, except where the extension of a white facial marking into the nostrils makes the skin pink.

For registration and membership apply to Mrs P. Howell, Penrhiwllan, Llandysul, Dyfed SA44 5NZ (Tel: 0239 75387).

The British Spotted Pony Society

The inaugural meeting of this Society was held on 1st August, 1976. Its objects are to encourage the breeding of spotted ponies, veterinarily sound, of good conformation and quality. These ponies have been bred in this country by a few enthusiasts for many years.

The question is often asked: 'Are Appaloosas and "Spotteds" the same thing?' The answer is 'No'. The origin of the name Appaloosa is probably only about a hundred years old and is thought to have been coined from the Palouse River in the Columbia Basin, USA. The true 'Spotteds' are of much older origin.

Height Ponies not exceeding 14.2 hh.

Markings eligible for registration 'Leopard' – spots of any colour on a white or light-coloured background.

'Blanket' – animals having a white rump or back on which are spots of any colour.

'Snowflake' – white spots on a foundation of any colour.

Piebalds, skewbalds and dappled greys are not eligible.

Characteristics White sclera round the eye. Hooves striped yellowish-white and black or brown in vertical stripes. Bare skin, often pink, is mottled. Manes and tails can be sparse.

Usefulness All-purpose animals.

106

Shows The Society holds its own annual breed show and classes for spotted ponies are staged at some shows, details of which are obtainable from the Secretary.

For membership and registration apply to Miss L. R. Marshall, 17 School Lane, Dronfield, Sheffield S18 6RY.

The British Appaloosa Society

The British Appaloosa Society was formed in 1976 to cater for spotted horses over 14.2 hh. It is affiliated to the American Appaloosa Horse Club and has adopted, in most part, the latter's rules and standards. The Society now has about 600 members and 500 registered horses.

Height 14.2 hh and upwards.

Coat patterns There are eight basic coat patterns with unlimited combinations. Many animals carry dual patterns, such as roan and spots. The basic patterns are:
  'Spotted blanket' – dark forehand with white over loin and hips, with round or egg-shaped spots; spots may vary from 6–4 ins (12–100 mm) in diameter. Blankets may be small patches on the rump to large ones.
  'White blanket' – dark forehand with a blanket without spots, or nearly void of spots.
  'Marbles (or roan)' – base colour is usually red or blue roan, at times described as bay, brown or black roan. Marbles usually have 'varnish' marks.
  'Leopard' – base colour pure white with evenly distributed dark spots over the entire body from head to hoof.
  'Near leopard' – born with leopard-coloured body markings but with different coloured head and legs, or head and shoulders and legs. As the animal matures the dark colouring generally fades.
  'Few-spot-leopard' – has the basic colour of white with blue or red roan 'varnish marks' and just the odd spot.
  'Snowflake' – the base colour is dark with white spots over the body.
  'Frosted hip' – dark base colour with either frost or white spots on the loin and hips.

Characteristics Hardy, with a tractable temperament; sure-footed and active; good 'doers'; exceptionally versatile.

Parti-coloured skin is always evident in the genital region and frequently seen around the lips, muzzle, nostrils and eyes. The eyes should be surrounded by a white sclera.

The mane and tail are often sparse; and the hooves often striped.

For membership and registration contact Mrs Anne Howkins, 2 Frederick Street, Rugby, Warwickshire, CV21 2LN (Tel 0788 860535).

The British Morgan Horse Society

Though well known in the USA, the Morgan is a relative newcomer to the British Isles. Its breeding dates back to the late 1780s, when a 14.1 hh stallion was given to Justin Morgan in settlement of a debt. This small horse proved to have exceptional strength and stamina, and excelled in everything he did during his long life. Eventually given his owner's name, he worked on farms and in forests, pulled carts and won all kinds of races. His innumerable offspring inherited his intelligence, courage and equable temperament.

In the 1850s the world's fastest trotting stallion was Justin Morgan's bay great-grandson; and in the American Civil War, the Vermont Cavalry was mounted on Morgan horses.

The Morgan goes equally well under saddle and in harness. It is elegant, attractive and versatile; and its ease of management makes it an excellent all-round horse for the whole family.

Height 14–16 hh.

Colour Black, bay, brown, chestnut, with some white markings, socks or a star. Grey is not permitted.

Characteristics Small ears, large eyes, well-arched neck, long feet (unlike any other horse).

The action is high and rounded.

The mane and tail are full and flowing; and the tail sweeps the ground.

The general outline and aspect is classical, reminiscent of the horses depicted in old sporting prints.

For membership enquiries and details of the special displays put on by members of the Society during the summer months, contact Mrs A. Conner-Bulmer, George and Dragon Hall, Mary Place, London W11 (Tel: 01–229 8155).

The Haflinger Society of Great Britain

Haflingers were first imported into Great Britain in the 1960s. They are the native ponies of the Alpine farms of Austria and have a long history on the Continent. These versatile all-rounders make excellent ride and drive ponies and are said to possess kindly temperaments. Their most striking feature is their colour: the body is always chestnut with a flaxen mane and tail.

Height at three years Mares: 13.1–14.2 hh; colts: 13.3–14.2½ hh.

Characteristics Tough, adaptable, hard-working ponies. The face has a slight dish and the neck is well positioned and not too short. The chest is broad and deep and the back is short with strong quarters. The limbs are clean and sturdy with a good amount of bone. The chestnut colouring can vary through shades of light, middle, liver to red; the mane and tail colour must be flaxen – no other colour is acceptable.

For membership and registration contact the Secretary, Mrs Helen Robbins, 13 Parkfield, Pucklechurch, Bristol, BS17 3NR (Tel: 027582 3479).

12 British Mountain and Moorland Breeds

There are nine breeds of native ponies which have inhabited the British Isles since the Celtic invasion, if not before. They have inhabited much the same areas (such as Dartmoor, Exmoor and the New Forest), known as 'haunts', throughout the centuries. All are now also bred in innumerable studs throughout the country and overseas.

These ponies should not be regarded simply as juvenile mounts. Many of them are capable weight carriers and have carried adults for generations. Above all they are a national heritage, are invaluable as foundation stock for breeding both horses and ponies, with an increasingly big export value.

Considering the amount of alien blood which has been introduced over the years, it is remarkable and indicative of this prepotent blood that the individual characteristics, described later, have been retained. They even remained safely tucked away on mountains and moors when Henry VIII ordered all equines under 15 hh to be killed. They were listed in the Domesday Book along with wild animals.

It is obvious that breeders of whatever stock breed to demand unless they indulge in it purely as a hobby. Just as massive horses were imported and bred from – useful not only to carry knights in full armour but to provide meat in times of siege – so breeders throughout history have cut their cloth to suit their coat.

Before wheeled traffic was introduced, everyone rode on horseback and all merchandise was carried on pack animals. Cattle and sheep were also herded over the old drove roads – along which modern trekkers now ride – by drovers astride horses and ponies of substance, and, of necessity, hardy.

When roads, however rough and ready, replaced the drove roads and tracks, and wheeled vehicles came in, again horses and ponies were bred to meet demands, namely with substance but more active than in the past. Coach and pack horses performed prodigious feats pulling heavy vehicles in bad weather over appalling surfaces, sometimes at the gallop. Professional men of all categories sat behind fast-trotting cobs and stout ponies.

Again breeders met demand by mating our hardy native stock with Norfolk Trotters and Roadsters (believed to have been imported from Scandinavia). Our famous hackney horses and ponies are descended from crossings of Thoroughbred and native blood dating back to 1775. More and more active horses, cobs and ponies were bred to meet the demands of the highways: faster, lighter, more quality (and therefore with better performance) horses were bred as hunters and hacks.

Then came the internal-combustion engine which was to sweep equines off the road and streets and out of the fields.

Two World Wars followed when, of necessity, breeders cut down production to a minimum and our native ponies went in thousands to the slaughter-houses under the most unsavoury conditions. The toll of the knacker trade went on right until approximately 1959, with the peak period between 1952 and 1955. Gradually riding as a pastime staged a comeback. Money changed hands. Britain had never had it so good. People who previously could not afford to do so became owners of horses and ponies, and thousands took up hacking and trekking. The latter recreation has undoubtedly saved the larger native breeds from virtual extinction.

Luckily a number of dedicated and astute breeders had retained their foundation stock through thick and thin so that the individual breed characteristics were not lost, but all our mountain and moorland breeds were not really universally known, let alone appreciated.

I am ashamed to confess that I had never even heard of Dales and Fell ponies when in 1952 I founded the Ponies of Britain with the late Miss Gladys Yule. I am glad that this organisation was able to put British native ponies on the map, and to make not only breeders but also the general public appreciate and gradually come to recognise our natives as the basis of all ponies and very many horses.

Again breeders looked ahead and foresaw that lighter-boned, even more active, larger, and better riding animals would be in demand.

Increasingly too, the USA and Continental countries were taking an interest in our ponies. Only in comparatively recent years have American children been mounted on ponies instead of horses and this change of attitude is gradually developing on the Continent. There is an increasingly large demand for our native ponies and those upgraded from them overseas, and that these should be 'registered' ponies is essential.

I cannot emphasise too strongly the need to retain our native ponies as foundation stock. It is absolutely essential that we also keep the individual breed characteristics. Many breeders upgrade successfully by selective breeding inside the breed, thus retaining

111

both the substance and the characteristics, at the same time breeding a proportion to meet modern needs. This seems to be an ideal policy.

No one appreciates more than I do the need to introduce fresh blood, whether it be the equine or human race, but I feel that the result should be kept in a separate register. Every stud book should have a part-bred section and the progeny with alien blood should not be eligible for the stud book proper for several generations, and then, of course, only if by pure-bred registered stallions of whatever breed.

How many generations should elapse before qualifying for the stud book proper is a controversial subject. Some argue that all our native breeds admit to infusion of other blood, but it is only of comparatively recent years that proper stud books have been kept but it makes nonsense of these if alien blood is admitted, certainly within less than three generations. The Ponies of Britain stipulated that ponies with alien blood in their pedigrees should not be eligible for *mixed* mountain and moorland classes and championships until the fifth generation, while they could compete in their own breed classes if their society permitted. This ruling was only reached after much thought by knowledgeable unbiased breeders. It could only be implemented where show executives were prepared to check the entries and this is the reason why nearly every other show shut its eyes. So long as other exhibitors did not object and purchasers of native stock were not misled, this was their affair.

Division of Breeds for Mixed Classes
For the guidance of show secretaries the native breeds are usually divided into two categories for Mixed M and M Classes as follows:

Large Breeds. Connemara, Dales, Fell, Highland, New Forest, Welsh Ponies, Section B; Welsh Ponies of Cob Type, Section C; Welsh Cobs, Section D.

Small Ponies: Dartmoor, Exmoor, Shetland, Welsh Mountain, Section A.

NB: A number of shows put the Welsh Ponies, Section B, in the Small Ponies Section, but as these ponies go up to 13.2 hh whereas the largest of all the small ponies is 12.3 hh, this is not popular. I recommend the above classification as the fairest.

The English Connemara Pony Society

Location Ireland – on the wild country between the Connaught coast on the west and Galway Bay in the south.

Origin Tradition has it that Spanish Barbs and Andalusian stallions from the Armada wrecks mated with the native ponies. Rich Galway merchants are said to have imported the finest Arab strains 300 or 400 years ago. Certain Connemara ponies show Arab tendencies, but these ponies undoubtedly existed before these dates.

Height 13 hh to 14.2 hh.

Colour Grey, black, bay, brown, dun, roan and chestnut, though the latter two are comparatively rare. Predominant colour: grey.

Characteristics Real pony type with small, quality heads and well-set-on tails. Some Arab characteristics. Free, easy, low action. Good, sloping, riding shoulders. Depth through the heart. Good bone. Great staying power. Hardy constitution, and intelligent.

Usefulness Excellent mounts for adult or child. Good all-round performers that can gallop and jump; revered for centuries by the most critical of horsemen. Excellent foundation stock when crossed with Thoroughbred or Arab blood for breeding larger animals, especially hunters.

Qualifications for registration in the Connemara Pony Breeder's Stud Book of Ireland:

(a) The sire and dam must be entered in the Connemara Pony Breeder's Stud Book in Ireland.

(b) Regardless of breeding, all ponies have to be inspected and passed as suitable for registration after they have reached the minimum registration age, namely two years.

(c) As from 1967, a pony in respect of which a foaling return was not duly furnished within one month of the date of foaling, may not be accepted for registration.

Registration in Ireland is effected through the Secretary of the Connemara Pony Breeders' Stud Book.

Qualifications for registration with the English Connemara Pony Society:

(a) Connemara ponies from Ireland and the UK, must be by a registered Connemara stallion out of a registered Connemara mare, the names and registered numbers being inscribed in the Stud Book.

(b) Any application to register in the colt, mare or gelding section an animal whose dam is registered in the ECPS Stud Book, must

113

be made by the breeder within six months after the birth of the animal.

(c) Any application to register in the colt, mare or gelding section an animal whose dam is registered in the CPBS Stud Book (in Ireland), may be done at any time if accompanied by the necessary documents.

(d) Additional rules for the stallion section: colts, regardless of breeding, have to be inspected and passed as suitable for registration as a stallion at the age of two years by CPBS or ECPS inspectors, have a veterinary examination and be blood-typed.

Horses and ponies with one parent in the ECPS Stud Book are eligible for inclusion in the Part-bred Connemara Register.

Registration The English Connemara Pony Society was founded in 1947 and started its own stud book in 1978. Until that time ponies were registered with the National Pony Society.

Shows The ECPS holds two shows a year: the breed in-hand show in July, and the ridden show in August. It also operates a highly successful performance award scheme, which runs throughout the year, and there is a system of mare and stallion premiums to encourage continued improvement in the breed and progeny performance.

The CPB Society annual show is held at Clifden, County Galway, Ireland, in August.

Membership details of ECPS membership and registration can be obtained from Mrs M. V. Newman, 2 The Leys, Salford, Chipping Norton OX7 5FD (Tel: 0608 3309).

For information concerning the CPBS contact the Secretary, 73 Dalysfort Road, Salthill, Galway, Ireland (Tel: 010 353 9122909).

The Dales Pony Society

Location The Upper Dales of the Rivers Tyne, Allen, Wear and Tees.

Origin Together with the Fells, which are, so to speak, their cousins, they date back probably to the Celtic invasion or before. Both breeds carried the lead ore and other merchandise from the mines in the far hills down to the seaports and smelting works, along the old drove roads used today by modern pony-trekkers. For centuries they have done all manner of work on the grassland farms of the North Country, and still carry their owners out shepherding today.

When used as pack ponies, they could carry as much as sixteen stone on each side of the body and averaged 240 miles a week. They became famous as trotting ponies and matches were held. Now they are used extensively as ride and drive ponies and are still valuable on North Country farms.

Height Not exceeding 14.2 hh.

Colour Black, brown, bay and grey, very occasionally roan, with white markings only as star on face, snip on nostril, and up to the fetlocks on the hind legs only.

Characteristics Smart, cobby appearance with stylish action, but must be of pony type. Short, strong back (shorter than the Fells); good loin and quarter. Any amount of bone with a lot of 'feather' of silky hair. Pony head with abundance of fine hair on mane and tail, which should not curl. Noted for their good, open, hard feet.

Usefulness A real utility pony.

After the war, the Dales pony, in common with some other of the native breeds, hit a bad patch. Tractors superseded them on the farms; farmers no longer wanted fast-trotting ponies to take them to town; milk floats were electrified; mines were mechanised; and while many were, and still are, used for shepherding, many ponies went to the meat market and the breed was in danger of extinction. Luckily, a few dedicated breeders carried on, and today the Dales Pony Society is a very active body, full of enthusiasm for the Dales pony which has made a great comeback in the last few years.

This is also first-class foundation stock when crossed with Thoroughbred blood. The fillies, again put to a Thoroughbred, produce excellent hunters and utility animals of all kinds.

These ponies have sensible, generous temperaments and are easily handled and broken.

Demand now exceeds supply and registrations with the Society are increasing every year.

Qualifications for registration:
Section A: Ponies of fully known parentage only are allowed into the Stud Book, and then only provided they comply on markings and height.

Section B: Ponies by fully registered parents but of incorrect height or markings. Also ponies upgraded from Section C if by a registered Dales stallion.

Section C: Ponies that are upgraded from Section D if by a registered Dales stallion.

Section D: Ponies of unknown breeding but of Dales type, provided they were accepted by inspectors nominated by the Dales Pony section. This section closed in 1971.

Stallions: All stallions must be Section A.

Measurement All Dales ponies competing at the breed shows may be measured at three years old.

Shows Dales Pony Society hold the following shows annually – a spring breed show in May at Barnard Castle, and an annual breed show in August.

For membership and registration apply to Mrs J. C. Ashby, c/o 196 Springvale Road, Walkley, Sheffield S6 3NU. A Stud Book is issued by the Society.

The Dartmoor Pony Society

Location A high tract of roughly 122,000 acres of moorland, lying between the English Channel on the south and the Atlantic Ocean on the north, known as Dartmoor. Altitude in parts 1,000 to 2,000 feet above sea level. Now bred all over the British Isles, and in Germany, Scandinavia, France, Holland and America.

Origin The breed dates back over 2,000 years.

Height Not exceeding 12.2 hh (127 cm).

Colour Black, bay or brown preferred, but no colour bar except skewbald and piebald. Excessive white markings discouraged.

Characteristics Small head, well set on and blood-like, with very small alert ears. Strong neck but not too heavy and in proportion; stallions moderate crest. Back, loin and hindquarters strong and well covered with muscle, but back inclined to be long. Tail set high and full.

Action Low and free and from the shoulders. No knee action.

Usefulness Superlatively good children's ponies, having good temperaments and intelligence without vice, and being easy to handle and break. Very good foundation stock for breeding larger ponies,

116

especially if crossed with Thorougbred blood.

Qualifications NB: Ponies can only be registered in the Stud Book if both parents are registered. Only ponies bred in Great Britain are eligible for inclusion either in the Stud Book or in the Supplementary Register. Ponies foaled in one year must be registered before 31st December in the year in which they are born.

For five years a Supplementary Register was opened for the entry of mares inspected and approved by a panel of Breed Judges. The first grade (SR I mares) have no pedigree. The second grade (SR II) are ponies by full registered stallions out of SR I mares; these also have to be inspected and approved as above. All ponies in the Register are marked with the DPS brand when accepted. THIS SR I REGISTER CLOSED ON 31ST MARCH, 1966. SR ponies are NOT eligible to compete in classes for registered Dartmoors.

Stallions at stud A list of these is available from the Secretary.

Shows Dartmoor Pony Shows; The South of England; Devon County; Bath and West; Royal Agricultural; National Pony; Ponies UK; Three Counties; Great Yorkshire; EANP Show.

Secretary Mrs M. Danford, Fordans, 17 Clare Court, Newbiggen Street, Thaxted, Essex (Tel: 0371 830178).

The Exmoor Pony Society

Location The moors in Somerset and Devon.

Origin The Exmoor Pony Society claims that the ancestors of its present ponies evolved in an ice age about a million years ago. Certainly it is one of the oldest breeds.

Height Mares not exceeding 12.2 hh; stallions not exceeding 12.3 hh.

Colour Bay, dun, or brown only. No white markings or white hairs anywhere.

Characteristics Deep, wide chest, slightly long backs but powerful loins. Shoulder should be set well back. Inclined to have short, thick necks. Grand limbs and feet.

Mealy muzzle, the colour of oatmeal; wide forehead with prominent full eyes, slightly hooded like a hawk, known locally as 'toad

117

eyes'. The eyes are surrounded by the same mealy colour as on the muzzle. The ears are short, thick and pointed.

The coat is a different texture from any other native breed: i. e. harsh and springy, in winter carrying no bloom but in summer close and hard and shining like brass. It is dense, and above all, weatherproof. Foals (or suckers) have thick woolly undercoats with a top coat of long, harsh hairs which act as an overcoat to keep out rain.

Action Straight, smooth, with no exaggerated knee action.

I would warn you, however, that all ponies with mealy muzzles need not necessarily be pure-bred Exmoors. A few ponies graze on the moors which are not true Exmoors; they are just 'ponies of Exmoor', though most probably have more than a touch of pure blood in them. *All pure-bred ponies are branded.*

Usefulness Hardy ponies – an asset which, however, should not be exploited – make splendid children's ponies provided they are properly broken and handled. They are becoming increasingly popular as strong driving ponies, easily matched for colour and stride. Good foundation stock to provide a line of sturdy and intelligent larger ponies and horses which are wonderful hunters and jumpers, by crossing them with Thoroughbreds. They endow their progeny with stamina, soundness, performance and intelligence.

Qualification Fully registered parents on both sides (also see under 'Inspection').

Registrations and amendments are issued yearly in January to holders of the stud book, which is thereby kept up to date. The complete book, in loose leaf form, can be obtained from the Secretary.

Produce from ponies exported to Europe are included in a separate section, provided they are the produce of imported registered stock.

Inspection Foals are inspected in the autumn by two inspectors. Prospective purchasers are encouraged to visit the herds during the short time that they are on the farms for the inspections.

Register of first-cross ponies A pony having one registered Exmoor parent is eligible for entry in the First-Cross Register.

The Society's star This is a four-pointed star affixed to the near shoulder.

Shows Exhibitors in Exmoor breed classes must be members of the Exmoor Pony Society or become members within a month of date of show. All ponies must be registered. They must be shown in a natural condition (this rule does not apply to ridden classes.)

All shows receiving financial or other support from the Exmoor Pony Society must have their Exmoor classes judged by a judge on the Exmoor Pony Panel.

Registered ponies entered in ridden classes at any show at which such classes are held under EPS rules, shall be three years old or over.

Sales There are no public sales of registered stock.

Sweden, Denmark and Holland are the main importing countries. In recent years a few ponies have also been exported to the Falkland Islands and America.

For membership and registration apply to Mr D. Mansell, Glen Fern, Waddicombe, Dulverton, Somerset (Tel: 03984 490).

The Fell Pony Society

Location The fells of Cumbria, Westmorland, and the northern end of the Pennine Range, 1,000 to 3,000 feet above sea level.

Origin Much the same as the Dales but less contaminated by other blood. Run very true to type and, like the Dales, have been used through the centuries carrying lead ore and merchandise, as drove ponies and general-utility animals on grassland farms in the north of England.

Height Limited to 14 hh. – not more.

Colour Black predominates, with browns, bays and very occasional greys. Broken colours do not exist in pure-bred ponies, and chestnuts are also barred. White markings, unless very slight, are most unpopular.

Characteristics Small pony heads with a lot of quality. Good length of rein. Good limbs with plenty of bone, feathered with fine silky hair. Massive, long, fine manes and tails, which must not curl. Good hard open feet. Delightful temperaments, easy to break, handle, and maintain.

Usefulness Ideal all-purpose, no-trouble pony for both adults and young people. Able to live out like all the native breeds provided they are fed extra rations and hay in hard winter. Excellent foundation stock for breeding larger animals, especially when crossed

119

with Thoroughbred blood, thus providing more quality and better performance plus the attributes of the native pony. Prominent winners at all the leading shows. Patronised by HM the Queen.

Qualifications

A Stud Book is published annually by the Society in the following sections:

(1) Main section containing ponies that have two fully registered parents.
(2) 'A' – Filly foals from IS mares by a registered Fell stallion.
(3) 'B' – Filly foals from 'A' mares by registered stallions. (Filly foals from 'B' mares by registered stallions to go into main section.)

On the registration certificate the ponies will carry 'A' and 'B' after their names to indicate the different sections.

NB: The Dales and Fell breeds are partly reciprocal. Dales accept Fell stallions but Fells do not accept Dales stallions.

Shows The stallion show is held in May; a breed show in August; and performance trials in June and September.

Annual sale At Wigton in October.

For membership and registration apply to Mr C. Richardson, 19 Dragley Beck, Ulverston, Cumbria (Tel: 0229 52742).

The Highland Pony Society

Location The Scottish mainland and the Western Isles. Also now in studs in England.

Origin It is possible that antecedents of these ponies inhabited Britain before the Ice Age. The breed's basis is thought to be the North European horse, but throughout the ages there has been introduction of foreign blood which has blended with the original to produce the Highland pony of today. Thus they became known originally as (1) the Scottish mainland pony; and (2) the Western Isles pony, which was smaller.

Comparatively recently this division ceased to be recognised by the Highland Pony Society, and there are now two types: (1) the Island type, which tend to be smaller and more active; and (2) the Mainland type, which tend to be larger, heavier and stronger.

Modern ponies derive from two famous strains: (1) the Atholl

120

13.2 hh riding pony – Cusop Heiress.

12.2 hh riding pony – Drayton Caraway.

Cleveland Bay broodmare – Knaresborough Welcome.

Arab stallion – Golden Samurai.

Connemara broodmare – Copper Beech.

Dales – Galphay Supreme.

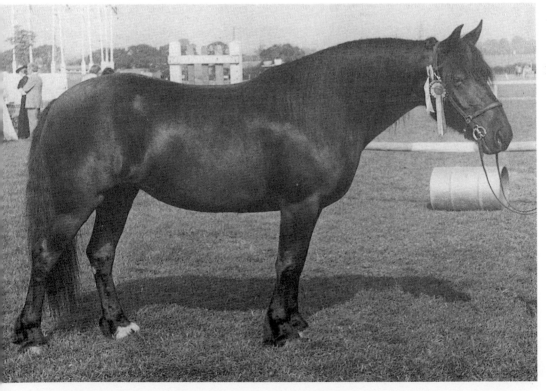

Dartmoor stallion – Hisley Salvo.

Exmoor stallion – Dunkery Buzzard.

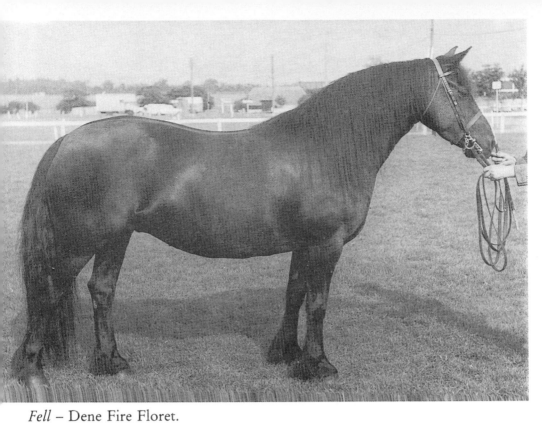

Fell – Dene Fire Floret.

Highland stallion – Swinton Dene.

New Forest – Fijal Prelude.

Shetland stallion – Bincombe Venture.

Welsh Section A – Stoatley Moonlight *and* Stoatley Primula
(*being driven by Anne Muir*).
Welsh Section B stallion – Twyford Signal.

Welsh Section C stallion – Synod William.

Welsh Cob (Section D) stallion – Llanarth Flying Comet.

strain from the Duke of Atholl's Stud, and (2) the Rosehaugh strain from the Avoch Stud. Both descend from two famous stallions, Herd Laddie and Bonnie Laddie.

Height Must not exceed 14.2 hh. Most Island ponies are about 13 hh.

Colour The most usual colours are grey and various shades of dun, that is, mouse dun, yellow dun, and cream dun. Black and brown were common but are not seen much today. There should be no white markings anywhere, other than a small star.

Characteristics An eel stripe along the spine and zebra markings on the forearm and second thigh are typical, but are not necessarily present. Head small and of pony type, well set on, with small ears, broad between bright, large, kind eyes, short between eyes and muzzle, with full nostrils. Neck strong and not short; arched, with profuse mane. Throat clean and not fleshy. Shoulders should be well set back, but this is not always so. Back short, with natural topline. Deep chest and ribs, which should be well sprung and close coupled. Quarters and thighs powerful. Limbs have good flat bone, with slight fringe of straight silken feather; forelegs placed well under weight of body, forearm strong; knees and hocks broad; short cannon bones but not too short pasterns. Feet, good, open, dark horn. Tail well set on, profuse but not curly.

Usefulness Famous on the moors for carrying deer and game. Used for all purposes on crofts and farms. Is now in tremendous demand as a trekking pony, for which it is ideally suited, being very sagacious and sure-footed, and up to a lot of weight. If properly schooled makes a good ride and can jump. Larger ponies are up to carrying sixteen stone; small Island type are suitable for children. Riding type greatly improved in recent years.

Qualifications Before being eligible for the Highland Stud Book proper, a Highland pony must have a recognised sire and dam already fully registered.

Only mares three years old and over, and stallions and geldings two years old or over, can be registered.

Appendixes The Appendix A Register was open to ponies of unknown pedigree and was closed to further entries in December, 1975.

Appendix B Register is open to female or gelded progeny of an Appendix A mare and a registered Highland stallion. Inspection is required for admission to Appendix B.

Appendix C Register is for the female or gelded progeny of an Appendix B mare and a registered Highland stallion. Inspection may not be required. The female or gelded progeny of an Appendix C mare is eligible for the Stud Book proper but inspection is required if it has white markings.

Progeny register This is open to Highland ponies of all classes and is only used an an initial record. When a Highland pony filly becomes three years old she is eligible either for the Appendix Register or the Stud Book proper, according to her qualifications.

Geldings may be registered at two years old. They then appear in the Stud Book under the heading of Geldings, but, unlike stallions and mares, are not allotted Stud Book numbers.

Grant This Society receives a grant direct from the Horserace Betting Levy Board, which is used as premiums for stallions standing at stud, to help all breeders.

Shows The Society holds an annual show at the Royal Highland Show at Ingliston, Edinburgh, in June, and a breed show every two years, in Scotland. For other shows, apply to the Secretary.

Exports Many are exported, notably to France, but the home demand is such that there are not many available and prices are high. The Society keeps a computerised record of sales.

For membership and registration apply to Mr I. Brown, Beechwood, Elie, Fife, KY9 1DH (Tel: 0333 330 696). The Society issues its own Stud Book.

The New Forest Pony Breeding and Cattle Society

Location the New Forest, Hampshire.

Important note Hundreds of these ponies are killed annually on the roads, and hundreds more are injured by fast-moving traffic. It is no kindness to stop your car and feed ponies that roam by the roadside, as this only encourages them to keep near the roads.

Origin Mentioned in the Charters of King Canute and listed under 'Wild Animals' in the Domesday Book. In the late 1800s and early 1900s stallions of various other breeds were turned out with the idea of enhancing the stock. The breed improved dramatically between

1959 and 1967, which can be put down to a number of breeders who took the trouble to breed selectively within the breed, also, only registered New Forest stallions have been permitted to run in the Forest since 1935. A vetting scheme was introduced in 1967.

The present Society was formed in 1938. Now all ponies are checked by the registration committee before being accepted into the Stud Book. When there is any doubt about the parentage not being true Forest, the application is refused or put back for further inquiry. Every help is given to those wishing to trace a pedigree.

When, however, mares are running in the Forest, it is not always possible to say exactly which stallion is the sire of their progeny, any more than it is possible to do so on a Welsh mountain. The agisters are, however, very quick to observe. In a case where it has not been possible to identify which stallion has served a mare, but since all stallions have to be registered, vetted and approved, the words 'Forest Horse' are used in the Stud Book. In this connection the word 'horse' is used instead of 'stallion'.

Height There is an upper height of 14.2 hh; no lower limit exists but not many New Forests are under 12 hh.

Colour Any colour but piebald, skewbald or blue-eyed cream, which are not registerable.

Characteristics and usefulness The demand for Forest-bred and reared ponies has largely been usurped by those bred and reared in private studs all over the country. Only the top Forest breeders can hope to compete against these.

The breed characteristics are much less apparent than other breeds, due to so many stallions of alien blood having been turned out on the Forest.

The good ones, whether Forest or privately bred, make excellent ponies of all-round riding type, honest, friendly, natural jumpers and, if Forest-bred, almost certainly traffic-proof. They have had innumerable successes both under saddle and in harness in county and even international shows.

Shows The stallion show at which premiums are given to stallions; successful stallions then have districts allotted to them. Held on August bank holiday Saturday.

The breed summer show is held on bank holiday Monday at New Park, Brockenhurst. A competition for Forest-fed mares that have never been off the Forest is organised each year.

Point-to-point races are held on Boxing Day each year, over 3 miles of open Forest.

Sales Six of these are held annually at Beaulieu Road, in April, August, September, October and November.

Brands and tail markings All ponies running on the Forest are required to be branded for identification purposes. They are also tail-marked by the agisters to show that the marking fee has been paid to the verderers by the owners.

There are four agisters – each with his own district and pony tail-mark. They are appointed by the Verderers Court – which incidentally is one of the oldest existing courts in the country – to look after the animals in the Forest. Ponies in private studs do not require to be branded, but all should be registered.

Overseas branches Many countries now have their own stud book societies, including Holland, Denmark, France, Germany, Sweden and Australia.

For membership and registration apply to Miss D. MacNair, New Forest Pony Breeding and Cattle Society, Beacon Cottage, Burley, Ringwood, Hants (Tel: Burley 2272). The Society issues its own Stud Book.

The Shetland Pony Stud-Book Society

Location The Shetland Isles in the far north of Scotland. Now in innumerable studs all over the country and worldwide.

Origin Thought by authorities to be the oldest of the breeds and almost certainly of prehistoric origin. Probably the purest of all native pony breeds.

Height Not exceeding 42 ins (106.6 cm). The over-riding height limit is applied to all entries and no pony exceeding 40 ins (101.6 cm) at three years of age or 42 ins (106.6 cm) at four years of age or over, can be registered, even if out of a registered dam by a registered sire.

Colour Any colour acceptable, but not spotted.

Characteristics The smallest of all the breeds. Tremendous strength for their size. They should have small, refined heads, small neat ears and large kind eyes. Strong necks. Short well-ribbed-up backs are essential. Strong quarters and high-set tails. Plenty of bone for their size with very short cannon bones; knees and hocks close to the

124

ground. The latter should be neither cow-hocked nor sickle-hocked. Coats thick as bears' in winter but like satin in summer. Plenty of straight silky hair on manes and tails. Hard, round, open feet.

Usefulness For centuries the only means of transport in the formerly roadless Shetland Isles. When properly broken and schooled, they are excellent for small children. Very fast, and with great staying power.

Qualifications Ponies which are out of registered parents on both sides are accepted, provided that they are registered by 30th September in the year following year of birth. No registered numbers are allotted until:

(*a*) Colts are registered as stallions at two years old or over.
(*b*) Fillies are registered as mares when they have had their first foal.
(*c*) Geldings can be registered at any age.

Until the entry as a stallion or mare is made, youngstock are simply referred to by the volume and page number of the foal entry.

A listed number of mares are accepted for registration upon inspection, even although their ancestry cannot be traced. These mares, known as IS mares, must be of high standard and must have foals at foot by registered stallions. They must be passed as true to breed type (and as breeding true to type) by an inspector appointed by the Council.

This breed should never be crossed with any other breed.

Sales Sales take place annually at Baltasound and Lerwick in the Shetland Isles, Aberdeen, and Reading, in October.

Shows This Society holds an annual breed show which is held in a different area each year. Classes are also staged at all the major UK shows and at many local shows.

Performance awards The Society runs schemes to encourage participation in riding and driving. These are very successful and are expanding all the time.

Shetland Pony Grand National Registered ponies from all over the country compete in a mini 'Grand National' to raise substantial sums of money for Great Ormond Street Children's Hospital.

Exports Ponies are regularly exported to Europe, USA and many other countries.

For membership and registration apply to Mrs B. M. McDonald,

Shetland Pony Stud-Book Society, Pedigree House, 6 King's Place, Perth, PH2 8AD.

The Welsh Pony and Cob Society

This Society Stud Book contains the following sections:

Welsh Mountain – Section A of the Welsh Stud Book

Location Welsh mountains, 'on the hill'; also in studs all over the British Isles and the world.

Origin Much debated, but certainly of Celtic origin, if not earlier. While Arab, Thoroughbred, and other blood has been used throughout the centuries, it is fair to say that improvement within recent times has been mainly achieved by breeders using selective breeding inside the breed itself.

Height 12 hh maximum.

Colour Grey dominant, roan, chestnut, brown, bay, dun, cream, palomino or black. Piebald and skewbald not eligible for registration. Heavy white markings are not liked but wall and blue eyes are not uncommon and are permitted.

Characteristics Great similarity to Arabs, especially among the best which have fine heads, full of quality, slightly dished muzzles and full, dark eyes, also a gay head and tail carriage.

Strong, level, short backs, with strong loins and well-sprung ribs. The old-fashioned type were rounder of rib under the saddle than the type being bred today, which have better riding shoulders and whose ribs are flatter under the saddle. Good, full quarters with knees and hocks close to the ground, but with a tendency to sickle and cow hocks. Hooves dense, round, and open.

Mane, tail, and fetlock hair very fine and straight. Whole outlook, bright, alive, and full of presence. Action darting, vigorous, and extended. High knee action, which was encouraged in the past, is now the exception rather than the rule. Fast and showy in harness. Not suitable for adult riders.

Usefulness First-class children's ponies and wonderful foundation stock.

The Welsh Mountain pony is the foundation stock of all Welsh ponies, namely Welsh Ponies (Section B of the Stud Book).

Qualifications (for entry into Stud Book proper).
Ponies by fully-registered Section A stallions out of fully registered or FS II mares, Section A.

Sales All over Wales and in Hereford.

Welsh Ponies – Section B of the Welsh Stud Book (Derived from the Welsh Mountain Pony)

Location All over the British Isles and abroad.

Origin Either Welsh Mountain ponies which have outgrown the 12 hh maximum; or Welsh ponies which have at one time been crossed with Arab, Thoroughbred, and other bloods, but notably Arab, which have been inspected and passed by inspectors authorised by the Society.

Height Up to 13.2 hh.

Colour As for Welsh Mountain.

Characteristics Larger, with more scope than the Welsh Mountain, and generally more quality, dependent on their breeding, and with low riding action and good fronts. Hocks tend to be sickle but again the whole appearance is most attractive. Some make top-class show ponies; others, utility types, may have larger, less-quality heads than the show specimens.

Usefulness First-class riding ponies: the best are capable of holding their own in any class, whether in hand or under saddle. All are useful utility ponies with good performance.

Qualifications (for entry into the Stud Book proper):

(1) Ponies by fully-registered Section B stallions out of fully registered or FS II Section B mares;
(2) Ponies by fully-registered Section A stallions out of fully registered or FS II Section B mares;
(3) Ponies by fully-registered Section B stallions out of fully registered or FS II Section A mares.

Sales. All over the British Isles.

Welsh Ponies of Cob Type – Section C of the Welsh Stud Book

Location All over the British Isles.

Origin The Welsh Mountain Pony.

Colour As Welsh Mountain.

Height Not exceeding 13.2 hh.

Characteristics Strong, thick-set, cobby appearance, with good bone. A compromise between the Welsh Mountain pony from which it is bred, and the Welsh Cob.

Usefulness Fast trotters with high knee action. Used to be seen put to harness but now mostly used for riding and trekking. Excellent foundation stock.

Qualifications (for Stud Book proper):

(1) Ponies by fully registered or FS II parents, Section C;
(2) Ponies with one parent registered in Section C and the other in Section A, B, or D.

Welsh Cobs – Section D of the Welsh Stud Book

Location All over the British Isles and increasingly in Europe.

Origin The Welsh Mountain pony, interbred with Hackney, Roadster and other blood at one time.

Height No height limit.

Colour As Welsh Mountain. Piebald and skewbald barred. Excessive white markings not popular.

Characteristics Smart, stylish appearance, with substance and quality. Good bone and silky feathers. Small, alert head, good tail carriage (the tail was always docked until a law was passed preventing this). Great goers, with knee action. Good fronts. Mostly round-barrelled, short-coupled, with powerful loins and quarters and grand hocks. Hooves open and of good horn.

Usefulness Superlatively good riding, jumping and harness animals. Used extensively in light trade turnouts, where they were and still are big winners. Excellent for trekking. First-class foundation stock for breeding hunters and jumpers, crossed with Thoroughbred blood.

128

Qualifications (for entry into Stud Book proper):

(1) Cobs by fully-registered or FS II parents on both sides;
(2) Cobs registered in Section C that have outgrown it, subject to certification of height by a veterinary surgeon.

Section E – Geldings

All geldings are registered and numbered under this Section, in the Stud Book issued by the Society.

Height If Cobs, unlimited; otherwise, heights are as for mares and stallions.

Shows These ponies are not eligible for all in-hand classes, though a number of shows do accept Geldings. They appear extensively in ridden classes, when some shows insist upon their being by fully registered parents or at least out of FS I or FS II mares. It depends on the classification of the particular show. Exhibitors should watch for this carefully and inquire whether their animals are eligible or not.

Registration Any gelding by a fully registered Welsh stallion out of a fully registered, FS, FS I or FS II Welsh mare, is eligible for registration in Section E of the Stud Book proper.

Appendixes of the Welsh Stud Book

There is an appendix for each section of the Stud Book A, B, C and D, as already described – for mares (only) which are not eligible for registration in the Stud Book proper. Originally mares were passed by inspection as FS (foundation stock) and registered in the FS appendixes according to their type, and thereafter upgraded by being mated with fully registered Welsh stallions. Originally this Register was only for mares of Welsh type whose breeding was unknown but in recent years animals have been inspected and passed which were known to be by Arabs or Thoroughbreds. These conditions applied until 1959 when this Register was closed.

Qualifications Mares not eligible for the Stud Book proper must be inspected and passed by inspectors nominated by the Welsh Pony and Cob Society. Progeny of FS mares by fully registered Welsh stallions from the appropriate section become FS I. If fillies are then

129

mated to fully registered Welsh stallions from the appropriate Section the progeny become FS II. Fillies which are again mated with fully registered Welsh stallions from the appropriate Section are eligible for the Stud Book proper.

FS I and FS II fillies are accepted at most shows.

Welsh Part-Bred Register Animals are accepted for entry to this Register at any age, provided the breeding shows not less than 25% of Registered Welsh Blood. This is calculated from either sire or dam, or cumulative from both. Welsh Part-Bred Horses and Ponies are becoming increasingly popular because of their ability and variability in the competitive disciplines.

Welsh Pony and Cob Society Area Associations There are a number of Area Associations in existence around the British Isles. They stimulate interest in the breed by arranging a wide variety of activities, which include shows, stud visits, lectures and evening functions.

For information, and names and addresses of Association Secretaries contact: The Welsh Pony and Cob Society, 6, Chalybeate Street, Aberystwyth, Dyfed, SY23 1HS (Tel: Aberystwyth 617501).

PART 3

Showing and Judging

13 Showing in Hand

There is a considerable art in showing in hand. I could name one or two exhibitors who have learned it to such a degree that you can be pretty certain they will be in the money. Likewise, I have seen rosettes thrown away by bad production and poor showmanship.

While it is a valuable experience for foals and youngstock, it is not a good thing if overdone. Too often youngstock get ring-crafty, round of their joints and one-sided in their mouths. Over-showing also tends to turn them sour and nappy, but some public experience does no harm and in fact is good. Use discretion.

It is essential, if you are not going to exasperate the most patient judge, to have your animal under control. This particularly applies to colts. Any judge will excuse a youngster having a buck and a kick but not one which upsets everyone and is never on its legs. It is also a waste of time, and time is an important factor at every show.

The art of showing in hand is something almost anyone can learn, while not everyone is experienced or competent enough to ride their own animal. To begin with, there is not the problem and worry, often expense, of finding a child to ride a pony, when one then also has to cope with the parents! There is not half the work involved and, in nine cases out of ten, the owner can not only do the chores but take the horse or pony into the ring. This is much more fun than handing it over to someone else while you stand agonised on the ropes. It also gives added interest if, as often happens, you have bred the animal yourself.

Nothing puts a judge off quicker than presenting both your animal and yourself looking messy and untidy. Spit and polish have won as many prizes for mediocre animals as have been lost by slovenly presentation of good ones. Well-handled, well-mannered animals, skilfully 'carved out' (to use a horsey expression), led by a neat competent attendant who knows how to show the animal to best advantage, catch and hold the judge's eye, whereas he or she may well either miss altogether a good one, presented in a slovenly fashion, or may at once decide to have nothing to do with it. Horses and ponies which in hand are never on their legs, which refuse to run out or, when they do, carry their heads at an angle thus giving the impression that they are short in front, may attract a judge's attention, but not advantageously. Here then are some practical tips.

Handling Youngstock

Handle your young horse or pony from a foal. Put a foal slip on him quite soon and accustom him to having your hand passed over his body and his legs.

Teach him to lead out sensibly. At the first lesson place one arm under his neck low down by his chest and the other arm round behind his buttocks, then ask an assistant to invite him to lead on when, with a little encouragement from behind and restraint from in front, you can prevent him racing off and getting a straight neck, or worse still, from rearing up and coming over backwards, when he may injure himself. Always do this on a soft surface, never on concrete or any hard ground where, if he does come over backwards, he may be badly injured.

Get him used to meeting other people so that he will greet the judge politely instead of with a snort. Teach him to stand still and four-square while you stand right away from him, thus giving him as much front as possible. The nearer you stand to any animal the shorter his front will appear to the judge. Encourage him to stretch his neck and drop his head from the poll by offering him a titbit (but *not* sugar, which makes them greedy and grasping).

Walking Out

Teach him to walk out in hand quietly and freely. As the human arm is not long enough to reach round and touch a horse's or pony's flank, it is now necessary to have additional aid, such as a fine cutting whip, long cane or even a light long twig. Some people express horror at the sight of such a thing when handling a foal. This is nonsense, for you should not have to use any of these to *hit* the pony. It should simply be used to guide him and to *indicate* what is wanted. No pony that has been properly treated and handled should fear a whip or stick, for it should be used only to touch and never to strike. It can also be used to remove flies or to give the foal that little scratch it dearly loves, proving to it that this is merely another piece of equipment, and not an instrument of pain.

This aid should be used lightly on the pony's side, carried in the left hand and behind the leader's back. In this way the pony will not realise that you, his handler, are doing this to get him to move off without hesitation. If at the same time you say firmly 'Walk on', he will soon not require this artificial aid.

When leading a pony you should never look back. For some reason, all equines seem to dislike this. So when you are leading in hand, always remember Lot's wife and look ahead, not back. To have another person 'chase him up' is worse than useless.

Never, under any circumstances, should a horse or pony be hit over the head or neck, at any age or at any stage.

Trotting Out

This should only be asked when the animal, of whatever age or size, is walking out freely and has been taught to carry himself.

The leader should walk (or run) just behind the animal's elbow, never in front of it. This is the centre of balance. Should you get in front of this centre the animal will tend to stop, even run back. If you let him get too far in front of you, he may play up and then contrive to get what is called a 'sraight neck'. This means that instead of bending his neck and giving to the pull on the rope, he will stretch his nose out and away, straighten his neck and take off. If he achieves this to the extent that the rope is in a straight line you will find that you have great difficulty in holding on to him at all. His neck must bend towards you if you are to have control when he plays up.

At all paces he should be *light* in the leader's hand, for this is the only time when his true action can be seen. If his head is twisted right round towards the leader, this will tend to throw his opposite leg outwards and develop muscles incorrectly. If he is pulling on the rein he may throw his feet anywhere and may even take control, and also will develop the muscle on the lower side of the neck which tends to make his head look as if put on upside down, and which once formed is difficult to remove.

Bitting

There are different opinions upon when a young animal should first have a bit placed in his mouth. I think this should be delayed as long as possible, up to two years old. But if the time comes when you cannot really control him properly without it, then it should be a

135

fairly thick, straight bar, half moon, or, better still, a rubber snaffle with small keys (not a jointed snaffle as this is too severe). *It should definitely have a coupling under the chin to which the lead rein is attached*, so giving an even pressure on both sides of his mouth. To lead from one ring of the snaffle or to pass the lead rein, attached to the ring of the snaffle on the far side, under the chin and through the ring on the near side, is thoroughly bad and will very quickly render a young animal one-sided. Or the neck muscles may be made stiff on one side, or over-developed on the lower side, causing the head to look as if it were on upside down.

Many a young animal comes into the ring worrying more about the bit he is so obviously unused to, or which is causing him discomfort – even pain – than paying attention to the business on hand. Clearly if he is nervous about his mouth he will not put up a good performance, and will certainly be behind his bridle when asked to run out. On these occasions I long to suggest, and sometimes do, that the bit be removed in order that I can see how, on the walk and trot out, he really moves.

Ring bits are disastrous. They should never be used on any young animal, whether horse or pony. By ring bits I mean those heavy metal ones shaped like a baby's comforter. They are a menace and should be completely barred, as should comforters!

The bars of an equine's mouth are very tender; the skin is easily broken or calloused, thus rendering the mouth insensitive.

It also horrifies me to see a chain used under a pony's chin, especially in the case of small, perfectly harmless yearlings. No wonder they hang back when asked to run out. A web rein or light rope is the correct thing, and this should be attached by strap and buckle (not a clip, which can open) to a coupling under, but not even touching, the chin groove.

Standing a Pony Up

To get a young animal to do this needs patience. Here again, a light touch of cane or whip on a leg to be moved is more effective than taking an uncomfortably firm grip under the pony's jaw and proceeding to twist its mouth and head about, or forcing it backwards, in an effort to move its leg. Directly the leg is moved, appreciation should be shown in the usual way by an encouraging word or a pat on the neck. Generally speaking, it is much better to get a pony to move forwards rather than backwards in order to achieve

136

the correct stance. So many exhibitors push them back on the bit, which has the effect of shortening the neck and spoiling the line of the shoulders.

Once the horse or pony has learned from clear indications what is wanted of him, he will put himself on his legs whenever you stand in front of him.

Care should be taken, when standing a pony out, that he shows all four legs – in other words, his forelegs and his hind legs should not be together. The foreleg on the side the judge is looking at should be slightly in advance of the other and the hind leg slightly behind the opposite leg. Above all, they should not be extended like hackneys'. This, in a riding horse or pony, is an abomination.

They soon learn to stand still as you gradually step back from them, to keep their stance and to stretch their necks and drop their noses without moving. As I say, a cube or peppermint in the pocket achieves this better than grabbing grass.

Lungeing and Schooling

Every animal needs to be disciplined sooner or later in its life. When I say sooner, I certainly do not mean a lot of lungeing before its bones are set and its muscles strong, causing joints to become round and even producing ring- and side bone in front and curbs behind. Handle well but only lunge lightly.

Few young horses or ponies should be backed before they are three years old, and then in the autumn of the third year and ridden on lightly. All owners are in a hurry; they simply will not give their animals time. And time makes all the difference in the long run. Whatever it costs, it pays not to produce animals in the ring before they are ready.

Never lunge on the bit, which, alas, is too often seen. To correct a pony by jabbing its mouth is disastrous, whereas a sharp jerk on the lunge rein, provided this is attached to the ring on the front of the cavesson, is an excellent corrective which can do no harm. I cannot see how a young animal can be schooled without a cavesson. Some have a short stem attached to the front of the noseband, at the end of which is the ring for attaching the rein. This gives even more leverage and therefore control. A long whip – to be used as a guide and not for punishment – is also essential.

It is painful to watch the bad lungeing to be seen on showgrounds. There is an art in this, the main thing being to keep the animal going round just in front of the centre of gravity, with the lunge rein taut.

137

The minute the horse or pony gets behind this centre he will either stop or come barging in on top of you, when flipping the lunge rein is useless. Your objective should be to keep him between the rein and your whip hand, and by holding the whip out in a line with his quarters, to keep him going forward with light but firm pressure on the lunge rein. In short, you should keep him going on between your two hands.

It is important that his head and neck should be bent the way he is going, and he should lead with the inside leg. If, however, he should lead with the outside, it is better to let him adjust himself rather than to keep stopping, and so disappointing him.

Again I say, beware of over-lungeing young animals. Exercise is essential and it is much better to turn him out in a field or paddock or, in bad weather – if you are lucky enough to have one - in an indoor school.

The more youngsters run out the better. If in a field, it is essential to give him/her a suitable companion; in an indoor school he/she can be on his own, but preferably not.

I know breeders who keep their youngstock confined far too much – even rugging them up. The result is lack of bone, substance, general development, and hardiness.

If there is nowhere to turn them out they must be given walking exercise daily, but it really is essential that youngstock should have their liberty.

Feeding

All youngstock should be fed extra rations, except possibly native ponies on good grazing (and this should not be too good, especially in the spring, or laminitis will result). I have found some of the well-known brands of horse and pony cubes excellent for youngstock.

Animals that are going to be shown should be fed on 'puddings': namely, well-boiled barley mixed with bruised oats, bran, well-soaked sugar-beet in small quantities, soaked flaked maize mixed with boiled linseed (which must never be left standing or it becomes poisonous), sliced carrots, mineral salts, etc. Mountain and moorland ponies can be kept out right up to the show day but may also require to be fed extra rations, according to their condition. The ideal for them is a field with not much keep where twice-daily short feeds can be given. Unless they have some hard feeding and are brought in at night for a period before the show, their droppings will be loose like a cow's – and therefore messy – and they will 'fade' and run up light at the show.

But for youngstock, good grazing is the breath of life. This, and freedom, anyway for part of the day.

Broodmares

Mares should be taught to walk out briskly and to trot back freely and in a straight line. It is essential that they should be agreeable to leaving their foals while doing this. Foals, too, should be accustomed to having their mothers taken away from them, as well as themselves being taught to walk and lead sensibly, preferably on their own but if not behind their dams. All this needs time and patience, and the earlier you start, the better.

Mares should, of course, go out to grass every day before and after foaling, but the better-bred ones, and certainly Thoroughbreds, should be stabled at night. On the other hand, mares of the native breeds are better out all the time, but should have some shelter or at least a windbreak. They are better also to foal out, except of course in very bad weather when they may have to be brought in. The less mares are fussed over, the better, though of course they should be watched for any sign of trouble or abnormality. While no horse or pony should be allowed to get poor, it is even more important that mares should be well looked after and fed. They will need extra rations before a show or they will run up light. It is essential that they have plenty of grass, otherwise they will have no milk. At the best shows this is provided whenever possible. Mares should not be over-fat before service.

Equipment

All show equipment, be it in hand or under saddle, should be designed to show off the animal at its best. It is as important as a new hat to its owner.

Whether it be a bridle, a show headcollar, a stallion bridle, or a foal slip, it must be made of good leather, narrow, finely stitched, and, of course, immaculately maintained.

Buckles must be small, neat, and of brass (riding bridles have stainless-steel buckles). Browbands should be attractive; either brass chain link on plain leather, or plaited or diced (never plain) coloured patent leather, or, better still, diced ribbon with little tabs. Hunter bridles, however, should have plain leather browbands.

139

Stallions should be shown in specially made and fitted stallion bridles with either a straight bar or jointed snaffle and a *long* white web lead rein. The use of brass chains at the end of the lead rein has increased in the last few seasons; this is possibly because of the number of women and girls now leading stallions and colts. When used also as curb chains these are very hard indeed on any animal and especially a young one, as they bruise and cut in under the jawbone. In my opinion, and that of many others, this is the greatest mistake. The possible exceptions are stallions of the heavier breeds of native ponies which can be too strong for women to lead without this aid, or on a mature Thoroughbred *if all else fails*. There is no harm, of course, in using a chain at the end of a lead rein provided this is attached to a coupling under, but not touching, the chin, or if the portion touching the chin – if it is attached to the ring of the bit on one side and under the chin and through the ring on the other – is covered with chamois leather. Or the chain can be divided and attached by a spring hook to each side of the bit. This, and the use of a coupling, ensures a level pressure on each side of the mouth. Also, chain used in this way at the end of a lead rein prevents the possibility of chewing through a rein.

Contraptions of any sort – and I include severe bits that act too sharply – only create reactions and evasions. They also invariably shorten the animal's stride when run out, which of course counts against it.

Bits should not be too wide; rather than this they are better too narrow but neither is right or comfortable for the wearer. They should fit and be fitted correctly, that is, placed on the bars of the mouth just below the back teeth and not rattling on the front ones or curling back the lips, nor resting on the tushes of a male animal. In the case of a horse or pony with a very soft mouth who is reluctant to face the bit, it can with advantage be covered with chamois leather or a rubber or vulcanite one used.

Again, if the animal is to have any future under saddle, every endeavour should be made to avoid jabbing in the mouth. Try also to avoid pulling the animal's head back so over-developing the muscle under the neck, which gives an impression of a ewe neck and is very hard to disperse.

Strapping

This entails hard work whether the animal be stabled or out at grass. Nothing beats a good strapping but results only come with practice.

Good health is a great aid to show success. Clean skins and coats full of bloom derive from inside far more than from patent additives or rugging up. Animals in good health are infinitely easier to produce than those that are not. There are some coats which, however much you strap them, exude grease, which is largely constitutional and which no amount of strapping will improve. Horses and ponies with coats like this either want 'Dr Green' (that is the summer grass), or their insides need cleaning out.

Stallions kept stabled and fed on hard food are, of course, easier to dress than mares and youngstock which, as I have said before, are much better shown off grass. But even stallions should have their daily 'run out' in a paddock. Nothing upsets me more than to see stallions kept perpetually stabled. If it is not possible to put them out daily in a paddock for at least two hours, they should either be led out or ridden, preferably the latter.

Provided the animal is fit, rain water is a good cleanser and puts on bloom. Some animals have a tendency to exude grey scurf, usually as a protection against inclement weather. They will need a strapper with a strong arm, willing to spend a lot of time. There is nothing to touch elbow grease. For removing scurf, a body brush, hay whisp and stable rubber are better than soap and water, as the former stimulate the oil glands at the root of every hair. Only rarely should horses and ponies be given a shampoo, when care should be taken to ward against chill. It should certainly not be done on a day with a cold wind blowing and the animal should be lunged or its bloodflow otherwise stimulated afterwards. It must then be well dried and strapped, especially its ears. It should never be left when these are wet or cold and *never* left wet and shivering. A final polishing with a silk cloth produces a sheen.

Actually, washing does the coat no good. It is to be avoided if possible, especially if the animal is being shown continuously. The exception is apparently the Shetland, whose owners I have seen every year washing them from head to foot and then throwing buckets of water over them. As they go to numerous shows, this is surely another proof of the hardiness of Scottish products!

Feet

According to the dictum 'no foot no horse' this paragraph should have come first, but perhaps placing it at the end of the chapter will put even more emphasis upon what is one of the most important points in production.

141

A judge is at perfect liberty to pick up a hoof and look inside, though I have to admit that I have never yet seen one pick up a *hind* foot! It is therefore of the utmost importance that feet should be carefully watched and cared for from birth. It is no use doing so at the last minute before taking an animal to a show. Just as with children, any tendency can be helped, if not actually cured, by early treatment. So many defects in a horse's or pony's feet, any turning in or out of the fetlocks, even slight crookedness emanating from the knee, can be improved if not actually cured by the skill of a good farrier called in in time and giving regular attention.

A forefoot that turns out slightly but only too obviously can be rectified by allowing the inside horn to grow and paring the outside. Pigeon toes can be improved by doing the opposite. In extreme cases it may be expedient to put on special shoes. If a mature pony has a slight deviation from the true in either of his forelegs, or if he does not move absolutely straight, the clip of the shoe placed judiciously will often create a satisfactory illusion. A tendency to forge can be stopped by cutting back the hind hoof and fitting the shoe well back and with a rolled toe.

A tendency to over-long pasterns should be noted early in life and the animal's feet kept short. Long pasterns behind can be made less noticeable by shoeing with a wedged shoe, which is better than calkins.

An animal that does not really move can be improved by working him in ordinary or slightly heavier shoes and replacing these with light plates on the show day.

All show ponies (except mountain and moorland) are best fitted with very light iron or aluminium plates. Some producers put these on only in front, using light iron ones behind. Aluminium behind tend to spread and twist, besides which, being expendable, they are expensive. All feet must be washed but the greatest care should be taken not to allow any water into the heels. The hooves should be well dried and oiled if the show is on grass. If on tar or cinders, just wash and dry. Use oil on black horn, and vaseline on white, and for obvious reasons never put black oil or any other stuff on a hoof opposite a white fetlock and/or hoof.

Condition

While a show animal has naturally to be shown in first-class condition, I deplore the number of young horses and ponies which appear in the ring showing signs of unnatural living. At each and

142

every show one sees youngstock too fat, even gross. Judges are largely to blame. Too many tend to put up these over-produced exhibits. (Can it be because, as I have said, fat covers a multitude of evils?) While it is right to judge on the day, surely 'potential' should play a large part when judging young stock. (This particularly applies to young hunter classes.) Here a young horse with 'scope' should surely be placed over his more mature but 'stuffy' rival. By 'stuffy' I do not mean only that the animal is fat. It almost invariably has not only a short back, but straight, narrow shoulder blades and lacks length from hip to dock.

Exhibitors with animals which fall into the second category may well decide that they stand a better chance if shown fat as they have no 'line' to lose. Exhibitors of young animals that have range and scope and which will *when mature* undoubtedly deserve the description that they 'stand over a lot of ground' will be well advised not to show them so fat as to hide this excellent potential.

Ponies with a tendency to laminitis should be turned out only at night and brought into a stable from 8 a.m. to 8 p.m. during the early summer months and given only water. To find poor pasture can be inconvenient, sometimes impossible. Water meadows, however, should be avoided. But the ideal, especially for native ponies, is pasture which has not a lot of protein. Oats, of course, must be avoided.

If rationing fails then the only other thing to do is to sweat off the fat. This is done by rugging up with a layer of polythene sheeting or rubber under a rug both in the stable and also when lungeing. This obviously cannot be done in very cold weather or you risk a severe chill. Simply to exercise an over-fat animal only turns fat into muscle and the same applies to strapping.

This problem affects Dartmoor, Welsh and Shetland ponies more than any other, though other sizes and types can be affected, but not to such a degree as the natives which for centuries have been bred and reared on moorland.

Remember, a good skin and coat are produced by good feeding, so that it is not necessary to keep youngstock stabled with the idea that this is good for their coats. Even rain will do more good than harm, and nothing could be better than the sun on their backs.

Plaiting Manes

All manes should be plaited except in mountain and moorland classes, in which they should never be, with the possible exception of Section B Welsh. I am often asked what exhibitors should do when they have a native pony which they have just shown in its own breed class and which is then due in an open class, or vice versa. All I can say is that as they must be unplaited in a native class, they must take their chance in an open class, when it should make no difference whether the pony is plaited or not.

Always use a needle and thread, never an elastic band. Plaits should be as neat and tight as possible, except when the animal has an over-lean neck or one which tends to be upside down, then the plaits should be 'bunched' – to give more depth to the neck – before starting to stitch.

An uneven number of plaits, including the forelock, is usual. The mane should be well pulled from *underneath*, and shortened, before attempting plaiting. Never cut a mane.

Tails

All tails, other than native breeds, look best either pulled or plaited. Broodmares should be plaited unless of course they have recently been, as in the case of some maidens, in ridden classes when this is not possible because they have previously been pulled.

Native ponies must be shown naturally.

Foals, other than native, I think should certainly have their manes and tails plaited.

The length of the tail depends on the animal's natural tail carriage. When held out by hand, at the natural angle at which it normally holds it when in motion, the end of the tail should reach the seat of curb on the back of the hind leg. A slightly longer tail is favoured by some hack exhibitors, but I still think that the above is about the correct length when the tail is carried.

Equine Influenza Immunisation

As a condition of entry, many more shows now require the production of a valid certificate of vaccination on arrival at the showground. It is essential therefore to ask your veterinary surgeon's advice as to which course is most suitable for your horse or pony, and to arrange for its administration well before the start of the season. In some cases, if the certificate is not produced, or found to be out of date, the animal will not be allowed to compete and you will probably be asked to remove it from the showground.

This rule applies equally to ridden animals.

14 Notes on Ridden Ponies

Breeding

The definition of a riding pony is anything of pony character not exceeding 14.2 hh. It can include ponies registered with any one of the nine native breed societies, but the large majority of riding ponies are cross-breds.

Very rarely are there registered Thoroughbreds of this height and even they are liable to be small horses rather than ponies. If they are Thoroughbreds which are of pony type, they are obviously valuable.

Arabs are a thing apart and while they can be bred to 14.2 hh and under, the best are larger. They cannot compete successfully in open classes and therefore have classes of their own.

Pure-bred native ponies, especially those 12.2 hh and under, have competed successfully in open riding pony classes, both in hand and under saddle. They have even won the championship at the Royal International Horse Show.

However, the large majority of ridden and in-hand show ponies are cross-bred.

Except inside the nine native breeds, breeding riding ponies is 'fluke breeding', just as in the breeding of hacks and cobs.

In my opinion, and in that of many breeders, the two most important bloods are small native and Thoroughbred, with a soupçon of Arab. It is the proportion of blood that matters.

The first-cross, whether it be TB x native or Arab x native is too strong, but a start has to be made somewhere, and it is in the further generations that one hopes to achieve the ideal.

Before starting to breed ponies, it is essential to have the aim clearly in mind.

The more TB blood (without producing a little horse) the better, as from this blood comes that essential 'quality'. Too much Arab blood and you risk too short a front, an indifferent hind leg and Arab quality, which is not quite the same thing as TB quality.

There is nothing worse than a bad part-bred Arab, but while it is possible to have too much of a good thing it is wise to have some.

145

Some of the most successful breeders stick to two original bloods and breed further generations of these two bloods – for example Arab and Welsh or TB and Dartmoor.

Others favour the three-way cross, that is TB x native x Arab. This is what I myself favour – for example, putting a small TB pony stallion to an Arab x Welsh mare, especially if there is more Welsh than Arab in her pedigree. One-eighth of Arab blood is generally sufficient.

The best cross-bred stallions have a larger proportion of TB blood in their veins than any other. Native blood is, of course, essential, as this gives a pony character plus substance, hardiness, and temperament. Good limbs can come from both the Arab, TB and native elements.

The mare is all-important. Above all, she must have bone and substance, and at least some quality if the foal is to be a top-class show specimen. If possible, try to see her dam and grandam, the sire's dam and if possible grandam, though I realise one has to be very dedicated to go to these lengths.

At the same time, it is essential that a study should be made of a stallion's progeny before he is used. Many a stallion who is not himself a show specimen has thrown beautiful stock, just as a winning stallion can be a poor stock-getter.

Likewise, because a mare has won under saddle, it does not necessarily mean she will make a good brood mare. Indeed, many proven brood mares have never won a rosette under saddle. While it is not wise to breed indiscriminately, the most surprising results have been achieved from haphazard breeding and from indifferent mares and stallions; but this is tempting Providence.

I could never, for instance, advise breeding from mares with indifferent conformation, crooked action or difficult temperament, or which have unsoundnesses which could be inherited. Even more so, I would not breed from a stallion with the same deficiencies.

It is always a risk to use either a stallion or a mare of unknown breeding because one can never know when there will be an undesirable 'throw-back'. In my opinion, and in that of more successful breeders than me, the stallion above all should be as near pure-bred as possible.

If the mare is a good one by all standards, it can be risked, but using a stallion of very mixed breeding – in other words a 'mongrel' – is making breeding even more of a fluke. True, the best cross-bred stallions have native Arab and TB blood in their veins in varying proportions, and the most successful have a larger proportion of TB than any other blood.

146

Some breeders have tried having a pure-bred native stallion to a TB mare registered in the GSB, sometimes with good results, sometimes not. The first-cross is, as I have emphasised, too strong (the progeny frequently have too large heads) but, again, a start has to be made.

Today there is a craze for small heads and this is where Arab blood comes into its own, and one of the chief reasons why I say that some Arab blood is most beneficial.

But while we have gained on the swings, by smaller heads and more pony character, we have undoubtedly lost on the roundabouts, by lack of bone.

Far too prevalent in the show ring today are lack of bone, long cannon bones, hocks up in the air, forelegs coming out of the same hole and round lymphatic limbs instead of flat, flinty bone. Action, too, has lost that very necessary elevation and suspension which is the mark of a truly beautiful mover.

It is essential to look at a mare with a critical, dispassionate eye, and, having decided on her bad points, to choose a stallion which by his conformation, etc., may, with any luck, correct these. It is obviously stupid to put a mare that is short in front to a stallion with the same fault, and if a mare has a sickle hind leg or is cut in above the hock, it is essential to mate her with a stallion with a good hind leg and well-developed thighs.

Too strong a proportion of native blood will provide substance, but a return will have to be made to TB blood to obtain the necessary quality and action without which no pony is top class. Animals which show quality as one- and two year-olds can grow 'stuffy' and lacking in quality as they mature.

And if there is too much TB blood then it will be essential to go back to native blood to retain pony character.

The breeder wanting just that something the others have not got may do well to introduce some Arab blood. If, however, the aim is to breed a hunter or utility-type pony, where quality is not quite so important whereas performance is, then a preponderance of TB blood will be an asset. It also gives that very necessary courage without which no animal can be a success in any sphere.

Ponies Under Saddle

The conformation and performance of a show pony under saddle is, or should be, the same as its larger counterpart, the show hack. The only differences are that (1) hacks are not usually asked to gallop whereas ponies are, and (2) judges do not ride the ponies but always ride the hacks.

Natural balance is even more important in a child's pony than in an adult's mount, as obviously a child cannot be expected to create balance. You will indeed be fortunate if you find yourself with that rare asset, a 'natural'. You will be doubly lucky if you can find a child that is likewise. But this ideal situation is rare indeed and you therefore have to produce both, and this *from the ground*, which is of course much more difficult than doing it yourself by being able to get up and ride.

Consider first the pony's good and bad points. Be ruthless in your criticism, for only thus can you hope to succeed. Having decided what needs putting right, your job then is to know how to do it.

I cannot of course describe here all the faults that you may find, nor their cure. I can only hint at the more common ones – such as a head that is on upside down, the pony that does not really use its shoulder but moves only from the elbow, is not happy about its mouth, lacks free forward movement, etc. There are, if not cures, then at least means of improving all these faults and of dealing with the countless other problems with which you will meet. One thing is certain; it will take time. Too many producers suffer from owners who expect their sow's ears to be turned (overnight almost) into silk purses. It may take weeks, months, even years. I have watched ponies being literally re-built by clever producers to win at the top. Equally, I have seen those only half-way there removed by owners who had not got either the knowledge or the patience to wait until the job was finished. The same applies to owners of young animals. They hurry them and thereby ruin them. If conformation has to be altered and action produced, it is obvious that this takes time. Likewise, young animals must be given time to mature.

You cannot hope to obtain improvement, especially in 'action', if the animal is either immature or weak, or both. Do not, therefore, in your eagerness, over-school the young and turn good temperaments into nappy ones by asking the impossible.

Lungeing and long-reining are essentials in the schooling of ponies, and the latter is more essential with ponies than with horses because an adult is unlikely to be light enough to ride a pony himself and few children have the strength or the skill to produce what is wanted. It will obviously be necessary, however, for the producer to learn how to lunge and to drive in reins correctly, or untold harm can be done. There is an art in both which has been described by better pens than mine, as has the initial backing and breaking-in of horses and ponies.

148

What I want to emphasise is that too much schooling does more harm than good. Twenty minutes twice a day is quite enough, and much better than forty minutes once a day. Avoid all shouting, jerky violent movements, use of the whip except as a directive, and endeavour always to proceed from one place to another as smoothly as possible. Never, either on the lunge, in reins, or from the saddle, pull up sharply – fade out. Encourage free forward movement. A pony should not, however, be in front of its bridle any more than it should be behind it.

Accustom the pony from the start to various sights and sounds. When he is going quietly under saddle, take him out hacking, either alone or with others. Jump him over small obstacles; better still, take him out hunting. There is no better cure for a nappy animal. Equines get as bored as do humans repeating the same thing day after day. Perpetual circling turns them sour, and no wonder, as well as doing young joints no good. Accustom them to the company of dogs, children, pigs, donkeys, music, clapping, anything.

Teach them to stand still from the beginning. Train them to run out readily and straight in hand. One of the hardest things for a young or weak horse or pony to do is to walk or trot in a dead straight line.

Obviously you cannot expect results from animals that are immature or weak for any reason. It is essential to feed well. So many pony owners and producers say, 'We dare not feed oats.' I do not believe this, though naturally the quantity varies with the temperament of the pony and the work it is doing. If a pony lacks presence you will jolly well have to feed oats. This sort of pony is one of the hardest to produce because it lacks presence if not fed oats but may well play the fool if given them. Herein lies one of the arts in production.

There are any number of things you can feed and should feed, but above all be sure you are not just feeding worms. Remember that teeth will need regular attention.

Do not give a lot of exercise. Obviously, the more exercise you give a pony the fitter it gets and therefore the more likely to get above itself and to play up. Your aim should be to achieve a happy medium, which is a pony that is well in himself and in his coat, in superb condition, but on the fat side and therefore inclined to be lazy rather than hard and fit and therefore full of himself. Good strapping plays almost as important a part as good feeding.

Combine the above with wise, patient short training sessions and give the animal plenty of time. Above all, study each one individually and school and feed according to your findings.

15 Judges and Judging

It has always struck me as remarkable that so many mature men and women crave to be invited to judge, be it horses, dogs, cattle or cats. It seems all the more extraordinary when you realise that this not only entails considerable inconvenience (early rising, long journeys, irregular meals, indifferent food) but also physical discomfort in pouring rain or hot sun, cold, and long hours of standing. Add to this the unvarnished truth that a judge is inevitably criticised by a proportion of the spectators and that every time he comes out of the ring he has made himself unpopular with the majority of exhibitors and gained only one friend.

What is there so attractive about the phrase: '. . . hope that you will do the honour of judging . . .'?

Firstly, it is flattering, and most people enjoy flattery, Secondly, it is a challenge. In some cases it panders to a sort of power complex, because what the judge says goes. This type of person, needless to say, makes a bad judge.

Good judges are oblivious to spectators and exhibitors alike. They are absorbed and genuinely concerned only with technicalities. The dedicated judges enjoy every minute, though it can be worrying when there is a near decision to be made or when anything goes wrong. Mostly they are people with a life-long love and experience of whatever type of animal they are judging. Some are judges by tradition – their forebears were judging when they themselves were still in the cradle.

Judges undoubtedly render a service, for by lending their knowledge, dedication and unbiased opinion they are helping to maintain and improve the standard of British stock. In the horse world they are extremely important because only if our judges are first-class will our horses and ponies remain at the top in world competition. It is indeed a blessing that these excellent people do not flag because, let us face it, who are coming along to replace this age group, whose names appear on nearly all the judging panels but who cannot, alas, be with us for ever? Who are the judges of the future?

I have to admit that at the time of writing I am unable to answer this question.

There are a large number of people who aspire to be judges but from my experience they lack the practical knowledge that former generations *absorbed* in their everyday life. Past generations of horsemen and women, because they had the money, responsible domestic and stable staff, and more time, were able to indulge in hobbies of which one, among most country-breds, was more often than not horses. Now money has largely passed into other hands – to people who have never had any contact with animals, let alone horses. What used to be called the 'working class' today have the means to own horses themselves and to give ponies to their children. The *nouveaux-riches* buy ponies regardless of price, whereas the higher-income group of previous generations mounted their children on the lawn-mowing pony. Today, horse-owning – and especially pony-owning – has become a sort of status symbol. Whereas in previous generations children were seen and not heard, youth today is given an importance out of all proportion. While it is praiseworthy that parents are prepared to slave for and lavish money on their children, is it wise?

In fairness, I must add that whereas the majority of parents in the past had everything done for them, modern parents do the job themselves. This must help, for by looking after their own animals the modern owners must have an advantage over those of the Victorian and Edwardian eras. As a result, never before has there been such a demand for instructional books and courses.

Until the beginning of this century, horses were the only means of road transport; everyone, therefore, even the maiden aunt sitting in her chair, had at least some contact and some knowledge of them – knowledge which had been handed down from generation to generation. The present generation will never have this background which enabled their predecessors to absorb horse knowledge and parlance; hence the lack of all-round, practical knowledge of basic conformation and everything that goes with it and the ignorance of horsy expressions. For example, whoever heard of describing a horse's extremities as 'lovely thin legs'? Yet this description has appeared in examination papers I have corrected. Only practical experience can teach the potential judge equine terminology and how to distinguish good points from bad *in the flesh*.

This same lack of practical experience is apparent in the veterinary profession. Before the advent of the internal-combustion engine they either rode or did their rounds in a dog-cart; they probably drove the horse themselves. Many hunted. They were all-rounders, and horses had the priority. Now cattle have this. Some are small animal specialists and make no bones about it. Comparatively few have the necessary *practical* horse knowledge and experience; even fewer own their own horses. What happens when the 'old school' retire? What is the Royal Veterinary College doing about it?

Judges' Panels

This seems an appropriate moment to suggest that all judges' panels should come constantly under review. Some lists are so out-of-date they even include the names of judges who have passed on. I see how embarrassing and hurting it can be to remove names for any reason: the older ones obviously have the knowledge and experience needed much more than the present generation – they could hardly have less. While one appreciates the difficulty of removing names, and of turning down those not yet qualified, it is essential if we are to keep up the standard of horses and ponies in this country.

The method of selection too often seems to be that of 'I'll scratch your back if you'll scratch mine.' Could I suggest that every society, before compiling its judges' panel, should set up a sub-committee composed of one or two knowledgeable, unbiased judges of the type of animal concerned, together with two or three top, fair-minded exhibitors of integrity (and there are many) who could then discuss in confidence the pros and cons of each candidate, and that the decision of this tribunal shall be accepted by the society? Otherwise, one gets all the axe-grinders, the 'old boys and girls' attitude, and committee members who know nothing all having their say, so that one gets nowhere. And perhaps, on each panel, judges considered capable by the tribunal of judging at the most important shows could be marked with an asterisk, and the list revised annually. Show organisers could then at least be as certain as possible of getting the right judge for the particular classification. They, too, should appoint a sub-committee, the members of which know something of the subject; the choice of judges should *not* be left to the show secretary.

No panel is perfect but this method would certainly help to eliminate the less desirable elements. Above all, show executives should not then pick their judges haphazardly but should give a lot of thought to this matter, which can make or mar their show. This particularly applies to breed classes which, for obvious reasons, are important.

Mountain and moorland and type classes should if possible be judged by a judge on their respective panels. Some societies insist on this but it is not always possible, when it is up to the exhibitors not to show if they do not wish to do so.

152

Mixed mountain and moorland classes are a headache because there are so few capable of judging this difficult classification – people who not only know the characteristics of all nine breeds but who have no bias for any particular one. I urge native breed societies to encourage and add to this fast-diminishing panel, and would-be judges to study our native ponies' characteristics.

Some people maintain that judges are born with an eye for a horse and cannot be made. This is a rather sweeping statement. While the best judges are those who have learnt the hard way, and especially through their pockets, it is possible to learn by reading, looking, and listening, and above all by getting as much practical experience as possible. While basic conformation and all that goes with it – age, unsoundness, blemishes, etc. – can be mugged up in books, no amount of theory or diplomas gained can take the place of long, practical experience.

And just to make things more difficult, opinions differ even among the most knowledgeable. (Actually it would be very dull if everyone agreed.) It can be very confusing; you feel you are lost in a maze of contradictions. 'How, in Heaven's name,' you ask, 'can I, a complete novice, know who is talking sense and who is not?' Or again: 'What am I to conclude when one acknowledged top judge tells you a horse has a good shoulder only to be flatly contradicted by another of equal status?' What to believe when a judge calls a hunter a 'middleweight' while its owner, a most experienced dealer, insists it is a 'lightweight'. How often one hears a divergence of opinion on whether an animal has bone and substance, quality, and what have you.

Only by studying, and absorbing different points of view, can you begin to see daylight, let alone arrive at a definite conclusion. Only by experience and by listening to all and sundry can you ever hope to be able to stand by your own opinions. Even then there will be occasions when you will have your doubts. No animal is perfect, no judge infallible.

Speaking personally, I have learnt more from dealers than from any other category of horsemen. A good dealer's yard is undoubtedly a judge's academy. After all, a dealer depends for his bread and butter upon his knowledge and his decisions. I owe them a debt of gratitude for all they have taught me and for the fun I have enjoyed in their company.

Yet there has always been a deep-rooted objection to dealers acting as judges. It is felt, not without justification, that they may favour possible potential clients; that it places them in an invidious position when, having sold a horse for a large sum, they are faced with it in

153

the ring and have to decide either to risk their reputation and put it up or be honest and place it down the line to a better one. Or the animal may genuinely have deteriorated, but this will not help much when facing the owner after the class. Or they may face the very real temptation to put a horse, which they hope later to purchase, out of the money in order to reduce, or at least not to increase its value.

On the other hand, most top-class dealers – and I am not speaking of any others – are jealous of their reputation as judges of horseflesh. A professional is also more likely to have the courage of his convictions and will certainly be less diffident about putting down an habitual winner in favour of a less-known but, to him, better animal.

In past generations there were a number of extremely knowledgeable dealers operating on a large scale. They sold so many horses that it was not easy for them to judge, though many did. Today the situation is rather different: there are far fewer 'professional' dealers whilst a host of amateur ones have sprung up. Nearly everyone in the horse world now has horses or ponies to sell, on which they are keen to make a profit no matter how well or how long they have served them. For example, many more people are breeding ponies and find themselves overstocked. Perhaps the worst offenders are the racehorse owners; they think nothing of sending broken-down, even old horses – to say nothing of barren mares – to sales where their fate is the knacker's yard, or the riding school, which can be worse. For all they fetch, why not put them down at home? The reluctance to do this springs not always from mercenary motives but from squeamishness, whereas in fact it is surely the least they should do.

If they are capable and of integrity, I see no reason why dealers should not be elected to panels provided they do not judge animals in whose sale they have had any part. But undoubtedly judges with no axes to grind are preferable.

If a judge recognises an animal which he has bred or sold, he should not judge it. If and when he is faced with this dilemma he should inform the steward and ask him to request the show organiser to appoint another judge. The substitute then either judges the whole class or the original judge places all but the animal concerned, leaving it to the substitute to put it where he thinks it should stand. This, I feel, should be the recognised practice as it saves the ill-feeling inevitably caused by judges handling animals which they have either bred or sold or, worse still, both bred and sold. It may, of course, happen that a judge places an animal with which he has had to do previously but which he genuinely does not recognise. Sold as a youngster, it may look quite different under saddle or as a broodmare which has had a foal. This cannot always be avoided and people should be a little more generous in their comments when it happens.

Dealers are not alone in being placed in invidious positions. I doubt if there is a judge of any animal who has not at some time found himself faced with a bias, an influence, or a prejudice of some sort or another. Judges in whose integrity I sincerely believe maintain that they can and do divest themselves of all prejudice. I am afraid I do not believe them, but what I do believe is that they may be quite unconscious of it, anyway at the time. After all, we are all human.

On principle, a judge should not be influenced by any knowledge of previous performance or prize-winning records. He must – or should be – insulated and isolated from all outside influences. He should make his decisions solely upon what he actually sees before him on the day in the short time at his disposal. Speaking personally, I greatly resent anyone trying to influence me. The judge must also judge the 'ride' on the day, *not* from what he may either have seen or experienced on a previous occasion.

His opinion must be his own, not gleaned from or influenced by anyone else. Yet is he not influenced by a number of factors, subconsciously if not consciously? I rather think so. Otherwise, how is it that if a good animal gets put down a rot frequently sets in and it takes times to get its worth acknowledged, while an indifferent animal has only to win once or twice to get looked at and often, having got what is called 'established', it takes a brave judge to dislodge it. It is also reasonable to suppose that a judge can be influenced at one time or another by personal association either with the animal or its owner. Or there may be a bias against a certain conformation (such as a bump between the eyes or a sickle hock), or even for or against the rider or the person on the end of the string. Prejudice can be caused by some previous unfortunate experience concerning either the animal or its owner. But this is not to suggest that there are a lot of dishonest judges. On the contrary, I believe the majority do their level best to arrive at an honest decision, sometimes in difficult circumstances, and that they are often unfairly accused.

It should also be remembered that competition today is so hot that a judge can find equally good reasons for putting any of the first four animals at the top. It is perfectly legitimate to have a bias or a prejudice against an animal provided one can give a definite reason, whereas some people generalise. 'I can't stand a horse that shows the whites of its eyes,' or 'Defend me from all chestnuts' are typical examples, whereas a good judge considers all aspects and does not let his eye, and therefore his mind, concentrate on only one or two portions of the animal's anatomy. Too many judges look at either the fore end or the rear, and not at the whole. Some go nap on a pretty head and a flipping toe and forget the trailing hocks or that it goes wide behind. Others look only at a good pair of hocks and ignore a practically perpendicular shoulder. Or they may think an animal moves well when in fact it only moves from the elbow.

Stallion owners are often criticised for judging their horses' progeny. I feel that provided they have not themselves bred them, this is unfair and rather stupid. One should remember that stallion owners buy a stallion because they like him, his type, and his conformation. Provided he throws to type they will obviously like his progeny. Their opinion is, therefore, based not on the fact that they own the stallion but on the fact that his stock, having taken after him, is what they like.

The same applies to judging animals belonging to one's friends. If we bar dealers, stallion owners, anyone who has bred or sold, and finally friends, we shall be reduced to having no judges at all. Personally I think that if one exhibits one must take the rough with the smooth, however hard this may be. While a good grouse is permissible, to attack a judge at any time, let alone in the ring, is quite indefensible and I would never blame any judge for retaliating. It is much better, however, to ignore this rather than to become involved in a slanging match, though there are occasions when exhibitors deserve everything they get.

When a panel of judges exists, it is wise, especially for show organisers without knowledge to choose a judge from it.

It is unwise to select anyone to judge a type of horse or pony which is outside his experience. Otherwise, we see a hunter judge trying to navigate a well-schooled hack and someone judging breeding classes who has never so much as bred a donkey.

Judges should, as far as possible, be selected away from their own area. The obvious snag to this is travelling expenses, but a show will get better entries for a judge who has little or no prior knowledge of the exhibits; exhibitors naturally hesitate to enter under a judge who has previously put their animal down.

It pays at least to try to discover whether or not a judge has always been associated with a particular type or breed and, if so, not to put him on to judge a mixed class. For instance, it is unlikely to encourage entries if a judge known to be closely associated with Welsh, Highland, or any other native breed, is selected to judge a mixed mountain or moorland class; or if an Arab devotee is given a class of cross-breds, a large proportion of which are part-Thoroughbred and vice versa. An established all-round judge is indeed a blessing to a show organiser.

While organisers are naturally tempted to experiment because of the need for fresh judges, this is often a failure. While small shows should definitely be encouraged to give opportunities to newcomers, the larger, more important shows would be wise to stick to tried favourites, and this particularly applies to breed shows.

For the same animals to go on winning all through the season becomes very boring for spectators, and if an honest judge refuses to judge on form and breaks the sequence his courage should be acclaimed. Instead, he or she is often dropped.

Whether to have one, two or more judges per class is largely a matter of expense and the difficulty of finding two who will get on together. Some show secretaries ask the judges concerned if they are agreeable; others chance it. On the whole it works, but it is as well to make sure your judges are not at daggers drawn! If there are two, a *referee* must be available to make the casting vote if needed. Personally I prefer to carry my own can.

A judge may find himself in the position of having to reverse his decision from one show to another. Or he may think fit to put down the line an animal he knows full well is rarely out of the first three. He may even put up an animal he put down the line on a previous occasion. Why not? He is there to judge ON THE DAY. Equines, especially young ones, can alter out of all recognition between spring and autumn, from year to year, from show to show, even from day to day. He must have the courage of his convictions.

Judging Championships

This may present difficulties, especially when reserves are also allowed to enter the ring. Judges have been criticised for placing an animal that is only second in its class or reserve for a cup, over a first prize or cupwinner when it comes to a championship. Again he must be prepared to stand by his opinion and may well be justified by the fact that in the championship the second prize or reserve winner happens to put up a very much better show than does the animal previously placed above it.

In championships where the first, second and third prize winners come in, minus their rosettes, the judge must remember his previous placings or find himself in dire trouble. Here a good steward can

157

legitimately help. This particularly applies in native breed champion-ships, when the ponies are bred to type and may look very similar. The answer is that in this case all exhibits must wear their rosettes.

Judging Mixed Mountain and Moorland Classes and Championships

This is so specialised that I feel it requires a section of its own. These classes can contain nine different breeds and four different types of Welsh. They can be of all sizes and, worse still, all ages. How to compare a mature stallion with a yearling? How to judge a Highland or Dales against a Dartmoor, Exmoor, or Welsh Mountain pony? Two principles which will help are:

(1) Judge each animal on basic conformation, quality, action and performance, apart from its breed characteristics; then
(2) Judge each animal on its breed characteristics, that is, whether it is in fact typical, with the correct markings, and capable of doing the job for which it is meant.

This method puts a very necessary emphasis on conformation, limbs, and characteristics, and mitigates any prejudice for or against a par-ticular breed.

If the class is a very large one, your only hope is to stop the exhibitors round the perimeter and ask the steward to sort them into breeds, or do this job yourself. It is wise to place the breeds of similar heights together: large types, that is, Connemara, Dales, Fell, Highland, New Forest, Welsh Sections B, C, and D; and small types, that is, Dartmoor, Exmoor, Shetland, Welsh Mountain Section A (F S mares are not eligible).

Then send the class on round the perimeter again, when you will find the picture clearer, though still difficult. For instance, a good broodmare in one breed must be more valuable than a youngster, unless this is quite outstanding. But it takes a very good broodmare to justify placing her over a really good stallion. However, by using the principles which I have suggested above, it is possible to arrive at a conclusion, which need not necessarily be popular with the exhibitors!

Judging mixed mountain and moorland championships is easier, for then you have only the first prize winners of each breed to choose from, when you must decide which in your opinion is the best representative of its breed. Judges at Cruft's Dog Show achieve this from nearly a hundred breeds, so to pick the right winner from, at most eleven, should not be at all that difficult.

If you find yourself with two different types, namely those with bone and substance but possibly less quality and some knee action, and secondly the finer, lighter-boned ponies with more quality and little or no knee action, you have only a few minutes to decide which you favour. If one is obviously a better example of its type, the answer is easy, but if both are equally good of their type the decision still has to be made, and quickly. My own opinion, for what it is worth, is that if the show is a breed one and the class is in hand, then the animal which is most likely to be valuable to the breed goes up, which of course excludes geldings. If a ridden class, then the animal which is the best riding type should win. But it is a headache when these two different types appear in a mixed mountain and moorland class of championship at a show which is not primarily a breed show. It can only be left to the judge's opinion on the day.

The same problem, which can be almost insuperable, is posed by championships in which different types and breeds not only of horses but also of ponies come up. Again the judge's only hope is to try as far as possible to divest his mind of bias and prejudice and to decide whether the best horse is a better representative of its type than the best pony, or whether to favour the horses rather than the ponies, or vice versa. The difficulty in this sort of championship is to find judges capable of judging both types without some bias one way or another.

But I feel that a judge should bear in mind which breed or type is in his opinion the most valuable. Cattle judges, I understand, having picked a first-class cow as the best Ayrshire, for example, and an equally good Highland cow, base their final decision on whether they think the Ayrshire a more valuable breed than the Highland, and vice versa. This could work with ponies, however, only when judging native breeds. Value today, as I have said before, depends on what people are prepared to pay. Today, ponies frequently fetch a larger price than a really good young hunter.

Championship Judges

While it is preferable when possible for the class judges to judge their own championships, a difficulty arises when, at large shows, there is a supreme championship involving several different types or breeds. Obviously all the judges who have previously judged these classes cannot come into the championship, or you could have a dozen arguing for an hour. The show executives must then decide

159

which judges are to be asked to officiate in the supreme champion-ship. At the same time, they must do their best to see that all types and breeds are fairly represented. This is some task, and not all shows by any means achieve this. This is why it is important that animals in championships should wear their rosettes, otherwise a show may find itself faced with an irate exhibitor who, having been placed first by her breed or type judge, is then put down by a non-panel judge.

Looking After Judges

Having invited the judges and received acceptances, show executives should look after them. Some judges like being kept busy; others find four or five classes quite enough, and fewer if the entries are large. At the end of an over-long day the best judges tend to get horse or pony 'blind'. They can obviously judge more classes if these are not consecutive.

There is no fixed rule regarding remuneration. The large shows either pay a fee or give a fixed sum against expenses, and at all shows, of course, judges are the guests of the show on the day and receive a badge, car park label and meal tickets. Some shows also add a guest badge. Smaller shows are dependent on the generosity of the judge; fees are seldom paid but nearly all shows pay accommodation and/or travelling expenses. Shows run by societies that are registered chari-ties are in a strong position, since often the judges give their services free. Native breed judges, many of whom come from outlandish places and who are not always persons of means, cannot be expected to pay their own travelling expenses, though they frequently do. A show should state its policy clearly.

Procedure

A judge should acquaint himself with the classification of the class(es) he is judging, either through the schedule or through his steward but *never* through the programme (or catalogue), with which he should never be seen until his classes are over. He must know what specials, cups, and championships come under his jurisdiction.

The recognised method, whether in hand or under saddle, is for the exhibits to come into the ring and walk around the perimeter in single file.

As first impressions are often right, a judge should give himself time to form a general impression at this pace and if a large class he may call a halt and take a look while they are standing round the perimeter. If the class is in hand, he then either calls them in or he can have them trot past him in single file while still standing round the perimeter. If under saddle, he either himself signs, or instructs the steward, to proceed at the trot and finally at the canter.

It may well be that it is during the initial walk round the perimeter that he decides more or less to which animals he will give further consideration and which in his mind he has already eliminated. This almost instant decision can only be achieved after a lot of experience; it is an eventual 'must' for any top judge and it is remarkable how often it is right.

If the class is hunters under saddle they must then be requested to gallop on, but, while ponies must also gallop, this must be done singly after they have given their show. Galloping ponies as a class is now 'out'.

The judge then calls in the exhibits in any order; in order of the precedence upon which he at that moment has decided; or he can make a back row.

While it is rather fun – because it keeps people guessing – to call the exhibits in any order, there is a disadvantage to this. Under these circumstances, an exhibitor leading an indifferent, even quite useless, animal, finds himself standing in that much-coveted position, the top of the line. Surprise and delight are manifested on his/her face – never has such a thing happened before; life is good indeed! But when the judge, having looked over and run out all the exhibits, sends the whole class round again and then puts this competitor right down the line in his final placings, disappointment is registered in a big way. Add to this the public disgrace, for you may be sure that quite a lot of spectators were under the impression that the animal placed first in the original line-up was the judge's choice. However much he may be reassured that everyone realised there was no order in the first call-up, this will never compensate for the belief that the majority of spectators round the ring thought he was the winner.

On the whole, therefore, with some exceptions it is best to call in more or less in the order you think will be your final selection. But when dealing with very large classes you will be well advised to call in first what is called the 'ruck' – namely, those that you consider unlikely to be in the money. This enables you to concentrate on the better animals. The disadvantage is that no one enjoys being 'the ruck', and you must take a further look when lined up to make sure you have not missed one worthy of elevation to the front line.

A judge who is quick and workmanlike can do much towards

161

holding the spectators' attention, whereas those who dither can easily lose it. It should, for instance, not be necessary for a judge with an experienced eye to pass his hand down every limb – if any. This should really only be necessary if his eye alights on something suspicious or to confirm that a curb is in fact a true one and not simply a pronounced 'os calcis'. Even so, he should do his best to disguise what he is looking for. Many an animal with perfectly clean limbs has been made suspect by a judge fiddling about and peering at limbs which in fact have nothing the matter with them. Other exhibitors are only too ready to spread rumours of suspected defects. It is, however, equally important that he should not miss any definite unsoundness or defects.

It is a judge's responsibility to see that prizes are not awarded to lame animals. He may either place any animal he suspects of unsoundness quietly down the line and say nothing, or he can call in the show veterinary surgeon. Sometimes the vet may make the judge look a fool by declaring the animal sound, but the latter can be consoled by the thought that it is possible for an animal to go lame, especially when ridden, and yet run out sound. For instance, he can knock himself, causing temporary lameness, or he can be what is called 'bridle lame', that is, not happy about his mouth, not on the bit, both of which can affect his stride. Even a sore back can cause him to go unsound behind when the weight is in the saddle, but run out normally when the saddle is removed. No matter, you did right to question it. You would look a bigger fool if you put up a lame one.

When it comes to riding exhibits, again the judge must be as quick and efficient as possible. Twice round the ring should suffice; nothing is more boring to spectators than having to sit and watch a judge schooling a horse in the ring. On the other hand, there are occasions when a judge is justified in giving a horse time to settle, but exhibitors cannot expect judges to spend the show's time navigating their horses for them. Lucky is the judge for whom every horse goes well.

Whether every horse should or should not be ridden, or, when in hand, run out, is a vexed question. Exhibitors have paid their entry fees, many have come at considerable expense, and are entitled to a fair crack of the whip. On the other hand it is essential that the interest of the spectators be held and the show run to time. The judge will have to use both discretion and tact. Breed shows are different. Spectators of these in-hand classes are mostly specialists and even animals down the line have their interest. I personally endeavour to run out every animal regardless. If time is running short and a judge is instructed that he must make his decisions

162

quickly, the only thing to do is run them out in threes or fours. Or he can call in the back line, inspect it thoroughly, then ask the exhibitors to leave the ring, when at least they are not kept hanging about without a hope of being given a run-out. This applies particularly in bad weather.

A ride judge has to decide whether a horse whose conformation leaves much to be desired but which gave him the best ride, is to go above another with both good conformation and quality but which gave him a lousy ride. These decisions must be made, for better or for worse, and as long as they are made honestly exhibitors should understand. Personally, if any animal of mine misbehaves I prefer it to be placed at the bottom of the line rather than appear in a minor position in the press.

The run-out should consist of walking away and trotting back and *past you*. Walking away decides whether the animal moves straight (should there be any doubt have him also walk towards you), but do not utterly condemn a youngster if he turns a toe out slightly or plaits a little. Remember he is immature and to walk in a straight line in hand is very difficult for any young horse or pony. When walking from you watch to see if he is what is called 'a good one to follow', that his hocks are neither cow nor bent, whether he has good thighs and is not 'split up'. At the trot, you should also watch to see if he goes wide behind. This is a bad fault but is often caused by over-trotting.

When it comes to the final decision it may well be that two exhibits or more appear to be of equal or almost equal merit. One may have a better hind leg than the other, who, however, has a better head. One may be lacking in scope while the other is not a dead straight mover. It helps, in coming to a final decision, to have these two (or more) animals out to stand one behind the other, and certainly to have them run or ridden out again as the case may be. You may find yourself with animals of equal merit but finally, of course, having to place them. It at least sugars the pill if one tells the losing exhibitor so.

While you decide, never leave the tail of the class, especially broodmares and foals, wandering aimlessly round. Remember to tell your steward to line up the rest, and always endeavour to have another look at them, even if you have not time to run each one out.

By this time you may have decided that the animal which caught your eye when it first entered the ring is the one for you; on the other hand, you may have come to the conclusion that it is simply a flat-catcher, of which every judge should be wary. They usually have a lot of presence.

It is wise on principle to discard any animal if you find that your eye involuntarily wanders to certain parts of its anatomy, giving you a feeling of uncertainty. When buying, I may have liked everything else about an animal but have discarded it because my eye kept wandering to its forelegs or its eye, for instance. The same experience can happen to a judge. He may lay himself open to criticism but instinct often proves correct.

Having made a decision, the judge should stick to it and should permit of no delay over the allocation of specials, the rosettes, and any other awards, which can cause spectator interest to flag.

To summarise, the business of a judge is:

(a) To keep a clear, unbiased mind, fear and favour no man, but do an honest job.

(b) To give everyone as clear a picture of what his/her policy is and endeavour to achieve some sort of uniformity, however mixed the bag with which he is confronted.

(c) To judge quickly and competently without appearing to be either flurried or worried.

(d) To exude a good firm atmosphere.

(e) Not to keep exhibitors hanging about any longer than is absolutely necessary.

(f) Not to ask for breeding until the awards have been given out; but to ask for or look at the age of the animal is both permissible and advisable, as obviously an older horse or pony of whatever merit may well have to stand down to a younger one that is equally good, if on value alone.

(g) To set a pattern of good manners and to dress appropriately.

(h) To maintain a friendly and correct attitude to exhibitors without being over-bearing or over-intimate. All should be treated the same, whether personal friends or the reverse. An explanation when handing a rosette to an exhibitor placed down the line is often helpful but can be badly received, and it is better to say nothing than too much.

(i) To ignore rudeness, which is better than becoming involved in a slanging match either inside or outside the ring. To attack a judge at any time, let alone in the ring, in unforgivable, but if an exhibitor asks you afterwards for your opinion you are justified in giving it but may be well advised to refrain, as not many owners really want to hear anything adverse. Actually, exhibitors who get a name for criticising judges do themselves immense harm. Clever exhibitors arrange their faces and accept defeat with good grace.

Finally, remember that while on the racecourse or polo ground, or in the hunting field, or in show jumping, they 'go in all shapes', in a show ring you are there to judge what in your opinion is the best on the day, primarily on conformation, quality, movement, and type and, if a ridden class, also on balance, performance, and manners. Too often, the above saying also applies in the show ring, and it is quite astonishing how many exhibitors enter animals which could not possibly under any circumstances be deemed worth the entry fee, let alone the prize money. But what a good thing for show organisers that they do, and all power to them so long as they take defeat with good grace.

To be a real show animal, whether horse or pony, it should conform as nearly as possible to the standards I have tried to describe.

16 Lameness and How to Detect it

The best way of detecting lameness is to watch your horse or pony in his loose box or stall. Notice whether or not he is resting a leg and, if so, which one and how. Normally weight will be distributed evenly over all four legs, although a sound animal will frequently rest a leg, so that you cannot entirely rely upon this evidence. Resting a foreleg and a hind leg diagonally may be quite natural and normal, especially if this is done on alternate sides. But if he is pointing a forefoot only, be suspicious.

But a judge cannot use this method of detection. He has to decide whether or not an animal is going sound in the middle of the ring, surrounded by spectators, and faced with the possibility of a very irate owner. Moreover, he only has seconds in which to make his judgment.

Here, then, are a few simple guides to knowing whether or not an animal is going true.

If the lameness is in the shoulder the lame leg appears to hang down slightly, and/or he may carry it slightly behind the sound one. Shoulder lameness is far the hardest to diagnose and a judge would be ill-advised to make any definite statement. He should be able, however, to detect if the animal is not going level. However, shoulder lameness is so rare that for all practical purposes it does not exist.

Make the animal walk both away from you and towards you, then past and away from you on a loose rein. It is better when this is done on smooth hard level ground but is rarely possible in a show ring.

If the horse is lame at the walk then the trouble is severe. Even slight lameness is more apparent at the trot than at the walk.

When lame in front from whatever cause the animal drops his head as the sound foot comes to the ground and jerks it up as the lame one does.

If lame behind, he drops his head when the lame leg touches down and raises it when the sound one does, that is, the reverse. Also the side he is lame on drops as the animal goes away from you when lame behind; in other words, he will lean over towards the sound

166

side to take the weight off the unsound.

Lameness behind is more apparent when the animal is being turned sharply around, especially if it is a case of spavin or string-halt. It will at once be more apparent if the hock is flexed for a few minutes and the animal then trotted out immediately. This is especially so with spavins. A judge cannot of course flex hocks in the middle of the ring, or indeed outside it. He either puts the animal quietly down the line, or asks the exhibitor if he would like to take it out of the ring, if willing for a veterinary surgeon to examine it. This should be done outside the ring. The horse or pony will then be examined by the veterinary surgeon. If he decides it is not going level, it should be withdrawn or placed at the end of the line. If he passes the animal sound, the judge should accept the decision, whatever his own opinion, and should then place the horse where, in his opinion, it should stand.

I personally do not think that a good judge needs to run a hand down the tendons, round the top of the coronary band, etc.

It should be remembered that lameness can be caused by a splint, either already formed or beginning to form; by sprains or strains of the tendons and ligaments, when heat will be present; by a blow or knocking at fetlock joints when galloping round the ring; or the lameness may be momentary. Or he may have knocked a nerve in the lame leg with the hoof or the shoe of the other. I have seen a horse fall through hitting a nerve. This lameness may be very temporary. If it occurs in an animal that a judge is thinking of putting in the money, he should get on with judging the other animals in order to give the lame one a little time to recover. But no judge is justified in holding up a class for this purpose.

An animal can walk out sound and yet be 'on the nod' at the trot. The judge should insist that both paces be executed normally; there should be no slowing up or weaving in the hope of preventing detection. The animals should be run out straight, at a normal pace and on a loose rein.

Lameness does not improve if the trouble is a spavin, sore shins, corns or laminitis. It can improve in the case of navicular or rheumatism, and *sometimes* in the case of a splint.

If a stifle joint goes out the animal will be unable to move backwards without dragging his toe. He will also have difficulty in putting his hind leg to the ground moving forward. He will bend the hock and fetlock of the affected leg as little as possible.

The best time to detect lameness in the show ring is when, after the preliminary walk, trot and canter (and gallop if asked for) has been executed, and the animals have been standing while the judge looks them over, they are run out in hand. It is then that any lameness is likely to appear, that is, when the animal is asked to move again after being motionless for a time. If they are not sound, the longer they have been standing still, the more apparent the lameness will be. This is when the judge should have eyes not only in the front of his head but also at the back. I emphasise, when running out a horse for the detection of lameness insist that the animal's head be left loose.

17 Defects a Judge Should Look Out For

Appertaining to the Head

● *Influenza, cold, or catarrh*, detectable by a discharge from the nostrils.

● *Swollen glands*, under and below the ear (not to be confused with naturally over-large parotid glands), which may be strangles and, therefore, highly infectious. At the same time, the animal may have a dirty nose.

● *Conjunctivitis of the eyes*. Frequently caused by flies, making them water excessively, and the rims may become inflamed. Or the cause may be an in-growing eyelash, or a particle of dust, hay, or husk, or influenza.

● *Cut chin grooves*, caused by ill-fitting or twisted curb chain, or bad hands, and causing bit evasion.

● *Cut tongue*, again caused by harsh treatment, and again causing bit evasion.

Defects in the Neck and Throat Area

● *Coughs*. An animal brought into the ring coughing has no business to be there, and the judge has every right to request the steward to remove it. But there are coughs and coughs. A horse or pony can cough because of:

(1) laryngitis and pharyngitis;
(2) indigestion or stomach coughing;
(3) broken wind, distinguishable by a double flank movement;
(4) bronchitis;
(5) asthma, common in old, fat ponies;
(6) it has swallowed something irritating, or, to use human parlance, something has gone the wrong way down its wind-pipe.

169

As it is even difficult for some vets to be able to distinguish more or less between numbers (1) to (5), while number (6) may only be a temporary irritation which will right itself, it is even more of a problem for a judge. If he has doubts, he is at liberty to call in the show veterinary surgeon.

A rattling, wheezing cough occurs in bronchitis and asthma.

A soft, suppressed cough often marks the presence of inflammation of the lungs; the pain coughing causes makes the animal cough softly.

A dry, short cough denotes some sort of irritation of the respiratory organs, and unless it becomes chronic will usually pass off. If chronic, it can indicate broken wind.

● *'Making a noise,' 'whistling,' or 'roaring'*. The last is an advanced stage of the first due to varying paralysis of the left or right vocal cord(s) or both. It is unlikely to be met with in a show ring!

Whistling – as distinct from partial paralysis of the soft palate which is often intermittent, the vocal cord(s) normally are displaced outwardly on inspiration, but when a paralysis is present the synchronisation is lost and the cords vibrate in the air stream of the larynx, which accounts for the noise.

A direct cause of whistling or roaring is degeneration of the left recurrent laryngeal nerve.

A judge, if he suspects a horse of making a noise, is at liberty either to put it down the line and say nothing, or to call in a veterinary surgeon.

You should remember that a horse that is not fit will often make a very slight noise but will cease to do so when he is really fit. But you are judging *on the day*, and whistling is an unsoundness.

● *High blowers*. The noise that some horses make by flapping the alae of their nostrils can be mistaken by inexperienced people for roaring. It has, however, no connection with disease of any sort, and can be disregarded.

Injuries Appertaining to the Withers

● *Ill-fitting saddles*, or those with insufficient stuffing, or with a too-narrow tree, cause irritation, pain and sores. These in turn can affect the animal's temperament and movement. They can be the cause of bucking.

A judge has a perfect right to point out to an exhibitor when the tree of the saddle comes down on the wither in front, or the cantle presses on the spine at the back when weight is in the saddle.

•*Shoulder lameness*. This is very hard to detect. All a judge can do if he considers the animal is not going level is either to say nothing and put the animal down the line, or ask the exhibitor whether he has any objection to a veterinary surgeon being called in, or whether he would prefer to take the animal out of the ring.

Defects of the Pelvis

If one hip is lower than the other, the animal is said to be 'down of his hip', which is almost always due to an accident of some sort. It need not necessarily interfere with his performance, but is a defect in the ring.

•*Slipped stifle (or patella joint)*. The displacement of the patella (stifle) on the thigh joint can be seen through the foot being flexed back on the pastern bone, by a straightening of the hock, and by an inability to advance the leg, which appears locked. It is most commonly displaced upwards, whereupon the leg is in extreme extension and displaced posteriorly (left behind) and cannot be flexed. It is most apt to occur in young animals and the more often it happens the more liable it is to recur.

A stifle with this tendency can often be heard making a clicking noise in movement, while its replacement is indicated by a sudden click (common in worm-ridden or weak yearlings). Fortunately most animals grow out of it when their muscles strengthen. Obviously, if a judge detects this in the ring the animal cannot be placed that day.

Defects and Unsoundness in the Hock

•*Curbs*. This may be a sprain of the ligament which passes over and binds down the tendons at the back of the hock, due almost always to faulty conformation.

It is easily recognisable, either by standing at *exactly* right angles to the line at the back of the hock – when any deviation from the perpendicular is noticeable – or, better still, by passing a thumb down the back of the hock when any small lump, and certainly a large one, will immediately be felt. But be warned – should you not stand absolutely at right angles but slightly anteriorly, you may easily mistake a prominence of one of the bones of the hock for a curb. If you stand too far behind the right angle you will be unable to notice any deviation from a straight line down the back of the hock. In young animals it is best to leave things to nature and only resort to an artificial remedy when absolutely necessary. This is a definite defect and should penalise a show animal. A good judge can often tell when a curb has been treated (Fig. 8, page 36).

●*Capped hock.* This may simply be an effusion under the skin at the point of hock, caused by lying down or getting up on insufficient bedding, by kicking in the stable, or by a blow. It may be accompanied by a thickening, and inflammation of the bursae, or with fibrous deposit

It does not affect performance, except in rare cases, but is unsightly and, if pronounced, should definitely count against a show animal, especially when two are otherwise of equal merit.

●*Thoroughpin.* This is a bursal enlargement or secretion of synovia, arising from irritation of the flexor-pedis tendon.

It is discernible in the hollow of the hock, either on the inside or the outside. Should the puffiness appear just in front of the point of the hock on the outside and you press it with your finger, the bulge will appear on the inside and vice versa. Hence its name (Fig. 8, page 36).

It does not often cause lameness, but is a blemish and a weakness, and should count as such in the judge's summing up, except in working hunter classes, when it may be overlooked.

●*Spavin (bone).* It is not possible to define exactly, and especially on paper, the exact site of a bone spavin. Speaking generally, it is situated on the inner and lower part of the hock. Its importance depends on its position rather than its size. For our purpose, it is definitely an unsoundness and must cause the animal to be eliminated. Unless very pronounced, it is not easy to detect and is a judge's nightmare. It can be mistaken for a blood vessel.

It can be detected in certain cases by causing imperfect flexion. The hock does not fully flex, or may be carried round in a slightly circular way. Frequently the toe is dragged along the ground. If ridden on a hard surface this will, after a while, cause the shoe to be worn at the tip. A degree of flinching will also be noticeable if the animal turns sharply. Animals with this defect go sounder when warmed up, but there will again be stiffness if, after exercise, the animals stand still for even a short period. This, of course, is common to all lameness.

Detection is sometimes possible by looking at the hocks through the forelegs, when they will not appear to be a pair.

Should a judge suspect a spavin, he either uses his discretion or

172

calls in a veterinary surgeon (Fig. 8, page 36).

•*Spavin (bog).* Yet another bursal enlargement sited inside the hock (see Fig. 8, page 36). It is more often found in upright hocks, because this formation induces concussion and irritation. It should not be tolerated in a show animal, but often is! It is much easier to detect than a bone spavin.

•*Elbows (or ulna)* Capped elbows are similar in cause and effect to capped hocks. They do not cause unsoundness, but are unsightly and, therefore, a blemish. As such they have to come into consideration when judging animals of otherwise equal merit.

•*Splints.* These are a deposit of bone either between one or other of the small bones and the shank or upon any of the three bones of the foreleg, lying between the knee and the fetlock.

The cause of this abnormal growth is concussion or knock-on and inflammation, either in the ligaments or in the tough fibrous membrane forming the outer coating of the bones known as the periosteum, or in the bones themselves.

When inflammation is set up in a bone or its periosteum, morbid enlargement is likely to be the result.

Splints are easily felt by passing the fingers down the splint or cannon bone unless they happen to be situated near or under the knee, when detection is much more difficult. They are common in young horses, and many horse experts are suspicious that, if older animals have none, they have done little work. Even a very prominent splint can disappear in time, especially in young animals. If numerous in some young animals, they point to 'soft' bone, which will have a shorter life span.

They are the cause of much argument amongst judges. Some automatically put an animal with a pronounced splint down the line. Others ignore them. Some judges prefer to give young animals the benefit of the doubt. In hack or pony classes, which after all are beauty contests, a very prominent splint (i.e. the size of a walnut) should count when there are two animals of otherwise equal merit. Small splints can be ignored unless of course the animal should happen to be lame from this cause, when it is automatically eliminated (Fig. 8, page 36).

•*Broken knees.* Knees that are marked are not tolerated in a show animal. I would, however, qualify this in the case of working hunters when the cause could be wire or a slip-up on a tarmac road. As, however, the owner will give this as the cause, whatever the real reason, it is up to the judge to decide whether he thinks the injury was caused by accident or because the animal has faulty action, and judge accordingly.

Horses can come down through hitting a nerve on the inside of one leg with the hoof of the opposite leg. This may be caused by faulty action and is another reason why judges have to be critical of any blemishes on the knees.

•*Calloused legs.* These result when the structure of tendons and ligaments has suffered strain. All the tendons at the back of the leg appear thick, round, and hard. When legs reach this condition they rarely cause unsoundness, but are not acceptable in a show animal. It can be overlooked in working hunter classes if there is not a clean-limbed animal present with an equally good performance.

•*Windgalls.* These are bursal enlargements and vary in size. They are caused by over-exertion, concussion or irritation. They are soft and puffy, and are not acceptable in show animals, except possibly in working hunter classes.

•*Sidebone.* This is an ossification of the lateral cartilages or 'wings' of the bone of the foot. It is the red light in young animals of worse to come. Heavy cart-horses are prone to this disease, which can then often be seen by the naked eye.

If affected, the wings of the bone of the foot will feel hard and immovable instead of elastic. If the lateral cartilage is supple, it is normal. Usually they are caused by excessive concussion, but can be due to a blow or a 'tread' from another animal, that is, when travelling without a partition in a horse box, or from an over-reach.

The animal will not necessarily be lame in the early stages, though there may be a certain footiness apparent. They will always be more unsound on hard ground. It must militate against any animal, especially in the show ring.

•*Ringbone (high and low).* This is a bony formation, again caused by concussion, irritation, or inflammation. If it is round the pastern joint, it is called 'high ringbone'; it also affects bones within the hoof.

The best way to diagnose this is to pass your fingers down the front of the shin, over the pastern and so on down to the hoof, when slight bony enlargement may be felt. There will be no heat in the affected part. Pain and swelling may appear later. The animal may be only slightly lame, but usually persistently so. There may, however, be some heat round the fetlock joint.

NB Judges should, however, beware of making any definite statements when they have only seconds to decide unsoundnesses which may

174

take experienced qualified persons some time to name.

●*Stringhalt*. This is a nervous complaint, causing the animal to snatch up a hock, occasionally or, in advanced cases, almost invariably when moving. While unsightly, and basically an unsoundness, it does not necessarily affect performance. It cannot however, be tolerated in a show animal and must count against even a working hunter unless there is nothing better in the ring.

Defects and Injuries to the Feet

●*Laminitis* is the equivalent of gout in humans, and just as painful. In severe attacks, the animal can hardly be got to move. In less severe cases there is heat in the affected feet, and the animal will tend to throw his weight on his heels. If an animal, and this particularly applies to native ponies, has had a severe attack, this can cause a separation between the sensitive and insensitive laminae. This, by loosening the attachment, causes the coffin bone to descend and press on the sole, when it in turn also descends, loses its concave shape, and becomes convex. This is called a 'dropped sole'.

This disease also causes rings to appear *round* the hoof, especially emanating from the back of the hoof, while the toe tends to protrude, due to the animal taking the weight on its heels. These rings should not be confused with the normal rings that almost always appear on horses out at grass, which are much less pronounced, and appear round the front rather than the back of the hoof – nor of course with sandcracks.

Native breeds, especially Shetlands, are very prone to laminitis, and a judge should be on the watch for feet showing signs of having had this disease (see Fig. 10, page 39).

●*Navicular*. This, in its primary stages, is inflammation of the navicular bone, which lies at the back of the coffin bone, inside the hoof.

The first sign may be pointing a foot in the stable, followed by a shortening of the stride, and perhaps lameness. It will be intermittently lame in the early stages. Presssure on the hollow of the heel will often give pain and is symptomatic of the existence of the disease.

A marked feature is that the animal invariably goes on his toes in progression, and if affected in both forefeet he will have a short, pottering action. It is unlikely, however, that a horse suffering from this will be presented in the ring.

●*Thrush*. This is a common disease where stable management is bad.

175

It shows itself in the form of an acrid strong-smelling unhealthy secretion issuing from the sensitive frog through the cleft of the external frog. Again, it is unlikely that an animal suffering from this in any marked degree will be shown.

●*Seedy toe*. This is a separation of the horny and sensitive laminae commencing in the lower partition of the laminae and extending upwards. It can be the result of laminitis. More often it is caused by the pressure of the clip of the shoe, and is aggravated by dirt or gravel getting into the hollows so formed. It would count against an animal just like any other malformation or disease of the foot.

●*Over-reaches and treads*. These are injuries to the coronary bands or coronet, inflicted by the shoe of the other foot when in motion, turning, backing, or shying, or by the tramp of another horse. If there is a blemish it could count against a show animal.

●*Sandcracks*. These are perpendicular fissures in the wall of the crust of the hoof. In most cases they are due to brittleness of the wall because of lack of oil or too dry a wall. They can also be constitutional or caused by the stupid practice of rasping the wall, resulting in what one farrier described to me as 'distressed feet'. These cracks do not necessarily cause lameness until they become sufficiently deep to expose the sensitive laminae or extend to the coronary band. They should, of course, not be confused with grass rings or the rings caused by severe attacks of laminitis, both of which pass round the hoof, not up it.

●*False quarter*. Should the coronet be involved in any serious inflammation its ordinary secretions may be arrested. If the inflammation is long continued it may affect the band until it becomes wholly disorganised and its vitality destroyed, when a break or separation of the wall below the place where the injury occurred will result. This separation is called a 'false quarter'. Though the legitimate secretion of the coronet band is not restored, nature will throw out a species of spurious horn which will sufficiently protect the sensitive parts immediately under the seat of injury for the horse to go sound for all practical purposes. The foot may not appear normal and may be blemished. The horse is therefore not a show specimen although this blemish might be overlooked in working hunter classes, where there is not another sound unblemished animal of equal performance in the ring.

176

PART 4

Show Organisation and Duties of Officials

18 Councils and Committees

How is the average voting public to know who does or does not make a good committee member? How are you or I to know, for example, that Mrs Greatly Daring the minute she is elected will not settle down to propose legislation by which she alone will benefit? How can Captain Tiddlypush know that 'the Major', who used to be a tower of strength when they served together, is now so deaf he cannot hear the motion? In these circumstances, can it be wondered that under this voting system councils and committees up and down the country get cluttered with dead wood of which they cannot be rid without either pulling strings or being utterly ruthless, or that motions are passed which the secretary, for one, knows from the beginning are still-born.

Having 'got on', these people in the main are re-elected year after year, either through being 'a Name' or because the voters have no knowledge either of their abilities or of what they are required to do.

While there is something to be said for businesses that have a strict retiring age, ability is what counts.

There is much to be said in favour of dictatorship, but the dictator has to be a born leader, when it is up to the members to decide whether his influence is for good or for bad. If for good it is obviously in everyone's interest and will benefit the cause to follow, if not blindly, at least loyally, but always with the courage to disagree should the need arise. If for bad, the sooner he or she is unseated the better. But is it not always easy to decide, especially in the early days, which way the wind will eventually blow, north or south. Once a north wind has everyone in its grip, frozen stiff like mesmerised rabbits, it is too late - the dictator will be difficult to depose.

On the other hand, there is much to be said for dictators, for usually they are dedicated people. They have a one-track mind, which is the greatest aid to success, and 'drive' which makes things hum, and their position makes it possible for them more or less to pick their own team and so not find themselves cluttered up with dead-heads and anti-bodies chosen for them by other people.

179

To an astute leader the power to choose his own committee and staff is obviously valuable, especially if he is a good picker and able to place the right colleagues in the right place at the right time. If, however, he has not the perspicacity to distinguish between a 'yes-man' and an honest workman – if he puts a square peg into a round hole – if he tends to run the whole as a private party – the society will definitely suffer until someone has the energy or inclination to oppose it.

Even if a really dedicated leader of complete integrity has been found, a council or committee has to be formed. Alas, this is often done in a hurry or on the spur of the moment, and the ensuing committee then contains a number of members who either contribute nothing or who are a perfect nuisance.

How to avoid this, anyway in the initial stage? Someone has to start the ball rolling, but there is bound to be a diversity of opinion as to whom these people should be. There will be those who have been practically bludgeoned into standing and who, when elected, have little real intention of doing anything. These, however, are not such a menace as those who feel they must prove their worth, if not throw their weight about, but probably give the matter little serious thought before a meeting. Then there is the type who have not got a clue, but mean well. They think up the most impossible ideas, which they propound at a meeting, and, as no one likes to hurt their feelings, the motion may well be carried, when the secretary is left holding the baby, which, before he gives it its first bottle, he knows is a weakling and a sheer waste of his time. Then there are the 'axe-grinders'. They are the biggest menaces of all. They blatantly put forward ideas which are patently to their own advantage, and frequently only to theirs. Finally, there are the apathetics. They sit silent as the grave, confining their activities to voting when they more than probably have not got a clue as to what they are voting for or against. An astute chairman gets to recognise these people and deals with them. A dictator either gets rid of them or ignores them.

Good council or committee members are those who know what they are talking about, have the ability to put across their ideas, are prepared to devote time and thought, and grind no axes. Moreover, they are prepared to stand up for and vote for what they think is right, regardless of the 'Establishment'. They may not be right all the time, but at least they are live wires and not dead wood.

A clever chairman can, more often than not, get any motion he wants passed without the majority of the members being aware of what he is doing. At the same time it should be remembered that those dealing with the day-to-day working of the organisation, whatever it is, are, or should be, likely to know what is best for it.

Elections to councils and committees could be improved if voters took the trouble to find out the sort of people who are needed, the qualifications required, and then to find out more about the people they either propose or vote for, and whether they make good committee members. More often than not they just vote for names without taking into account the required qualifications for the job.

The same applies where a management, or finance and general purposes committee are elected by members of the council. The chairman, being only human, very naturally uses his influence to get people elected with whom he is in accord. If he is a good chairman this is a good thing. If not, it can be detrimental. It also leads to back-scratching and voting on the 'old-boy' basis. Incidentally, a number of societies claim to be democratic when, in fact, they are anything but.

Whether committee or council members automatically retire every year is a matter to be decided when drawing up the constitution. Annual retirement, which is not often the rule, gives a chance of getting rid of useless members, but leads to a lack of continuity. It is more usual for members to retire every three years, when they either do or do not offer themselves for re-election. While I am all for continuity, this system can mean that members who are past their best, or who have lost interest (if they ever had any!) get elected year after year, thereby excluding others who would be really useful. There are, moreover, societies whose council members are only rubber stamps, the society being run either by the management, finance and general purposes committee, or what have you.

I do feel, however, that people should be more conscientious when they have agreed to serve. They must be prepared to give some of their time and to do something – that is, if they are allowed to do so.

With regard to the number of council or committee members, a well-known platitude suggests that the best number is one. Undoubtedly, in the case of a small local society, or when forming new societies, it is advisable to start with a small select number, only adding more when the need arises and when the qualities and abilities of those selected have been tested. It is very unwise to elect a large number as they then form into groups, which can be troublesome. It is, of course, essential to have a quorum, which should not be less than five, and, I suggest, not more than eight. Permission to co-opt should be clearly stated in the rules.

19 Officials

President

A President is largely a figurehead. He can, however, exert a great influence for either good or bad, affecting the whole atmosphere. He should therefore be carefully chosen, not simply because he has money and can therefore be presumed – even expected – to be ready to part with some of it.

Primarily, he should be a man of integrity, well thought of by people whose opinion counts, and not necessarily with a title, though this can add authority and a certain glamour. He should never be pompous, but if he has influence in circles which are likely to be useful this gives added weight to his adoption.

He should make himself agreeable to all, and should be approachable not only by the council and committee and secretary but by any of the members, whether of high or lowly birth or importance. In short, he should be a good mixer.

On the day, he must be willing to present cups *ad lib* and sometimes *ad nauseam*. He should not interfere with the organisation or listen to tittle-tattle but should support its rules and regulations and its officers. He may, of course, give advice and make suggestions, and should be ready and willing to pour sand on fire should the need arise.

It is, alas, true that the more lunches he presides over – and pays for – the greater will be his popularity, and the more events he can get sponsored, the longer he will remain in office. To be fair, however, very many presidents are highly thought of and remain in office although contributing a minimum financially. Personality is what counts in this office.

It is both amazing and very fortunate that so many men and women deem it a great honour to be invited to become presidents. Long may this happy state of affairs continue; otherwise the time may come when presidents have to be coerced, even bludgeoned, into taking office!

Chairman

Even if the real incentive and organisation is in the hands of an *organising* secretary, a chairman of committee is necessary and invariably takes the chair at council or committee meetings at which the policy of the society or show is decided and the major decisions made, leaving the secretary to carry out the day-to-day duties. If the secretary is not the organiser, upon the chairman will largely fall not only the responsibility but also the task of ensuring that a policy is formed and maintained.

A chairman's responsibility varies, therefore, according to whether he has an effective salaried organising secretary, who will take most of the initiative and much of the responsibility off his shoulders, or whether he has under him simply a salaried or honorary, even part-time, secretary, who is there to take orders and to carry out the decisions of the committee.

Let us first take the position of a chairman who is lucky enough to find himself with an able organising secretary. I feel his first duty is to give every possible support to this rarity. He must, of course, make certain that the financial situation is sound so that there is no danger of committee members being involved financially. As chairman, he/she must be kept right in the picture; no important step should be taken by the organising secretary or by anyone else without consulting him, or at least informing him. If then the chairman deems it necessary to place the matter before the committee, it is up to him to instruct the secretary to call a meeting, or he may either decide to consult the member or members of the committee in whose particular province the matter lies, or that it is a matter with which he and the organising secretary can deal.

It is obviously advantageous to choose a person who has an interest in, or at least some knowledge of the 'end product'. Not only is it a strain on anyone to have to simulate this, but it means that on technicalities he is at a loss and has to rely on the knowledge or judgement of others. All the same, complete ignorance can be preferable to a *little* knowledge. The latter can be a menace.

Even when there is a good and dedicated organising secretary, the chairman must never become a figurehead, and an organising secretary would be very foolish not to work with the chairman at all times and, therefore, we hope, with the majority if not the whole of the committee.

If, however, a chairman is working with just a secretary (probably part-time), he may well have to have not only the ideas but also the 'drive' with which to implement them. While, as I have said, the

183

secretary is there to do the bidding of the chairman and his committee, the secretary must advise whether or not a proposal is feasible. When some motion in committee is carried which for sound reasons is just not practicable, it is a sheer waste of his time and the organisation's money to try to carry it out. This is very important. So often one serves on committees where vague or useless ideas, thought up at the eleventh hour are passed by a small vote by members who either have no knowledge of the subject or have not given the matter sufficient thought.

A good chairman is, next to a good dedicated organising secretary, the greatest asset any organisation can have. Look to the top of a first-class school and you will find a good headmaster. One only has to sit under a clever chairman to realise what influence he can exert. It is up to him to keep order at meetings, to keep the members from going off at tangents, to allow the rebels to have their say yet at the same time to direct their energies into other channels, and in extreme cases to deal firmly but tactfully with them. He must side-track the axe-grinders, discreetly silence the 'natterers', and control the temper and tempo of the meeting in such a manner that its business is dispatched efficiently.

A good chairman gives the impression that the committee, not he, is making the decisions, when in fact the opposite is often the case. How many votes can be obtained by a few well-chosen phrases, while quite a little oil poured discreetly upon troubled waters can avert a deadlock, if not open warfare.

He must learn to use the individuals on his committee to the best of their ability. In consultation with the treasurer he must decide upon income and expenditure. He must endeavour continually to make fresh contacts likely to be valuable and should keep an eye open for fresh blood, with a view to co-opting on to the committee anyone likely to prove an asset. He must cultivate what are commonly called VIPs and titled folk, because, whatever people may say, titles are still aces, and, like spades and hearts, are rated higher than other cards!

A good chairman 'inspires' his committee and his staff. The best are 'born leaders'. At all times he must be loyal to all who serve him.

Chairmen should not become personally involved in major or even minor disputes or complaints. These should be sent in in writing to be placed on the table at the next committee meeting. While the 'chair' should be readily accessible to the lowliest member and known to as many members as possible, he should not listen to or become involved in the tittle-tattle which invariably percolates through showgrounds. At the same time it is advisable that he should have

184

his ear attuned to the 'bush wireless' as this is sometimes a most useful source of valuable information.

A good chairman keeps his committee members loyal and happy and directs their talents and energies into channels best suited to them. He should not be above taking off his coat in emergencies, thereby setting an example. Too many people in high places are afraid of losing face if they condescend to menial tasks, when actually the opposite is the case, although admittedly they have to have that certain 'something' to carry it off.

If and when he has to ask any member of the committee or staff to resign, or if he has to give anyone the 'sack', he should make certain he has a majority vote and that the notice comes from the association/society and not from him personally. He, as well as the organisation he serves, should have a good lawyer in reserve, who should attend meetings when it is deemed necessary.

On show days, the chairman's duties are mainly social, although he must be readily available to the secretary to deal with any objections, or settle disputes, or make rulings in emergencies. While the president, even if he does not actually pay for the lunch, presides at it, it is the chairman, together with the secretary, who sees that everything runs smoothly.

A chairman must be ever alert to interest people in his cause, whatever it may be, either as members, exhibitors, spectators and, above all, as sponsors. Now that everything is so costly, sponsors are a most valuable and indeed essential asset to any organisation, and an alert, astute and enthusiastic chairman can do a tremendous amount in this field. It is essential that he should at all times present the organisation, or show, or whatever it is he represents, in the most acceptable and inspiring light. He must belong to that organisation body and soul, inspiring all those working under him with the same enthusiasm and loyalty. He should never forget what every chairman owes to the dedicated people who work voluntarily, whom it is therefore churlish to criticise and only courteous to thank.

I hope it does not appear smug to wish that this book may be of some help to, and show appreciation of, the numberless unpaid chairmen to whom exhibitors, spectators, and many charitable causes owe so much.

Honorary Treasurer

Of all the officials of a club or other organisation I suppose the treasurer, honorary or otherwise, is the least understood, mainly

185

because few people are interested in the financial state of any organisation and fewer still love 'figures' or even understand them. Members quite understandably want just 'to get on with it,' be it showing ponies or simply playing golf. They leave the chores of looking after the money and the books to a dimly apprehended individual who almost certainly wears glasses and whose name is scarcely known. As long as there is something in the kitty, and the show, or shows, can go on, they are content. And to a point, where such a situation exists it is really a compliment to the committee in general and, it is to be hoped, to the treasurer in particular because it should indicate a freedom from financial worries which betokens success for the organisers.

As far as I know, there is no set of rules to govern the activities of a treasurer. Apart from sheer dishonesty, it is possible to side-step the responsibilities of looking after other people's money to a degree which, in the eyes of a banker or of an accountant, is quite alarming. But whether an organisation is large or small the principles are the same, so let us take a look at them.

In outline, the chief obligations of a treasurer are the keeping of records capable of being audited, the custody of all cash and securities in as safe a manner as is practicable and the provision of money for the day-to-day running of the organisation and at special functions, e.g. shows. It entails making proper banking arrangements for all occasions and the signing of all cheques. He should make a constant review of reserves, if any, and of investments should these be undertaken, so that all relevant information may be available for committee meetings when held, and for the chairman at any time, even in the dead of night if the chairman is inclined to consider such matters at such an hour!

On show days the treasurer is of course at the beck and call of everybody, from first thing in the morning, when the sale of tickets is arranged and the provision made for cash 'floats' at all points on the showground where money is involved, to the periodical collection of surplus cash as it accumulates and the final analysis and 'balancing' of each and every activity at the end of the day. And before an evening meal can be contemplated the collected money must be lodged safely, preferably in a bank.

Some cynics say that a treasurer must be perpetually suspicious of everybody with whom he, or she, deals, and that a system of checks and counterchecks should be instituted which makes it virtually impossible for everyone, himself included, to be dishonest. This may be a doctrine of perfection, and it is certainly true that all reasonable precautions against loss should be taken. But we all realise that

186

occasions continually arise when individuals must be trusted implicitly. It is for the treasurer to judge and assess each risk, though it is as well to remember that one cannot be too careful with other people's property.

Here I might mention that the question of insurance is often overlooked; and that applies not only to property and assets of all kinds, but to third-party risks and to loss of profits due to various contingencies. The treasurer should at least be ready with an opinion as to which risk should or should not be covered.

Likewise, if a lot of the work is delegated and there is an office staff to consider, the treasurer should know what is going on. When he checks different aspects of the book-keeping, he may be misunderstood, though this is seldom the case. Actually, he is only doing his duty. He does not expect to unearth mistakes and when, as is usual, he finds everything in perfect order I suggest that he make suitable commendatory noises.

By and large, then, the treasurer is a lucky person. He carries some of the responsibility, which is to be expected, but he works mostly in the background, out of the line of fire of the ordinary members of the club.

Although he may help to mould policy, his is not the final responsibility. He can enjoy all the fun – and avoid trouble – from a discreet distance.

Show Director

This may be a separate individual, the chairman, or the organising secretary. One of the chief essentials in a show director is that he should have *vision*. He must be able to 'imagine', ahead of the show day, what is wanted, to see the showground layout as a whole, and what may or may not happen given various situations. He should be able to see the layout in his mind's eye when he walks on to either a bare field or an already established ground, such as one belonging to another organisation, or a racecourse, and, in the latter cases, he must be able to judge how he can adapt it to his own requirements. An organiser who is without vision is liable to errors and omissions which become only too apparent on show day. The more he can anticipate, the more successful he will be.

He simply must sense what exhibitors will expect and what they are liable to do if they do not get it. He should envisage how traffic will pile up, where the public are likely to wander, and therefore to get in the way, and how car parks should be sited to entail a minimum of walking; where the stabling should be located (as near as possible to the rings); and where the loudspeakers, the toilets, the restaurants and bars, etc., should be. He should imagine himself in various roles: for example, that of an exhibitor coming in late, in the dark, or a disabled member of the public, or an exhibitor with a number of animals to prepare and show in various rings.

He must in fact visualise and see that everything listed under 'good organisation' is under control. Needless to say, he must also have the very necessary authority.

Quick decisions are difficult in the heat of battle. It is not easy to keep a clear head when faced with an inflamed exhibitor or a disgruntled spectator, and it is amazing how angry they can get. All sense of proportion seems to vanish, I myself have been guilty, both as an exhibitor and as a spectator. Neither can a director show favouritism. Once a show becomes known as 'So-and-So's benefit', once it gets around that So-and-So is well in, this is a bad thing. While there are bound to be some extenuating circumstances, a show director should beware of creating dangerous precedents, or he will find himself in real trouble. As far as possible, all men should be equal in his sight. He should begin as he means to go on. He can so easily cause ill-feeling and resentment by making an unfair decision, by showing favouritism, or by failing to recognise a reasonable request.

Finally, he should be able on the day to sit back and if possible relax, ready to deal with any emergencies that may arise. That they will is a foregone conclusion.

Secretary

A good secretary (who can be either a man or a woman) is the most valuable asset of any association, society, or show. Upon him depends the efficiency and smoothness of the whole. (This position should not be confused with that of an organising secretary, whose duties are the same as those of a show director, but without holding any responsibility for policy, for which he has, or should have, the backing of his council or committee.)

A secretary has the job of running not only the showground but also the office. He is therefore more often than not in the best position to know whether a policy or decision of any kind is likely to succeed or fail. His finger is more on the pulse than that of anyone else. He has a more intimate knowledge of the members (if a members' show), of the exhibitors, of the general public, of the various departments, and therefore is more likely to know what their reactions will be.

He also knows or should know, the various contractors with whom he has decided to deal, and from whom he has extracted the best possible terms. It is up to him to see that all equipment is ordered, the show's property maintained and insured and extra staff engaged for the busy season and on the show day. He should also know the scope and ability of his own permanent staff, whether on the showground or in the office, and should keep the progress sheet under his thumb.

In consultation with the judges' selection sub-committee it is up to him to procure the services of judges and stewards, and if the best judges are wanted, this should be done six or eight months in advance of the show date.

Because he is so closely in touch with the everyday working of the whole, more often than not he is the best judge of what is or is not a right policy, and what is or is not practical. He should – indeed, he must – work in close liaison with his chairman, council, or committee, who in turn, if he is capable and straight, should give him their loyal support and plenty of rein. He should, of course, carry out policies and decisions passed in committee, whether he thinks them a good thing or not, but his opinion, whether for or against, must be worth having.

Frequently he may find himself having to do things of which he does not approve. He may even be left holding a baby for which he was not primarily responsible, in which case his loyalty will be taxed. A good relationship between chairman, committee, and secretary is essential, and give-and-take between them is therefore most advisable.

A responsible secretary should be allowed to pick his own staff and should be given the authority and responsibility and be left in peace to get on with the job without constant interference by members of the committee. He should have the complete confidence and support of the chairman. If, after fair trial, he fails, then he should be replaced but, given he proves himself, then the chairman and committee would do well to listen to his advice. He should be permitted to make suggestions and should certainly state when any proposition is not feasible, either from his own or his staff's point of view, or because of his inside knowledge.

His greatest value will be his ability to get on with all sorts of men and women; to organise his office, showground, and the staff of both. He should be able not only to maintain, but to increase membership, or, if not a membership show, public support. He should have the ability to buy well. If he has social attributes as well as organising ability, if he is able to get the most out of staff, then he is indeed a 'find'. Incidentally, he should be able to relax with his staff, while at the same time maintaining their respect (in public Christian names should not be used, whatever endearments may be used in private).

The efficiency of the office – the accounts, the filing system, and certainly the correct entering of exhibits – are his responsibility, and upon this efficiency depends the smooth running of the whole. If mistakes are made in the entries, either through ineligibility or omission, there will be TROUBLE, and double checking is therefore essential.

On show days it is up to him to see that the office is efficiently and intelligently staffed; that all queries and complaints, even objections, are dealt with courteously but very firmly. This will be one of his hardest tasks. He should never create a precedent, but the 'couldn't care less' attitude must be avoided. Should it not be possible to deal with the matter forthwith, the impression should be given that it will be, and it is up to the secretary to see that it is.

It is essential he should have a really efficient deputy (or right hand) upon whom he can rely, and who has the necessary knowledge and ability to implement his orders and to carry on the everyday routine of both showground and office in his absence. Dependent upon the size of the show, he must also have behind him a trained efficient office staff, and a reliable head groundsman with a good memory. If the showground belongs to another organisation someone must be authorised to carry out the secretary's instructions.

It is essential that he should have the ability to decentralise and not try to do everything himself. So many otherwise efficient people fall down on this score. They can even be a perfect nuisance.

He should work hard himself or the people he employs will soon see through him and slack off. His orders must be carried out, but at the same time he must be approachable, fair, firm and impartial. A sense of humour oils the wheels.

He will no doubt have to deal with some 'twisters' and may even be offered payment in cash or kind in return for contracts or privileges granted. To all of these he must not only turn a deaf ear but, figuratively speaking, use the toe of his boot.

He will be wise to realise that without exhibitors there will be no show and that they deserve every help and encouragement. There will inevitably be among them those who are never satisfied, who are even out to make trouble. With this fortunately very small minority he must deal very politely but very firmly. After all they need

190

not come again. Rules once made must be kept, otherwise there would be no respect for the show.

Finally, we will undoubtedly need that other great asset of any organisation known as 'drive'. He will find he will have to use this all day and every day or the whole thing finally drags to a halt.

These essential qualities may not lead to popularity, but personally I would rather be respected than universally popular.

It is always apparent when a show is blessed with an efficient secretary.

20 Shows

Schedules

On the front of the schedule (or prize list) is the name of the show, its venue, date, closing date for entries (and whether or not late ones are accepted); the name, address and telephone number of secretary should be clearly stated in bold type. If the showground is lent, due acknowledgement should be given. The name of the President may also be printed on the cover.

Inside, for the sake of authority and goodwill, the name of the chairman, council, or committee members may be included, and other office-bearers – but not necessarily. It is better to list the panel of judges rather than place their names under individual classes, as they can then be seen at a glance. If they can appear in both places, so much the better.

Rules and regulations should be clearly stated but it is no use making them if they cannot be implemented. Members' subscriptions, and privileges, admission prices, cost of car park, meals, and stabling, and details of prize money should be included. If late entries are accepted it should be stated on what terms; if not accepted, this should be in bold type.

The various types and breeds of horses and ponies should be kept together. In other words, in-hand classes should be followed by ridden classes in types, commencing with hunters, followed by hacks, cobs, etc. In-hand ponies should start with broodmares followed by youngstock; followed by ridden ponies. Mountain and moorland breeds should all be together and it is tactful to place them in alphabetical order.

Classification should be given much thought and be carefully worded if trouble is to be avoided. The classes chosen should be suitable for the type of show and the area in which it is held. If the show is to pay its way, classifications should suit the majority rather than the minority. All persuasions or tempting offers or influence which may be brought to bear, to put on classes to suit individuals, should be avoided unless some individual or society – notably a breed society – offers to put up the prize money, when the rosettes

192

may be given by the show. It all depends on whether there is time and space to stage a particular class. Other shows and breed secretaries are always ready to advise on type, height, age groups, sex, breeding, breeders, age of rider, nominations, substitutions, limited classes, open, novice, local and radius classes, and mountain and moorland classes whether in breeds or mixed, part-bred animals, etc. In all circumstances, whatever classification or ruling is printed in the schedule must be adhered to; should there be any discrepancy between schedule and programme, *what appears in the schedule takes precedence*. If registered numbers are required, these should be insisted on, and checked, but they are not required for open classes.

It should be clear to what particular type or breed the class refers: for example, whether pure-bred Arabs, or part-bred, or Anglo-Arabs; whether fully registered native breeds or unregistered (that is, ordinary utility ponies) – it is unwise to mix these.

Here are some ways of limiting classes:

(1) Confined to novices, which are usually described as 'not having won a first prize' (or prizes, with means to three places), followed by the type of class(es) from 1st January of the year of the show.
(2) A monetary limit, i.e. 'not to have won a first prize of more than £X'.
(3) A radius limit, i.e. for a horse or pony 'owned and ridden by an adult (or child) living within a radius of . . . miles of the showground'.
(4) Confined to children of farmers, or what have you.

Points (2) and (4) above are obviously difficult to check, but even if the show secretary has not got the necessary information he will soon be given it – by the other exhibitors!

In children's ridden classes the British Show Pony Society classification usually is, and should be, adhered to, and their rules followed. The same applies to shows staging classes for any other types of equines when the relevant society's rules should be used.

Some shows put on classes without mentioning whether registered numbers etc. are required, when unregistered animals enter and trouble ensues. This particularly applies to mountain and moorland classes. If unregistered animals are to be accepted, this should be stated in the schedule so that owners of registered animals need not enter if they do not wish to do so, but nearly all shows now limit their native classes to registered animals, and rightly so. However disappointing this may be to owners of non-pedigree animals, it not only raises the standard of exhibits – which surely must be the aim of every show organiser - but helps to maintain the breed societies.

There can always be a separate class for unregistered animals if funds permit, and any number of small local shows take field entries catering for ordinary utility ponies, which are by no means to be despised.

Riding pony broodmare and youngstock classes are always open. Part-bred Arabs, Palominos and Spotted Horses and Ponies should be registered but by no means always are. Here I would mention that registration of ponies in the National Pony Stud Book *proper* is desirable, and essential for closed classes, but registration in the *register* of this society does not necessarily qualify for closed classes and is not required in Open classes. For example, progeny from approved mares may not be eligible in certain instances, and Welsh FS and Appendix Highland mares are not eligible at most shows, even in their own breed classes. Show organisers would be well advised, and will I hope find it helpful, to study the various sections of this book before compiling their schedules.

Mountain and Moorland Classes
While every native breed pony is entitled to be judged under its own breed classification where show finances permit, they may be judged: (1) altogether in what is called a mixed mountain and moorland class; (2) divided into large and small types (large types are Connemara, Dales, Fell, Highland, New Forest, Welsh Ponies Section B, C, and Welsh Cobs Section D; small types are Dartmoor, Exmoor, Shetland and Welsh Mountain Section A); or (3) judged first of all in their breed sections followed by a championship for which all first-prize winners are eligible; (4) or shows adjacent to a natural haunt of these ponies, such as Dartmoor and Exmoor, the New Forest, or the North of England, may put on classes for these breeds only, as being virtually local.

Some shows insist that, while eligible for their own breed section awards, to be eligible for the championship exhibits must be by fully registered parents. These are the shows which are popular but this entails some office work checking the breeding, or contacting the relevant breed secretary.

See also page 68 for notes on height.

Open Classes
These include hunter, riding pony broodmare, and youngstock classes, working hunter pony and hunter pony, hacks, cobs, and riding horses. The number of classes staged for them depends on what the show can afford. The National Light Horse Breeding Society (HIS) advises on classification for their exhibits. The follow-

ing is the suggested classification for ponies if classes have to be limited.

(1) Yearling colt, filly or gelding unlikely to exceed 12.2 hh at maturity.
(2) Yearling colt, filly or gelding unlikely to exceed 14.2 hh at maturity.
(3) Two- or three-year-old filly or gelding unlikely to exceed 12.2 hh at maturity.
(4) Two- or three-year-old filly or gelding unlikely to exceed 14.2 hh at maturity.
(5) Riding pony yearling colt, filly or gelding, two-or three-year-old filly or gelding unlikely to exceed 14.2 hh at maturity. This latter will not be popular, however. Concessions to yearlings can be given by awarding one or even two Specials for the best of them.

At shows which can afford the time and money to give individual classes, the popular classification is to give a class to each height:

not exceeding 12.2 hh;
exceeding 12.2 hh but not exceeding 13.2 hh;
exceeding 13.2 hh but not exceeding 14.2 hh

in each age group, namely, yearlings, two-year-olds and three-year-olds. (Where very large classes are anticipated, some shows put on a class for under 12 hh as well or divide the sexes.)

While it does not matter to what height a hunter grows, it does when dealing with ponies. Indeed it is a burning topic. It may be a good thing, therefore, to mention in the schedule that pony young-stock should not exceed certain heights at various ages. This simply *acts as a guide* to exhibitors who are genuinely anxious not to show a pony likely to grow out of its class height limit. Borderline cases will always be a problem. The heights recommended are:

Yearlings not to exceed 12.2 hh at maturity – 11.3 hh
Yearlings not to exceed 13.2 hh at maturity – 12.3 hh
Yearlings not to exceed 14.2 hh at maturity – 13.3 hh
Two-year-olds not to exceed 12.2 hh at maturity – 12 hh
Two-year-olds not to exceed 13.2 hh at maturity – 13 hh
Two-year-olds not to exceed 14.2 hh at maturity – 14 hh
Three-year-olds not to exceed 12.2 hh at maturity – 12.1 hh
Three-year-olds not to exceed 13.2 hh at maturity – 13.1 hh
Three-year-olds not to exceed 14.2 hh at maturity – 14.1 hh

Obviously the owner of a 12.2 hh yearling hesitates to enter against those likely to reach 14.2 hh at maturity, yet few shows can be expected to stage classes for all ages of all heights. Actually a judge should not make any difference on the score of height; a good little one is just as valuable as a good big one and in the case of broodmares more so, as they can then be put to Thoroughbred and other quality stallions.

Obviously only the specialised shows can afford to give classes for all heights and ages.

Division of Classes

A class may have so many entries that it makes judging difficult, if not impossible, besides being discouraging to exhibitors. If the show can afford it they can be divided in the following manner:

(1) By dividing the sexes; only practical if these are pretty evenly divided.
(2) By dividing the age groups, that is, in a class for one-, two-, and three-year-olds; yearlings can be given a class of their own.
(3) Division by height. For example, should the original classification read 'Pony broodmare not exceeding 12.2 hh,' this can be divided into:
    (a) Broodmare not exceeding 12 hh
    (b) Broodmare exceeding 12 hh and not exceeding 12.2 hh
    This, however, entails finding out the height of all exhibits as many owners will probably have failed to fill this in on the entry form.
(4) By simply drawing a line half-way through the class, as is done in racing when a race is divided into divisions. If there is a championship, then either the winners of the two divisions have to be judged against each other and the best goes forward for the championship, or both qualify.

Cancellation of Classes

Should a class (or classes) be cancelled it should *not* be omitted from the programme as this is confusing. Instead, its number and nature should be left in, followed by 'Cancelled owing to lack of entries'.

The schedule should state how many entries there must be for the class to be staged and there should be a rule that a class may be cancelled at the discretion of the committee.

Amalgamation of Classes

It may be possible to amalgamate a class with too few entries with another class to make it a worthwhile proposition.

This is always very possible with classes for yearlings and two-year-olds, when the yearlings can be given a Special, or even two, as they obviously are at a disadvantage with older animals.

Ridden classes, too, can be either cancelled or amalgamated on the same lines, or in fact divided. If the original height limit was 14.2 hh it is usual to divide this into:

(1) 13 hh and under; and (2) over 13 hh but not exceeding 14.2 hh. But this again entails not only obtaining the heights from the owners but risking some of the ponies which should be in the 14.2 hh appearing in the 13 hh, and is therefore not recommended.

Special Awards
These are very popular and it pays a show to be liberal with them, especially if, when money goes with them, this is donated by others.

Specials can be awarded in the following manner:

(1) For yearlings, when they are classified with older animals.
(2) For mountain and moorland ponies when they are classified in open broodmare, youngstock, or ridden classes.
(3) Small ponies of, say, 12 hh and under, when classified with larger ones, whether in broodmare, youngstock, ridden or driven classes.
(4) For novices.
(5) For youngstock by or out of a Thoroughbred registered in the GSB, when Arabs should be excluded as some of these are in the GSB.
(6) For youngstock by or out of a registered Arab.
(7) For first crosses, when breeding has to be checked and both parents must be *fully registered*.
(8) Other part-breds, such as part-bred Dartmoor, part-bred Welsh, part-bred Connemara, etc.
(9) For the best child rider – but personally I do not approve of this.
(10) For the best child rider under, say, 12 years in classes where they are in with older children.
(11) For the best performance by the child of a farmer.
(12) For the best pony and rider domiciled within a certain radius of the show.
(13) For the best pony domiciled in Scotland, Ireland, etc.
(14) For the best pony from a riding school or trekking centre.

There is no doubt, however, that Specials are popular with exhibitors

197

while being yet another chore for the office staff and on the day for judges and stewards.

Cumulative Specials

These arise when some enthusiast offers a prize for the best animal in more than one class, for example, for the 'best registered part-bred Arab in classes 2, 4, and 6'. This means that owners of the best in these classes which are eligible have got to be notified and literally herded together to ensure that they are in the right ring at the right moment to compete with the winner of class 8 after that class. This may sound quite simple, but you would be surprised! To begin with, up to 80 per cent of exhibitors may fail to put their registered number in the part-bred Arab Stud Book on their entry form. As the schedule states 'registered', to be eligible registered they must be. The name of the sire, even the dam, may be given but, nine times out of ten, the secretary has no knowledge whatever of Arabs and he/she therefore either has to enter into correspondence with the owner – only to be told that she has gone on holiday – or with the secretary of the society concerned. Meanwhile a note has to be made both in the programme proofs and on the stewards' cards that this particular animal is only eligible if registration is forthcoming on the show date, or the entry form has to be returned.

It is wise to present a rosette to the winner of this Special in each class in order to make sure the right animal turns up to compete in the final. Otherwise winners of the eliminating rounds have a habit of getting lost, or someone who is not entitled to be there turns up in the ring and treats the steward with the most innocent-sounding reasons for being there. The best of the three qualifiers could have a slightly better rosette than those in the preliminary.

Other Societies' Rosettes

Should a society offer a rosette it may well be for something even more complicated, for example, for the 'best filly owned and bred by a member of that Society', or for the 'best exhibit by a Thoroughbred registered in the GSB'. It is patently impossible for show secretaries to know who are or are not members of other societies so that he either has to check with the secretary of that society, request those eligible to wear armbands (when half of them forget to do so), or trust exhibitors to give the right answer (when frequently it is found that although they were members at one time they no longer are). In the case of the second an objection may well be lodged because although the secretary does not know, one of the other exhibitors does, that the animal in fact is not in the GSB but in the American or French stud books.

These are the sort of things of which show secretaries should be forewarned. What at first appears to be an added attraction to the show and an incentive to more entries, can land them in trouble. Care should therefore be exercised before Specials of any kind are accepted, and if they are, the stated qualifications must be able to be checked, and not just on the show day. If other societies' rosettes are taken they should be obtained well in advance of the show, and should of course be mentioned in both the schedule and the programme.

Cups

These can either be challenge cups or cups donated outright, a difference which should be clearly stated in the schedule.

It greatly helps to avoid confusion and delays if every cup is given a name, for example, the 'Old Times Champion Challenge Cup for the best hunter under saddle presented by . . .' or 'The Beatrix Potter Challenge Cup for the best leading rein pony . . .'

In the case of an outright cup, it either has a name chosen by the donor or is simply described as 'Silver cup for the best . . . presented outright by . . .'

Where a cup is given for the best in two or more classes the winner of each class has to be brought forward for the championship. It must be decided before the show, and stated in the schedule and programme, whether or not first and second prize-winners are eligible to compete for the cup, or only first prize-winners. Whatever is decided should be stated on the stewards' cards.

The same applies to championship cups. It must clearly state in the schedule and programme and on the stewards' cards whether first prize-winners *only* are eligible or whether seconds, even thirds, are also eligible to compete. When there is a supreme championship, again it should be clearly stated whether or not reserve champions may compete for the supreme accolade. There may be trouble on the day if these important points are not clarified, and the secretary will be pestered by exhibitors asking whether or not they are eligible to compete and begging for reserve rosettes or prize cards.

It is inadvisable to let winners inscribe their own challenge cups. For the sake of uniformity it is better to have these returned to the cup tent after presentation, inscribed by the show jeweller, and sent on in due course. It also saves correspondence with winners regarding cost of inscription. Besides, not many are prepared to pay for this. Before the cups are despatched by the show jeweller, however, indemnity forms must be signed and returned by the winners.

Challenge cup maintenance and inscription is one of the heaviest commitments of any big show and those not financially stable should beware of accepting too many.

Actually, cups given outright are more popular than challenge cups and there is no upkeep cost.

In the case of membership shows, every member whether paid up or not, should receive a schedule, and, unless known to be a non-exhibitor, entry form(s), stable and catering forms and any other information, not more than six weeks or less than three weeks before closing date of entries. Potential exhibitors should also be sent membership forms and details. It is a good thing to advertise what classes are staged in the horse press, or, if they are local shows, locally.

Certificate of Service

Broodmare classes can either be worded 'with own foal at foot or with certificate of service' followed by the year of the show, or simply 'with own foal at foot'.

The latter classification is very much more popular as it is felt that:

(1) Mares if they are maidens are likely to have very much better figures than those that have had foals; and
(2) They may be mares which will never breed.

It is up to the show concerned to decide whether to include them or not. Those wishful of more entries usually put both. Major breed shows put only 'with own foal at foot', and they may give an extra class for mares without and/or foals at foot but with valid certificate of service for novice mares, that is, those which have never won a prize as a broodmare.

On the subject of age, it is preferable to put 'four-year-old or over', but some shows allow a three-year-old filly with certificate of service. Fillies under this age with foals at foot or certificates of service should definitely not be encouraged.

Entry Forms

Except at shows where animals are eligible for two, three, or more classes, it makes for more accuracy if there is an entry form for each animal, but if exhibitors have an animal eligible for several classes enough entry forms might not be sent, when exhibitors, who usually enter at the last minute, put these extra entries on a separate piece of paper, which means that the staff have then to copy them on to a proper form or they may get lost.

If, therefore, one entry form is sent to cover all entries, it should be of sufficient size and have sufficient space on it for details such as age, sex, height, dam and sire and registered numbers, to be placed against each class in which the pony is entered. It is most important that entry forms be very carefully laid out, and this especially applies to shows staging broodmare and youngstock classes, or mountain and moorland classes. The more classes an exhibitor can enter in, the more popular will that show be.

Numbering Entries

Some show secretaries number these as they come in, in a book, but this can lead to errors and omissions. It is much better if all numbering is done *after the entries close*, and then alphabetically and numerically (see page 208).

If a closing date is stated this must be adhered to in fairness to all and in order that the catalogue may go to press on time.

Entry Fees

The cost of entry fees depends on the amount of prize money.

Entries on the Day

These are not possible at the big shows. To begin with, they make a farce of the programme and with big entries it is essential to have everything cut and dried on the day. Every exhibit must have its number, description, and the class in which it is entered. The only exception can be classes held in a side ring for 'locals' or gymkhana events, etc.

Large shows, and especially breed shows where catalogues are virtually stud books, should certainly not accept entries on the day, for only by having a correct programme can any show hope to run smoothly and without trouble. Besides, it is very annoying for spectators if they are unable to find a number in a programme for which they have paid quite a considerable sum.

The bigger the show, the earlier must be the closing date for entries. This appears to be something some exhibitors are incapable of understanding, but they can have no idea of the amount of work entailed in getting entries not only entered in the ledgers (if it is a membership show), and/or in the account books, but also into classes. Every detail must be correct and legible for the printers' typesetters. One has only to have the experience of arriving at a show after a long and expensive journey to find one's animal is not entered to realise the importance of accuracy.

Another matter that holds things up is that so many exhibitors fail to send in their subscription with their entries or they hope or imagine that these have already been paid.

Entries for ordinary ridden classes of all kinds, jumping, or working hunters are child's play compared with the detail required for registered animals. All the former need is the name of the animal, its colour, sex, and sometimes height, name and address of exhibitor, and name and date of birth of the rider (in children's classes).

Every effort should be made to get the entries into their classes as soon as possible. Every alteration and cancellation entailing moving an animal from one class to another holds this up.

Late Entries

One rule above all others *must be made and kept*. No late entry can be accepted; this is the hardest rule of all to keep. Many and varied are the excuses proffered and intensive is the wheedling to which a secretary and his staff are subjected. The moment he weakens a secretary creates a dangerous precedent which if it leaks out – and it invariably does – will not readily be forgotten or forgiven, and there will be a shoal of such requests the following year. Besides, to accept late entries is not fair to those who took the trouble to be in time or to others who may have been refused. The only exceptions could be such classes as costume classes, gymkhana, and other similar types of class for which field entries are accepted.

Field Entries

These are popular as people need not make up their minds and risk their entry fees being wasted until the night before the show, or even that morning. They are not, however, advocated for large shows and are mostly only taken at very small shows or local gymkhanas where no proper catalogue is issued. I do know, however, of some very large shows that take field entries and get away with it, but they cannot be very particular on checking for eligibility.

Return of Entry Fees

Should two classes in which an animal is entered clash, as can happen at shows where they are eligible for several classes, it is only fair that the exhibitor should have his entry fee refunded for the class missed, provided that he writes in *after* the show giving the name of animal, number of class missed, and the times of the two classes which clashed.

There are some other extenuating circumstances such as a bad accident, even death, but the general rule should be that entry fees are not refunded. After all, if these have already been put in the programme the show would lose money on printing costs.

202

Nominations and Substitutes

Should the schedule state that these are not acceptable, this rule should be adhered to equally strictly. Indeed it is even more important, because nominations and substitutes are easily discernible in the programme by other exhibitors and are therefore a source, if not of actual objections, of ill-feeling.

Suggestions to an Intending Exhibitor

When you receive a schedule with classes which appear to be suitable for your animals, notice the exact conditions of each class, making sure that your animals are, in fact, eligible in every way. Make a note of the closing date for entries, and double check the requirements for equine influenza vaccination certificates, if they are required.

Before beginning to fill in the entry form read it through to make sure that you understand what is wanted. FILL IN ALL DETAILS REQUESTED, printing clearly. It is easier for the show secretary to discard surplus information than to acquire additional details, but surplus information takes time to cross out and not all the office staff have the necessary knowledge to judge what is and is not necessary. For instance, the youngster you are entering is by that Welsh Mountain pony sire known in every show ring, so you decide that there is absolutely no need to bother with the registered number of the sire. BUT THERE IS. This number will have to be printed in the catalogue, so there is space on the entry form clearly marked where the registered number of the sire is requested. Presumably your own private stud book is open in front of you as you make your entries and there is the number of the sire in front of you. Enter it on the form and so save the show secretary the extra, unnecessary job of looking up the number or of writing to ask you for it. You cannot expect a secretary to be a walking encyclopedia on registered numbers.

Again, colour is usually required. Perhaps you make a Shetland entry and, as most of these ponies are black, you ignore the colour question. But you have missed the fact that a special prize is being offered for the best pony which is not black. Because your pony is black, and you cannot win, why worry? Think for a moment of the long-suffering secretary. It is his job to mark on the steward's card prior to the show all the catalogue numbers of the animals eligible for this special prize. He comes to your entry form, finds no colour given. He may assume black but cannot be really sure. One more unnecessary postcard has to be written. All that was needed was for you to complete the colour column: 'Black'.

If height is requested then fill it in. Say you are entering a 12.2 hh pony in a class for which he must be 14.2 hh or under. You know he is so well under the limit that you just put 'under 14.2 hh'. You have failed to notice that there is a special prize for 'the best pony 12.2 hh or under'. How is the secretary to know whether your entry is eligible for this? This means yet another postcard and some more wasted time before the secretary can complete this part of the job. So enter the height of your animal.

Strangely enough, one of the most common omissions is the NUMBER of the class in which you are entering your animal. You yourself know so well which class concerns you that you completely forget that you have not written this vital piece of information on the entry form.

I repeat: FILL IN ALL DETAILS REQUESTED. The name of your entry, and the schedule number of the class or classes entered. The sex, age, height, and colour, also the registered number in the appropriate Stud Book where the class conditions require this, the name and registered number of the sire and of the dam, and the name and address of the breeder. BUT WHEN THE OWNER IS THE BREEDER IT IS UNNECESSARY TO REPEAT NAME AND ADDRESS; SIMPLY PUT 'OWNER' OR 'EXHIBITOR'.

In making entries for ridden pony classes, give the date of birth as well as the name of the child who will ride.

Should there be a Special in the schedule for which you know your entry is eligible, mention this somewhere on the entry form, unless the information already given makes it clear anyway. For example, 'Best Novice'. If your entry has not won a first prize prior to date of entry, say so.

The entry form may stipulate that a certificate of vaccination against equine influenza must be produced on arrival at the showground. If this is the case, check with your vet that yours will be valid. (See also page 144)

Finally, count up the number of entries and total up the entry fees, add stabling charges plus the amount of your annual subscription (unless this is paid by banker's order) and make out your cheque. Even here there are pitfalls! If you have followed all the instructions faithfully and made entries correct in every detail, do not then spoil the whole thing by putting the wrong date or year on your cheque, by failing to sign it, or by forgetting to include it with your entries.

And do please remember to check whether or not you are in fact a member and therefore entitled to the reduced entry fee or whether you are a member but have omitted to pay your subscription. Otherwise this means further correspondence and your entries are held up awaiting your further remittance.

An organiser MUST make rules and having made them see that they are kept. But, if a request is reasonable and provided it does not immediately create a precedent and other people follow suit, then it pays to be flexible. Unfortunately the real reason why an organiser cannot usually give in to an individual is because everyone asks the same privilege.

Compiling a Show Catalogue

I have always preferred catalogues which give the names of the exhibits in alphabetical as well as numerical order throughout. To achieve this, the entries cannot be given their catalogue numbers until after the entries have closed and have been filed under their respective classes.

The ideal is to have all information about each entry in every class. This is popular with both exhibitors and spectators. But where one animal is entered in more than one class – at some shows sometimes three or even more – this necessitates a great deal of typesetting and is therefore expensive to print. At shows where this happens, I suggest a compromise may have to be reached, by having a horse and/or pony index to show the pedigrees, sire, dam, and breeder, which are then omitted under the class entries. Particulars of breeding are thus printed only once for each entry.

But at only very few shows is there classification which permits of an animal being entered in more than one – or at most, two – classes, when the breeding, etc. should be put in the class entry.

The following loose-leaf indexes must therefore be compiled as the entry forms arrive, with one for the printers and one for office use.

(a) **Class index** Information required will vary with the conditions of the class, for example, it would be superfluous to record the age and sex of each entry in a class for yearling colts. As a guide, the first four items in the following list will certainly be required, and the remainder *may* also be needed.

(1) Number of class.
(2) Name of pony, with registered number and stud book concerned in a class requiring this.
(3) Name of exhibitor.
(4) Catalogue number (to be added at the 'numbering' session).

(5) Height.
(6) Colour.
(7) Sex.
(8) Age.
(9) Name of sire and, where applicable, registered number and stud book.
(10) Name of dam and, where applicable, registered number and stud book.
(11) Sire of foal and/or covering stallion together with registered number where applicable (in Broodmare and foal classes).
(12) Name of rider in ridden classes.
(13) Any additional information which will help the secretary to determine the eligibility or otherwise of the entry for any special prizes in the class concerned. (This item will only appear on the office copy as it is not required by the printer.)

(b) Pony index An alphabetical index of the names of all the exhibits, indicating:

(1) Name of horse or pony.
(2) Catalogue number (*to be added at the numbering session*).
(3) Class(es) in which it is entered.

NB If particulars or registered number, breeding, colour, sex and age are *not* put under the class index, they should be included in the pony index, but this method should only be used where an animal is entered in several classes (see above).

(c) Exhibitors' index An alphabetical index of the names and addresses of exhibitors, containing:

(1) Name and address of each exhibitor.
(2) Number of each class in which he/she has an animal entered.
(3) Catalogue numbers of all ponies being exhibited by this exhibitor (to be added at the 'numbering' session).

The printer will need his copy as soon after the entries close as can be managed, that is, as soon as the entries are filed under their classes and the numbering has been done.

Apart from queries arising after this, it is now that those eligible for the various Special awards will be worked out for the stewards' cards. It is therefore essential to have an office copy of the class index from which to work. It is also at this stage that the value of item 13 under 'class index' becomes apparent.

Where an animal is entered in more than one class there will need to be a separate sheet, in duplicate, for that pony *for each class.*

206

Where this happens, it is wise to make a cross reference at the foot of each *carbon* sheet that the pony is 'also in Class . . .' This will help when it comes to making out the timetable; it is remarkably easy to arrange classes at such times as to make an animal due in two rings at the same time.

Some show secretaries use card indexes, placing the above details on cards then filing them under their separate classes, but there are two big objections to this method. Firstly, it is very difficult – if not impossible – to take carbon copies on cards, and at least two copies are essential. Secondly, a printer's typesetter finds it very much easier to flip over sheets of paper in a file than to fumble with cards, which very easily stick together, so that some may be omitted. I have found that octavo files and paper cut to this size are by far the best and quickest method of getting entries into their various classes for the printer and the office.

To sum up. As each exhibitor's entries come in, you will need:

A duplicated octavo sheet for each class entered by each animal.

A sheet for each animal for the horse and/or pony index, of which only one is necessary, namely for the printer.

An octavo sheet for the exhibitor's index, of which again only one is necessary, for the printer.

An envelope addressed ready for the timetable and instructions, which should be sent later.

A large envelope for exhibitor's numbers.

In this way entries are not so likely to be omitted. Dealing, as many shows do, with large entries, many of them registered animals, I have found this the quickest and clearest method both for the printer and for office use.

Prize Money and Rosettes

The most usual procedure is to offer prize money and rosettes to three places, plus rosettes to six places, which is an essential in case of any elimination or objection affecting the first three places. Large shows can, of course, afford to offer more prize money than small ones, and increasingly the wisdom of offering more awards, even if this means slightly reducing the money awarded to the top three places, is being realised.

Moreover, there is not the slightest doubt that to win even a rosette sends the majority of exhibitors home happy. I strongly advise giving a good 'tail' rather than handing out disproportionately large prize money to the top three. As to how many places the awards should go, this depends entirely on the financial position and on how generous the organisers happen to be feeling. Quite ordinary rosettes in these days cost a lot, while specially good ones have gone up enormously in the last ten years. However, it pays to have the best rosettes as it's these the exhibitors remember.

The 'Numbering' Session

After the closing date for entries and as soon as all accepted entries have been typed and filed in the three indexes already described, the 'numbering' session can take place.

A large envelope marked with each exhibitor's name must be prepared in advance and, obviously, the actual numbers must also be ready. All that is now required is to assemble four individuals who are prepared to concentrate for a few hours (500 entries involving 420 ponies and 36 classes will take approximately three hours to number). We will call these people A, B, C, and D. Their jobs are as follows:

A has the horse and/or pony index which he numbers from 1 onwards as he goes. He calls the particulars of each animal to the rest of the team. He also has the exhibitors' index where, as each animal is called, he adds the catalogue number of that animal (in brackets) at the foot of the appropriate sheet.

B has the class index. As each animal is called he adds the catalogue number to that animal's sheet in every class concerned.

C has the exhibitors' numbers. He writes on the back of each number the name of the animal associated with that number, adding the classes involved.

D has the box containing the big envelopes, each of which has previously been marked with the name of an exhibitor. These are in alphabetical order and remain so throughout.

Method
C calls 'Animal number one' then turns the exhibitor's number over, ready to write on the back of it.

A writes '1' against the first name (which we will call AARON) in the horse and/or pony index and then calls 'No. 1, Classes 1B and 19B, AARON, exhibitor Mr C. Everyman'. As the class numbers are called, C writes them both on the back of 'One', adding the animal's name – AARON – whilst B looks up class 1B and marks the catalogue number '1' on AARON'S sheet. B then turns up Class

19B and marks '1' on the same animal's sheet in that class. Mean-while, *D* has found the big envelope for Mr C. Everyman and put the number (one) into it. *A* has also found Everyman in the exhibitors' index and has added the animal's number (1) to the other information already on this sheet.

This process is repeated until all animals in the index have been given a number. All that remains is to copy the numbers into the printer's copy of the class index.

Timetables

These, whenever possible – and certainly in the case of big shows for which entries of necessity close several weeks before the show date – should be compiled after the entries close so that the number of entries in each class is then known. How else can classes go in and out on time and the whole show run to schedule?

If the timing is done before the entries are known, the situation will undoubtedly arise when there are found to be either fewer or more entries than anticipated, and therefore either too much or too little time has been allowed. For example, class 1 has been allowed forty minutes, only to find there are only six entries, while class 10, given half an hour, has over twenty entries. This can mean that the class following class 1 has to go in early, upsetting both exhibitors and spectators and possibly entailing refunding entry fees to any who therefore missed it; it may even result in that ring running ahead of time for the rest of the day. Or, it will entail having a vacant ring for a time, which is a bad thing. In the second eventuality, the class runs late, again dislocating the whole show.

Then there are the shows that do not time individual classes, but instead put them *en bloc*, such as, 'Children's riding pony classes – 10 a.m. to 1 p.m.', with no mention of the order in which each size of pony – and therefore which class – will be judged. Or, 'Broodmares and foals – 11 a.m. to 1 p.m.', with again no height classifications or classes mentioned, so that this is not known until it is announced over the microphone.

I once judged at a show which made a cardinal error. The timetable simply stated that the riding pony broodmare and youngstock classes would be in ring X commencing at 10 a.m. There were two broodmare and two foal classes, and several youngstock classes ranging from one- to three-year-olds. In default of any other prior information, exhibitors took it that the broodmares, as they were mentioned first in the schedule, would be judged first. Imagine the

atmosphere when in fact the youngstock was called in at 9 a.m.!
Half the exhibits in these classes had not arrived and did not do so
until between 10.30 and 11 a.m., by which time they had estimated
the judging of the broodmares would be over. Many therefore missed
their class and, with transport costs as they are, fur and feathers flew.

The following timing is suggested as being approximately correct,
dependent upon whether the judge is a fast worker or a slow one.

Ridden classes (no preliminary ring)

Hunters	6–8	entries	30	minutes
	8–16	”	45	”
	16–20	”	60–75	”
Hacks	6–8	entries	30	minutes
	8–16	”	50–55	”
	16–20	”	60–75	”

Children's ponies and show hunter ponies – same as for
Hunters.

No class should be staged in a ring that takes longer than this or the
spectators will get bored. *Preliminary* judging is advocated if at all
possible for adult ridden classes of over twenty entries as the judge
should ride all exhibits. Unless so judged, the time allocated can
seldom be enough to permit the judge(s) riding more than six, which
is both unfair and disappointing to exhibitors who have, after all,
paid their entry fees.

This is, and always has been, a problem. All that can be said is
that as much time should be given to permit as many as possible of
the exhibits being ridden by the judge(s) without (1) boring the
spectators, (2) causing that ring – and therefore possibly the whole
show – to hang.

All exhibitors should be brought into the final judging, but only
the first three or so need then be asked to give a show, and the
judges do not ride them again.

The final judging and giving of the awards should not require
more than twenty minutes.

It will be appreciated that hacks have to be allowed slightly more
time than hunters and children's ponies, because after the preliminary
walk, trot, etc., they have both to give a show and be ridden by the
judge, whereas hunters have only to be ridden and the ponies have
only to give a show, before the saddles are removed.

210

Working hunter classes

These are usually pretty generously treated at the small shows, but at the large shows, unless they are given a *preliminary* ring, the time allocated seldom if ever permits the judge(s) riding very many. Some shows have the judging of the jumping in the main ring and then take the exhibitors to a preliminary ring for the judging of conformation and ride, before bringing them back into the main ring for presentation of awards. They thus avoid the necessity for two sets of jumps, which is one of the disadvantages of having a preliminary ring and the finals in the main ring, with fences in both.

The recognised time per exhibitor over the fences is two minutes and there should never be less than five fences.

Thereafter, the time allowed for the judging of conformation and ride should be only slightly less than that allowed the judging of a ridden hunter class, unless this is done in the preliminary ring.

Obviously, these classes take very much longer to deal with than any other, so they can drag. For this reason, preliminary judging is advocated, although this means two sets of jumps unless the method suggested above is adopted.

For working hunter ponies the procedure is the same except that they are not ridden. They are judged according to BSPS rules.

In-hand classes

The approximate timing of these is as follows:

Broodmares and foals

	6–7	entries	20	minutes
up to	14	”	45	”
up to	20	”	60	”
over	20	”	75–90	”

With over twenty entries, it is advisable, if time and money allow, to divide the class (see under Division of Classes) or to have preliminary judging.

Youngstock

	7–9	entries	20	minutes
up to	14	”	30	”
up to	20	”	45	”
	20–30	”	60	”
	30–36	”	60–75	”

Again, division of the classes is advocated where there are more than twenty-five, though this is very often not possible owing to lack of time and because of expense.

Leading-rein classes

If these have over eighteen entries, they should if possible be judged in a preliminary ring. Such large numbers proceeding at walking pace, however attractive, can become boring for spectators and are also very difficult to judge. By pre-judging them a judge can be given time. Also, parents of such small children resent not being allowed to show off not only the pony but the child, and it is obviously not always possible to allow every one to give a show when there is a very large entry.

Driving classes

These should be allowed approximately the same time as the hack classes – slightly more if the judge is to drive.

Show-jumping classes

Apply to the British Show Jumping Association (see page 77).

At shows where there is more than one ring, the best way to compile a timetable is to have a board into which it is easy to stick drawing-pins and on it to pin small cards upon which are typed the class number, a brief classification, the name of the judge, and the number of entries.

Example:

```
┌─────────────────────────────────────────┐
│   Class 1                    11 a.m       │
│                                           │
│             Working Hunters               │
│             not exc. 15.2 hh              │
│                                           │
│   (12)              Captain Snodgrass     │
└─────────────────────────────────────────┘
```

At the top of the board write the number (or the colour, if colours are used) of the ring. Then pin the cards one under the other, adding the time according to the number of entries in each class. This should be done in pencil so that it can be rubbed out if the time allowed is later considered either too little or too much or if any class(es) are found later to clash, either for exhibitors or judges. The number in brackets indicates the number of entries.

When a show's classification allows one animal to enter two, three, four – even five – classes, this system is essential, or you will have distraught exhibitors queuing outside the secretary's office asking for classes to be held up, or demanding the return of their entry fees for

212

	RING 1		RING 2		RING 3
9 a.m.	Broodmares 14.2 hh.	9 a.m.	Arab Yearlings	9 a.m.	Mountains and Moorland Small Type [these will not clash with 14.2 hh mares]
9.50	Broodmares 12.2 hh.	9.45	Arab 2- and 3-year-olds	9.40	Mountain and Moorland Large Type [these will not clash with 12.2 hh mares]
10.30	Broodmares 13.2 hh	10.15	Arab Mares and foals	10 a.m.	Mountain and Moorland Championship [this will not clash with 13.2 hh mares with any luck]

SAMPLE ENTRIES FROM SPECIMEN TIMETABLE

213

having missed classes through no fault of their own. When a lot of exhibits are eligible for two or more classes, the secretary and his staff are well advised literally to walk mentally through every class with each of the exhibitors concerned. This is done with the help of the carbon copies of the typed entries which have been compiled for the printer, at the bottom of which is, or should be, written, 'Also in Class . . .'

It is essential that the same check be made on the judges. Often at our shows, I am ashamed to admit, our judges can be seen jumping like grasshoppers from ring to ring! But shows with five rings going simultaneously, are, fortunately, pretty rare.

The timetable having been compiled and checked, it is then copied into type from the board, exactly; that is, with all the rings placed in line and with the various times as nearly level with each other as possible. An example is given on the preceding page.

When the timetables are printed, all exhibitors, judges, stewards, and other officials should be sent one. The envelopes for exhibitor's timetables can most easily be typed at the same time as the entries.

Exhibitors' Numbers

Exhibitors' numbers should be placed in large envelopes with the name of the animal written on the back of each and the exhibitor's name in capitals on the envelope. These should be given out either at the secretary's or stable manager's office. They should not be sent by post, when they are frequently lost or forgotten on the day.

Objections

It should be stated both in schedule and programme that objections must be lodged in *writing*, together with the appropriate fee, within the time limit mentioned, when it should then be brought to the committee table to be dealt with and either upheld or over-ruled, and the fee either returned or forfeited, or it may be handed on to another organisation whose concern it may be. Show executives should refuse to discuss the matter if the time limit has expired.

To exhibitors I say 'Don't', unless possibly over flagrant cases such as the misrepresentation of the age of a child or a registered pony, a false registration or ownership, all of which are facts which can be checked.

While there are some who will stop at nothing, I have found that

214

the large majority of exhibitors are both honest and sporting. A few, in their over-eagerness to win, may sail near the wind. Some are simply careless. A few cheat deliberately but they soon become well known.

Collecting and Show Rings

These *must* be large enough to contain the biggest class without endangering the exhibits through being over-crowded or kicked. It is preferable that rings should be oval in shape, thus giving a long side for lining up and running out the exhibits. A round ring is obviously inconvenient and corners are a waste of space. At shows with large entries, both should have separate entrances and exits, again to avoid kicking or jostling when passing in and out, especially with broodmares and youngstock, and also to save time. Entrances and exits of both should be opposite each other.

If collecting rings are not adjacent to their corresponding show rings, it means there can be little or no liaison between the stewards, necessitating much to-ing and fro-ing, or else telephonic communication has to be supplied, which is expensive.

While it is reasonable to ask mounted exhibitors to ride some distance to their collecting ring, exhibitors of in-hand animals cannot be expected to walk long distances, especially if they are showing a number of animals in consecutive classes. Should they have more than a few yards to walk from either their stable or their horsebox to the collecting ring, and again from the latter to the ring itself, it will mean that the timetable must allow for time between classes, so that the rings will be left vacant and the show run late. Besides, unless the exhibitors are young and energetic you will have tired and therefore disgruntled exhibitors on your hands. Remember that those in-hand classes may have a broodmare and foal, followed by a yearling, followed by two- and three-year-olds. It is therefore obvious that they must be considered. To do this at big agricultural and county shows may be difficult, but every effort should be made.

While it is essential for rings to be large enough to permit the judge viewing the exhibits from a reasonable distance and not to have them right under his nose, and for ridden animals to have enough space to show their paces, a show that sprawls never really 'goes' – any more than a cocktail party succeeds when a handful of people meet in a large room. An organiser's aim should be the happy medium between over-crowding and a show that rattles like a small packet of peas in a large pan.

The going is also important, and if show jumping is staged then it is essential that sand or peat is spread on the landing side of every jump; also practice jumps. These latter should be flagged red on right, white on left and taken *only this way* to avoid collisions.

Exhibitors should be told exactly where their collecting rings are, on arrival. I once searched for mine for over twenty minutes and, having found it, waited another ten before anyone arrived, including the steward. On another occasion I tramped over mud and duck-boards with a Dartmoor pony to the measuring block, only to be told what I already knew, namely that measurement within the native breeds was unnecessary as they were automatically covered by their registration!

Often shows have to be fitted into showgrounds and racecourses designed for other purposes, so that layout is made difficult, but whatever the circumstance control of spectators and exhibitors is essential. It is irritating, even dangerous, to be ridden down by mounted competitors, while the ignorance and nonchalance of the modern public is fantastic; they think nothing of allowing children and dogs to wander among a milling crowd of unbroken colts and fillies. Show jumpers, because they attract a gate, are, I am afraid, inclined to be rather high-handed and inconsiderate. They certainly do not mix well with in-hand classes.

All collecting and show rings, and in fact all offices, should be clearly marked with boards intelligently placed and readable at a distance. It is a good idea to have different coloured boards and posts for the different rings, because then even short-sighted people, unable to read a number, can at least see the colour – unless they are colour-blind. This idea also has a further advantage in that numbers hint at priorities whereas colours do not.

Chief Collecting-Ring Steward

The chief collecting-ring steward's tent must obviously be positioned as near to as many of the rings as possible. He should be able easily to keep his finger on the pulse of the whole show. He MUST be in telephonic communication with the commentator(s). At one show at which I judged, my ring was a quarter of a mile from the commentator; the only communication I had with him was by a field telephone which I located, half-way through the morning, buried under a thornbush by the ringside. In any case, he was unable to hear through it!

It is up to the chief collecting-ring steward to co-ordinate the whole show, especially if there is more than one ring. He should have before him the timetable, whereby he can see at a glance the whole layout and timing of the classes in relation to each other. This is particularly necessary at shows with three, four, or even more rings running simultaneously. It enables him to hold back a ring that is running ahead of time and to hasten on one that risks falling, or has actually fallen, behind time. He should be supplied with one or more assistants whom he can send out to the ring stewards when he needs any numbers checked, and he must be in constant radio contact with the commentator(s) in order to obtain their appraisal of the situation.

The chief collecting-ring steward is responsible for seeing that no class goes into the ring before its scheduled time, *except in exceptional cases*, when due and ample notification must be given more than once over the microphone.

If any hitch occurs, it is his responsibility – and his alone – to acquaint the show director or show secretary of the facts, and together to sort things out.

He should be notified of any absentees as soon as possible so that he does not keep calling up exhibitors who are not on the ground. Likewise, collecting-ring stewards, *where these are used*, should inform him of any laggards so that he can call up their actual numbers. His loudspeaker should, indeed, *must*, cover all corners of the ground, and certainly all stabling and horsebox parks.

It is also up to this official to see that those eligible for championships and cumulative special awards are ready in good time. He should note their numbers, which he obtains from the commentator, *or from the stewards' slips and from no other source*. Although ring stewards will, we hope, have instructed all eligible exhibitors of the ring and time of a championship – and although no exhibitor will be slow in coming forward for this crowning event – hitches can occur, and a chief collecting-ring steward looks and sounds foolish if he does not know the eligible numbers. He should also check that the judges are in their appointed places.

Any announcements regarding lost persons or property that affect the area covered by his loudspeaker should be given out by him rather than bothering the commentator.

He will probably find that the commentator is his best source of information as to the state of the rings, that is, whether they are running to time, before time, or late. But this information should not affect the time he begins calling up a class, which should be at least twenty minutes before its scheduled time, dependent on number of entries and whether it is ridden or in-hand. Obviously, in-hand classes should be given longer than ridden.

Upon the chief collecting-ring steward the whole efficiency and smooth running of the show depends. He must therefore be quick, efficient, tactful, and, above all, firm.

He will invariably be accused, whether he is to blame or not, if an exhibitor misses a class. He may also find himself involved in a controversy over what is considered an unjust adjudication or over a special award given to the wrong exhibitor, when his handling of the situation and his personality can do much to pour oil on troubled waters.

Collecting-Ring Stewards

Of all the jobs on a showground, that of a collecting-ring steward is unrewarding and quite the most boring. It is no wonder that volunteers are hard to come by, and once bitten, twice shy!

Actually, it should be perfectly possible, given an efficient public address system and an efficient chief collecting-ring steward, for exhibitors to present themselves in good time for their classes. The majority know – or by now should know – the ropes, and are there to inform the beginners. Therefore, provided the schedule runs to time, there is really no excuse for anyone to be late, let alone miss a class, if he is on the showground.

It seems very much fairer, instead of having collecting-ring stewards, to have three or more ring stewards, who then take it in turn to go out to the collecting ring.

The duties of a collecting-ring steward are to endeavour to get everybody in the class into the ring on time; to discover those that are missing and if possible to find out if they are or are not on the ground; to send the numbers of those which are presumed to have arrived on the ground but not yet in the ring to the chief collecting-ring steward for a final call over the microphone.

It is in the collecting ring that the checking of exhibitors' numbers should be done, not in the ring itself. So often exhibitors who are showing several animals omit to change the numbers they are carrying, which leads to confusion and high blood pressure on the commentator's part; this affects not just the exhibitor concerned but even the press, and therefore can result in a wrong name in the morning papers. This check for wrong numbers is a collecting-ring steward's main function.

When he discovers one, the steward should immediately query it with the exhibitor to discover whether it is simply that he has omitted to change it after exhibiting another animal, or whether in fact he has entered the wrong class, or – as sometimes happens - whether the animal is a 'ringer'. Any information he obtains should be passed on to the ring steward, who in turn informs the commentator who, if necessary, calls upon the organiser or show secretary to cope. If the mistake is only that the exhibitor has failed to change his number, this is comparatively simple to rectify. But occasions do arise which are ticklish, when the ring steward should not deal with the matter himself but should hand it over to the organiser. The judge should not be involved.

If ineligibility is involved, is it because this has escaped the notice of the office staff? It may be that the exhibitor has entered in the wrong class in error and this has been overlooked by the office staff. It is then up to the secretary to check the entry form and to decide whether to allow the animal to compete or to refund the entry fee. At big shows, I am afraid the answer is that the entry is not eligible, but smaller shows may possibly be less rigid. But if he accepts it, the organiser may have an objection on his hands.

To facilitate this operation, it is a good idea NOT to give the collecting-ring stewards simply a catalogue, through which he has to thumb to find the right class. Instead, he should have a board upon which are clipped, *in order of the timetable*, the classes in the ring for which he is responsible. This can be done before the show day by using extra galley proofs of the catalogue, pasting these on stiffer paper and clipping them on to a board in order of judging. At the same time, any animals known beforehand NOT to be coming to the show can be deleted by the staff. This saves a lot of unnecessary calling-up of exhibits that are not even on the ground.

A collecting-ring steward should be at his post at least twenty minutes before the time of judging. Having ascertained which exhibits are missing, and informed the commentator (whose public address system covers both stable and horsebox areas), he can return to his ring and check the exhibits as they appear and/or go into the ring. If they are then not forward, the exhibitors only have themselves to blame, unless a class is sent in before its scheduled time, when they have a legitimate complaint. If this has to be, very clear announcements must be made all over the ground and a close check made to see that no exhibits are missing.

If the show is running late, a collecting-ring steward may have to hold up his class to wait for exhibits from another class. In this he must use his discretion, or else await instructions from the commentator, who in turn receives his instructions from the organiser.

219

If classes are missed because of bad organisation, this is the fault of the organisers, who may well have to return entry fees, but a careful check should be made to make sure the case is genuine. Exhibitors who miss classes through no fault of their own should request a refund in writing *after* the show is over, when, if the claim is reasonable, the entry fee should be refunded.

If and when certificates of service or height certificates are required, it is up to the collecting-ring steward to see that these are forthcoming.

Ring Stewards

Ring stewards are almost as important as judges, especially at shows having a large number of specials and championships, and where various class winners have to be noted and brought forward to a cumulative special or a championship.

A good ring steward can make a show – a bad one can wreck it – and he can also make life easy or extremely difficult for the judges.

It should be remembered, however, that stewards give their time voluntarily and for free. They have all the dirty work and none of the fun. We therefore owe them a debt of gratitude, for we should be sore put to it to stage shows without them.

It is unfair to blame them for sins and omissions if they have not been properly briefed; if, for instance, they either have insufficient instructions or no instructions at all written down on their stewards' cards (or, if used, in the judges' books). Obviously, it is no use giving hurried verbal instructions to someone who has never done the job before and who knows nothing about horses and ponies. It is even more disastrous simply to hand him the catalogue and expect him to get on with it.

On the opposite page is an illustration of the type of steward's card I advocate. The number of the ring or, when colours are used, the colour, the name and year of the show, and the class number, are typed or written on both sides of the card – namely, main card on the left and a narrower duplicate perforated slip on the right. Then follows full classification on the left and an abbreviation on the right (slip) side, and the name of the officiating judge(s).

Below these details come the awards. The majority of shows give three prizes and a reserve only; at others, they can go to several places.

The awards should be checked with those printed in the catalogue and the superfluous ones on the stewards' cards deleted. If, on the

Show...19....

Steward's Card

Class no..Time.......

Description of Class

....

....

Judges............................and ....
and............................and ....

___

Awards
1st................ 2nd No......... 3rd No...........
4th No.......... 5th No.......... 6th No...........
VHC .... HC .... C ....
Reserve......... ....

Cups
The...
Eligible Nos ....
Winner No .... Reserve No.............
The...
Eligible Nos ....
Winner No .... Reserve No.............
The...
Eligible Nos ....
Winner No .... Reserve No.............

Specials
No..... Best..
Eligible Nos ....
Winner No..
No..... Best..
Eligible Nos ....
Winner No..

Other societies' rosettes
The.. Society
Winner .... Reserve.....................
Judges' Signatures...
....
Steward's Initials ....

Instructions to Steward

Show.........................19....

Steward's Card

Class no..............................
Description.....................

....

....

___

Awards
1st........ 2nd....... 3rd ....
4th .... 5th .... 6th ....
VHC ... HC ..... C ....
Res No............................

Cups
The.....................................
....
Winner .... Reserve........
The.....................................
....
Winner .... Reserve........
The.....................................
....
Winner .... Reserve........

Specials
No.... Best........................
....
Winner No........................
No.... Best........................
....
Winner No........................

Societies' rosettes
The..................... Society
Winner .... Reserve........
Judges' Signatures..............
....
Steward's Initials ....

Notes for Commentator

other hand, the awards printed on the cards are insufficient, more can be added by hand, for which space should be provided. In other words, if the awards printed on the cards run to only four places, and there are in fact highly commended and commended rosettes as well, these should be added by hand on the card, before the reserve.

Cups follow, then specials, and under each the numbers of the animals known to be eligible. For example, 'Special No. 10 for Best Yearling to No. 154. Eligible Nos.: 167, 280, 316 . . .' Whenever possible, the numbers of eligibles should be looked up and written on the stewards' card before the show. Only when it is not possible to know this information before the actual show day, should the stewards' instructions state 'Ask exhibitors'. It is by this preliminary office work that muddles and objections are made less likely, and time saved.

There follows space for rosettes awarded by other societies, and, at the foot of the left-hand side, clear but brief instructions to the steward, with even briefer notes on the right-hand slip for the commentator's benefit, whose duty it will be to call up those eligible for championships, etc. To do this, *he should always be guided by the judges' slips* (namely the right-hand slip of the stewards' cards sent up to him by the ring steward).

The card should also state in plain language the numbers of the exhibits eligible to go forward to compete in any semi-final or final of a championship; or for any special award involving exhibits from more than one class and for which, therefore, there may be two, three or more qualifiers, that is, from two, three or more classes. For example, the left-hand side of the card could read: 'Instruct class winner to compete for mountain and moorland championship in ring X with winners of classes 6, 8, and 10 at – p.m.'

It also helps greatly if the cards tell the stewards which animals are NOT eligible, and, if possible, why. It can happen that an animal goes forward and is actually handed a rosette for which it is not eligible, and then trouble results in a big way. Judges may make awards in all innocence, only to find that an objection has been lodged. It helps a judge if a steward can say at once why an animal is not eligible, for instance, because it does not belong to the age group required, is not eligible on breeding, or is not a novice.

Steward's cards at some shows have to be as large as 21 ins (53 cm) long by 8½ ins (21 cm) wide. (Judges' books are adequate enough for small shows or those with only three to five awards per class, and with few special awards.) These cards, when completed by the secretarial staff, are clipped on to a board by a bulldog clip in order of the timetable, with a polythene cover attached in case of rain. As each class is judged and the card filled in and signed, the larger, left-hand side is slipped under the unused cards and the right-hand slip (which should correspond exactly) is torn off and sent up *immediately* to the commentator who, when he has finished using it for his commentary, sends it on to the secretary's tent. There, the secretarial staff copy the winning numbers on to cards for the result board and mark up copies of the catalogue for the press.

I realise that some show secretaries, many of whom are part-time and voluntary, will say they simply have not the time to make out stewards' cards on these lines. But believe me, it is time well spent, even if it means burning the midnight oil. Hurried verbal instructions are apt to go in one ear and out the other, whereas written instructions, stating exactly what is required, save endless time and heartburnings on the day.

Never, under any circumstances, should a steward give height as a reason of elimination or for placing an animal down the line. This particularly applies to riding pony youngstock classes. In classes for mature animals, one of his duties may be to ask exhibitors for their height certificates, or, at shows where they are measured on the ground, for the veterinary officer's slip. Where youngstock is concerned, the ruling may be either (1) that height is a matter for the judges to decide (when on no account should the steward be inveigled, either in the ring or afterwards, into repeating the judge's opinion, which should definitely be confidential); or (2) that exhibits are required to be measured either before the class or in the ring, when a slip from the veterinary officer must be produced on request by the steward.

Should a ring steward discover any animal which is not eligible for any reason, he must act promptly but tactfully, by informing the commentator, or contacting the chief collecting-ring steward, who in turn should contact the secretary or office staff. He should on no account take it upon himself to make any decision.

The efficient ring steward arrives to collect his cards at the secretary's office at least twenty minutes before his first class. He or she is neatly but suitably dressed, wears a hat, and is prepared not to smoke while on duty.

He finds his ring and looks carefully through his card, noting the various Specials and cups for which exhibits have to be brought forward to the finals. If he has a catalogue, he keeps this to himself and never uses it in the ring, let alone when with the judge.

He hopes his judge will appear on time. If he/she fails to make an appearance and there are only, say, ten minutes to go before the scheduled time of class, he informs the commentator and chief collecting-ring steward, and both in due course put out calls over the loudspeaker. The steward has previously looked to see if the collecting-ring steward is in his place or, if the ring stewards are to take turns at collecting, he contacts his colleagues and arranges the rota.

When the judge arrives, the steward asks if he or she wishes to call in the exhibits or whether it is to be one of the steward's duties.

When the exhibits enter the ring, sent in by the collecting-ring steward, a good ring steward endeavours to space them out evenly, to prevent crowding and to see that they keep to the outside of the circle and do not crowd in upon the judge(s), so making it impossible to see them properly. In ridden classes, there will inevitably be the competitor who tries to catch the judge's eye by shooting past the animal in front of him and as near the judge as judiciously possible. While overtaking another competitor is permissible under certain circumstances (such as another's animal napping or being very much behind its bridle and therefore holding up the class, or, in youngstock classes, a young colt playing the fool), the correct procedure is to keep well to the outside of the ring and to overtake only on the side furthest from the judge.

A judge should never peruse the catalogue. The steward should therefore immediately tell him the number of entries, the time the class has been allotted, and, if the judge has not received or studied a *schedule*, the classification and any cups or Specials which will have to be dealt with.

Should a judge instruct the steward to call in the exhibits, the latter should listen carefully to the descriptions but should certainly not repeat them in a loud voice, especially if they are likely to be, for example: 'the female with the sticking-out teeth', or, 'the grey pony with the head of a battle-axe', or 'the popsy in the mini-skirt!' Personally I think it much better if the judge calls in his own choices, leaving the steward free to position the exhibits ready for inspection. He should keep them in line, and, above all, *with plenty of space in between*, otherwise the judge finds himself wedged between exhibits, quite unable to get a proper view, and in considerable danger of being either trodden on or kicked. Invariably exhibitors will crowd together if allowed to; this happens in every class at every show.

It is also essential that the steward thinks out beforehand where he is going to make his front line. This should obviously be facing the most spectators, and of sufficient length to make it possible to give a good show whether in hand or under saddle. By the way, the nearer it gets to the bottom of the front row, the more congestion and the more jockeying for the final places there will be. Anything rather than go to the back row, which is regarded as ignominious,

224

though often it is simply a matter of space, or the judge may for the moment have failed to spot a good one. The steward must make up his mind if and when a second line is needed and then insist upon its being made without argument.

Psychologically, it is not a good thing to have a back row at all, though often necessary. Here a tactful steward can help by suggesting that it would be appreciated if the judge would visit the back row, should he show no signs of doing so.

When the judge has finished looking over all the exhibits, the steward should *immediately* be ready to send forward the front line for further inspection and the run out, or, in the case of ridden classes, the individual show.

While the judge is inspecting the walk and trot, the steward should have the next in line ready to move out at once, while the one inspected returns to its place in the line from the back, NOT from the front where it is likely to collide with the next in line moving out. In large classes, involving two lines, much time is lost because stewards are hanging about doing nothing instead of being active in moving up exhibits ready for the individual inspection.

It may be that the judge wishes all exhibits sent round the ring again, to be called in more or less in their final order. Or he may simply change over one or two places, when it is the steward's duty to see that this is done as quietly and efficiently as possible, and with no argument.

Another problem facing ring stewards is when they find their rings running late. This, especially at big shows with very large entries and a very tight schedule, can only mean trouble ahead. A good steward will do his best tactfully to approach the judge to point this out and ask if he can possibly accelerate. If this is impossible, or if the judge, as sometimes happens, refuses to be hustled, it is then up to the steward to contact the chief collecting-ring steward, who in turn may have to contact the show organiser. It is at such moments of crisis that good stewards and a good organiser can, by quick thinking, create calm out of chaos. This is not easy when the pressure is on. At such times, officials can do much not only to clear things up but to keep the temperature down, which is apt to rise alarmingly.

The judge having made his decisions, the steward should then get cracking, writing the winning numbers down on both sides of his steward's card or, if books are used, in these. This is quite one of the most vital of his duties. One wrong number and there is chaos and confusion. It is at this moment that it is so important that competitors should be wearing their correct numbers.

Having got his prize-winners down, he must then go into the

question of any Specials and cups. If these entail carrying a competitor forward to a final or even semi-final, he must be meticulous in obtaining the correct number and in instructing the exhibitor concerned as to when and where the final judging of a Special or championship will take place.

Some time before the judge makes his final placings, the ring steward should make quite sure that the rosette/cup steward is ready to enter the ring. He should of course be briefed to come forward the minute he sees the ring steward writing down the winning numbers. No show should ever be held up for such an avoidable detail.

Finally, the steward obtains the judge's signature and adds his own, to ensure that, should there be an objection or other trouble, the secretary can at once contact those concerned in order to seek their advice or opinion.

Having checked that everyone has received his just awards and instructions regarding championship or accumulation specials, having attended the presentation of any cups and, in the case of challenge cups, seen to it that these are forthwith returned to the cup tent for inscription, he then sends the exhibits round the ring again, past all spectators, and out.

Many are the tales one hears of stewards interfering or offering their opinions to the judge. Sometimes this is not their fault, the judge having asked for it. But in fairness to both, the fact that a judge and steward are seen conferring does not necessarily mean they are discussing the merits or demerits of the exhibits.

It is, for instance, permissible, especially when dealing with a very large class, for a judge to say to the steward: 'Remind me that No. – does not move quite straight.' Or: 'Make a note that chestnut threw a buck,' etc., etc. When animals are entered in more classes than one, again it is permissible to check with the steward that in fact it stood fourth or what have you in a previous class *judged by the same judge*. In championships again, a judge is at liberty to check with the steward whether in fact he placed a certain pony second in its class. I know of many first-class judges who have difficulty in remembering all placings when they are judging a large number of classes. This difficulty presents itself quite often in classes of native ponies; for instance, in any breeds that are all black without even a star or snip to help one out, it can be quite difficult for a judge to distinguish one from the other in a large class, though not many would have the moral courage to admit it!

What is completely 'out' is such information from the steward as: 'That pony has been winning everywhere,' or 'That chestnut won the championship last week,' or 'When I was stewarding at — — last

226

week Mr Blank thought that grey was nappy.' Nor is it a good thing for a judge to put a steward in a fix by asking: 'Is that the Major on top of that flashy bay?' Or, 'Has Count Popoff got something in this class? I hear he's bought another world-beater.'

At many of the big shows etiquette demands that the judge instruct the steward to call in the exhibits rather than do it himself. Where there are two or more judges, using the steward is essential as one cannot have more than one judge hailing the exhibitors. For *one* of two or more judges to do so immediately gives the spectators the impression that he is the dominating judge. (Actually, in nine cases out of ten one judge does dominate, either by force of character or greater knowledge.)

When disagreement arises, tact on the part of the steward(s) may do much to keep the peace, and when there is a request for a referee judge it is his business to see that this is forthcoming immediately. This task may be ticklish; he may have to pour oil on troubled waters without appearing to interfere. Where speech is silver, silence is often golden.

Finding the referee judge is frequently like looking for sixpence in a plum pudding, so any steward finding himself with an even number of judges would be advised to find out beforehand who is to be called in as referee in case of a deadlock.

After preliminary judging, a judge cannot always be expected to remember which animals he has decided to qualify for the final. If only these are to come into the final judging, he must see that his steward writes down the numbers of the qualifiers to hand to the collecting-ring steward for the final. The commentator should also get a copy, otherwise animals which are not eligible may, frequently do, appear in the ring. If all the exhibits come into the final, the judge is well advised to write down during the preliminary the numbers of the animals which interest him, and should the steward know these, he should keep the information to himself between the preliminary and final judging.

I try never to forget that stewards offer their services voluntarily and am most grateful to them. Besides, I am quite sure that I myself would be the worst steward that ever entered a ring and have always taken care never to find myself in this position!

Class Boards

These should be sited in the middle of the rings and should not only display the number of the class but its classification, that is, '14.2 hh

Riding Pony', 'Yearlings', '2–3-year-olds', 'Highland Mares', 'Exmoor Stallions', 'Welsh Mountain Yearlings', etc. Only thus will interest be aroused and maintained, because, let's face it, the average spectator today does not know the difference between an Exmoor and a New Forest Pony, a small hack and a small hunter, and certainly not between the different weights of hunter. He may just be able to distinguish the Shetland classes.

Class numbers and lettering should be large enough to be read at a distance.

They should also display preliminary judging, championships, etc.

Result Boards

These should be placed in prominent positions and it should not be forgotten that exhibitors are just as anxious as, if not more than, the public, to see who and what have won. They cannot always find the time to go to a spot on the showground which, while it may suit spectators, is a long way from the collecting rings, stables and horse-box parks. A board should therefore be placed and serviced for exhibitors.

At small shows with only a few classes, the task of the press is comparatively easy, but at the big shows they have a monumental job – I know because I have done it – and should be given every assistance. The numbers of the various classes should therefore be pinned prominently on the result boards in numerical order, and the result cards – on which Specials and cup winners must also be clearly inserted – pinned on exactly under them and kept right up to date so that there is no delay and the press can be kept informed throughout the day.

Anything which makes easier this very difficult job is reflected in the press notices.

It is well worth while obtaining labour – voluntary if possible – to mark up the result board slips and the catalogues with the results which come in throughout the day, so that they are immediately available to the press only a few minutes after the show ends.

Marked Copies

This is a much appreciated service, again reflected in the press notices. Anyone with secretarial training or average intelligence can do this job as and when the stewards' slips come in from the rings.

It is of great importance that markers check with the office staff that the winning numbers in fact are correct. Should they notice any mistake they should immediately query it.

Judges' slips given to the markers should never be posted up on the result board or borrowed by anyone, but should immediately be returned to the secretary's office.

Rosette and Cup Stewards

It definitely creates a favourable impression, and certainly adds to the smooth running of a show, if rosettes and cups are forthcoming 'on the dot'.

Cups

All cups should have cards placed in or beside them on the cup table, stating name of cup, what it is for, and the class in which it is given. It is for the cup stewards to see that all challenge cups, after presentation, are brought straight back to the cup tent, as these will have to be inscribed. Some have been known to disappear between the presentation and the return to the cup tent. Outright cups naturally are taken away by the winners.

All challenge cups should have prize cards, that is, coloured cards giving the name and date and location of the show, and with spaces for the name of the cup, the winner, and sometimes the judge. These are retained by the winner when the challenge cup itself is returned.

Indemnity forms must be sent to all challenge cup winners before the cups are despatched, and obviously all cups must be fully insured. In view of the damage they often suffer in transit, due either to inadequate packing or to the Post Office, it is a good idea to insure them also for fair wear and tear.

Rosettes

These should NOT be left in the boxes in which they arrived from the makers, entailing fumbling for them while a class is held up. Nor should they be put in bags, envelopes, or bootboxes, when the steward or judge invariably pulls out the wrong one. By far the best method, and especially where awards go to several places, is to hang them on a slatted board. It is easy and cheap to make this out of ordinary hardboard with a slat for each class. The class number is stuck on beside each slat and the class rosettes are then hung on to the slat, together with the cup and special rosettes and any of those given by other societies. Where there are many specials, their number (which should correspond with the number in the catalogue) and a brief description should be written on a sticky label and fixed to the back of each, so that if it should fall off or if the stewards are undecided, they can tell exactly what any rosette is for. The same applies to the cup rosettes.

By this method, all the rosette stewards have to do is to pick the rosettes off the slats while the class is being judged and place them in a wire tray.

A cellophane cover should be provided for wet days. The steward on duty then takes the tray to the ringside, where he should watch keenly for the moment when the ring steward commences writing down the winning numbers on his card or judges' book, when the rosette steward should be ready immediately to take the rosettes into the ring, without having to be called up by the commentator, shouted to by the ring steward, or beckoned to from the ring.

The rosette order should be placed in good time, together with a clear order for all Specials and cup rosettes. All should be insured.

Organisers should remember to contact other societies with regard to their special rosettes they offer, should it be decided to accept these.

Commentator and Public Address System

The efficiency of the commentator largely depends upon the equipment he is given, the placing of loudspeakers, and adequate telephonic communication. Every show organiser should test the audibility of the loudspeakers for himself. Very often the acoustics are so bad that one cannot hear a word the man says.

Commentators can make or mar a show. When giving out results, a list of numbers is irrelevant: names must be given, including rider and owner when necessary.

I realise that in some situations it is not possible for the commentary to be heard in every part of the showground or hall; on one occasion at Wembley I could not hear one word the commentator said. Often they are either too loud or too low, or there is an echo, in which case one is either deafened or straining to hear.

The placing of the loudspeakers is of paramount importance and

230

the commentator should try out the instrument with the supplier, who can often adjust it to his voice or advise him on how best to use that particular instrument. It may be something to do with the pitch of his voice; he may speak too fast or too near or too far from the microphone.

It is up to the public address service to site loudspeakers on a showground so that they can be heard all over the stable and horse-box areas as well as by the rings where, however, spectators should not be deafened. They should also see that adequate telephonic communication between various points as detailed by the organiser, have been tested and are working at least half an hour before the show opens.

Badges

All paid-up members must receive their badges, car-park tickets, etc., well before the closing date of entries for the show. Those who do not pay their subscriptions cannot blame the organisation if they do not receive these, but they invariably do. Badges for those in any honorary capacity, such as vice-presidents, honorary members, sponsors, and all officials should be sent, together with car-park tickets, timetables, etc., just before the show, or they are liable to be mislaid. Big shows can afford to have special cases to hold these badges, others would do well to place them between pieces of cardboard to be sure they arrive without damage. Whether to give gift badges and free meal tickets to the friends and relations of the above is up to the organiser, but such gestures can pay dividends.

Honorary Medical Officers

It is essential to have a doctor and an ambulance (St John or Red Cross) on the ground – more than one if a large show. At very many shows the medical profession give their services free. This should be acknowledged by letter and of course badges, guest badges, car-park and meal tickets should be sent before the show.

Honorary Veterinary Officers

Again, these officers are essential but they rarely find it possible to give their services free. At large shows, of course, several are needed,

231

but one must be on every showground all the time. He may not be called but he must be there. If measuring has to be done, he must be informed of the time and place to do this and given every facility to do so as correctly as possible under the circumstances. Badges etc., as for medical officers, should be sent before the show.

First Aid Post

Usually, the St John Ambulance Brigade or the Red Cross will staff this in return for a donation, dependent on the size of the show. They must be provided with a room or tent equipped with table and chairs, and if they ask for it, a bed. Access to hot water and a toilet is essential.

An ambulance should be available.

Farrier

At all shows where there are ridden or driving classes, a farrier must be engaged and be on the ground from opening to closing time. If only in-hand classes are staged (which is unlikely) he should not be necessary. If show jumping is on the programme, he should also most certainly be there and readily available. He will have to be paid a fee by arrangement.

Ringside Parking

Undoubtedly, this makes life easier for spectators and exhibitors alike. It is also a source of revenue.

The reason for its popularity is obvious. You do not have to trail from car park to stable area or ringside – often a long, long trail, carrying handbag, umbrella, overboots, mackintosh, picnic basket, or what have you. You do not then have to sit on a hard seat or bench or a soggy straw bale.

Moreover, you do not find yourself sitting in too close proximity either to a complete stranger or to the owner of an animal you have been describing vividly, but not necessarily favourably, to your friends!

In your car, you have all your needs within arm's reach. You can sit warm and comfortable and sheltered from the elements, you can entertain your friends and, blissful thought, criticise the exhibits to

232

your heart's content without risk of mortification or libel.

You can, moreover, bring your own lunch. You can treat your friends to a drink. You do not have to find the marquee, where food of a sort is provided and where you either sit at a table and wait interminably for some cold collation to be handed to you by a reluctant waitress who calls you 'ducks', or stand holding a metal tray and watch someone ahead of you in the queue take the last portion of the one dish you decided you could face.

And if you are a connoisseur, or think you are, the nearer you get to the exhibits the better. What, I ask you, can you see from a grandstand? If you are anxious to learn you have to be able to see, and this certainly applies to in-hand classes.

Worse still are the shows where one fails to find a seat at all. I marvel at those where I frequently see hundreds, if not thousands, of the public, standing sometimes six or eight deep, rubber-necking round the ringside for hours on end. Is it surprising that attendances fall? Indeed it is a wonder to me that anyone, without hope of obtaining a seat, comes at all. Yet I know from personal experience that the majority of the general public would rather stand, even in pouring rain, than pay extra for a seat in a covered grandstand. This is what show organisers are up against.

I realise that at the big county and agricultural shows ringside car parking is not possible. But organisers of smaller shows, where the space is available, would be well advised to make available for cars every possible space round the rings.

Some organisers object to ringside car parking because they say it spoils the look of a showground, but can we, in these days, afford to turn away an obvious source of revenue which will please both exhibitors and public?

There is, however, one snag, and that is that, having paid for this space, you will find the general public not only obstructing your view but actually sitting on your car. This is why I feel that seats of some sort (which should be low) should also be provided.

Exhibitors' Cars

It is important that exhibitors (and I am only concerned with exhibitors in equine classes) should be permitted to park their cars as near as possible to their horsebox and stabling. While some have really no valid reason to expect this – namely those whose animals are produced for them and who therefore have no equipment with them

233

– it is difficult to make exceptions, and the majority have a very real argument in favour of being allowed to park their cars near the exhibits. They may have to 'do' their own animals and, therefore, have to transport equipment in their cars, and it is very tiring to keep running backwards between car and stabling. They may also have had to bring children, even dogs, with them, to say nothing of food for all. Obviously, to have to walk across a large showground every time you have to go to the horse-lines, is enough to try the patience and temper of a saint, and few exhibitors are this.

Cars at the large county and agricultural shows must of course be parked outside the perimeter of the show itself, but so often the parks are sited unnecessarily far away. One dreads traipsing backwards and forwards as this saps one's vitality and takes the edge off one's enjoyment before one ever enters the ring.

At other shows it should be possible to allow exhibitors this amenity.

Horseboxes and Caravans

The same principle applies to horseboxes. The nearer they can be parked to the stabling the better, for obvious reasons. It is not unreasonable for exhibitors to wish to have them nearby along with their caravans, especially on wet days when they need to change their clothes. They also have often to cook hurried meals, keep an eye on children, and let the dogs out for a run.

Just as every hostess should sleep at least once in her guest-room bed, so every show organiser benefits by having at one time been an exhibitor. This particularly applies to exhibitors showing animals in hand.

It is, however, often necessary, even essential, to be adamant regarding parking of vehicles. Should exhibitors or their staff refuse to comply, an organiser has no alternative but to be ruthless and, believe me, exhibitors can be extremely exasperating. There are, however, two sides to every argument.

Stabling

Having said that about some exhibitors, for the majority who behave themselves everything possible should be done.

For instance, there can be nothing more depressing than to arrive after a long journey along traffic-jammed roads, having possibly had

234

breakdowns, punctures, and other hazards to overcome, only to find someone else occupying the stable allotted to you. It is for this reason I strongly advise show executives to allocate stabling *for the duration of the show*, even if this entails more cost to the exhibitor who only wishes to stay one night. The majority would rather pay a little more and know for certain they will find their stabling awaiting them and that they have not got to hand it over probably at some inconvenient moment to an impatient fellow exhibitor, who then has the job of mucking it out and setting it fair.

It is also much appreciated if all boxes are set fair, especially when a predominance of the occupiers are women, some of them not in the first flush of youth. It is not conducive to goodwill for an exhibitor to arrive at a showground, probably late in the evening, more than probably in bad weather, and be unable to find the stable, or having located it, to have to find an implement with which to cut the wire round the straw bale, and pitchfork before setting about making it ready, probably without even the light of a torch.

To avoid irritating and frustrating delays for exhibitors, and worry and time-wasting on the part of show officials, every block of stabling should be lettered, and every stable have the name of the exhibitor on the door.

It also makes for goodwill if there is an official at the horse gate to tell you where your stabling is, where you may park vehicles, where food can be obtained, and where the toilets are. Also the location of the secretary's office, where more often than not the exhibitors' numbers are to be found. Personally, I prefer these to be given to the stable manager who hands them out at the horse gate the first night, when they may then be transferred to the secretary's office on the show day(s). Without these little touches, the show starts off with disgruntled exhibitors, and success depends largely upon having as few of these as possisble.

The stable manager should be posted at a focal gate, supplied with a tent, table and chair and a stable book, and as I have said before, with exhibitors' numbers (see page 214).

The stable book should be alphabetical so that all that need be done is look up each exhibitor's name under the applicable letter and to inform him that he will find his loosebox(es) in Block – and that on the end of that block he will find a list telling him which boxes have been allocated to him.

It may be that an exhibitor has booked so many boxes for his animals and one or more in which to sleep himself, or for the staff. It is obvious that these 'sleepers' must be provided with curtains or some sort: sacking serves.

235

Stabling should be situated as near as possible to the ring, especially with a tight programme and where in-hand classes are involved; otherwise the schedule is held up waiting for exhibitors, or else they miss their classes.

Organisers who find a permanent ground with stabling are fortunate. At the same time, I have always found a supplier of temporary loose boxes both efficient and obliging, and their boxes are popular with exhibitors as they do provide this canvas screening.

Manure

Mucking out should be done early in the morning and exhibitors requested to put this neatly outside the boxes for clearance, which if possible should be done before the show opens.

In some areas – but by no means all – horse manure can be sold to firms growing mushrooms, etc., but it stands to reason that boxes that have only been used for one night are unlikely to provide much manure and it is therefore unsaleable. Some firms agree to pick it up for free, but mostly it has to be burned.

Forage

If hay and other forage is provided, times of issuing this should be sent (together with the timetable) to all exhibitors and they should pay for this direct.

I have actually known of exhibitors, incredible as it may seem, bundling bales of straw or hay secretly into their trailers and getting away with it, but provided it is made clear to them before they come that they either have to bring their own or pay for forage provided, the majority will do this.

At shows where there are classes for mountain and moorland ponies and broodmares, cut grass should be provided if at all possible, but it is no use sending this and piling it up in big heaps on a hot day as it will inevitably heat, when it is extremely dangerous and will almost certainly cause colic. The mounds should be very small and the grass fed quickly before it heats, or it is best not to have it at all. I have found that it is useless to try and get payment for this as there is no means of measuring it. Supply depends upon the goodwill of local farmers. Most exhibitors now bring their own hay, etc.

236

Litter

Again exhibitors should be encouraged to leave the ground tidy, by supplying litter-baskets, or litter-bags can be obtained from the local authority.

Fire Precautions

This is the organiser's nightmare, as it should be of any horse or pony owner. I can imagine nothing worse than a fire in the stables, especially in temporary stables, which being made entirely of wood and sacking are highly inflammable. Therefore rows of stables should not be less than twelve yards apart, and no vehicles should be permitted to park in this area.

Smoking. Smoking, let alone lighting fires or stoves, anywhere near the stabling, should be *absolutely forbidden*. The difficulty is that habitual smokers are liable to forget. If one finds oneself committing this sin, the cigarette should be well stubbed out, away from all straw.

I once discovered exhibitors huddled over a Primus stove inside a temporary loose box, cooking their breakfast. The stove was well banked up with straw. Is it that some people have no imagination or are they just downright careless?

Fire-extinguishers must be provided and the location of the nearest fire brigade and telephone must be known to officials and night watchmen.

'No Smoking' notices should be erected though I doubt if anyone reads them.

Night Watchmen

Apart from the danger of fire, night watchmen are unfortunately a necessity in these days because of vandalism. Not only do people steal, they cut tent ropes, slash tents, remove telephone wiring and so on. Television and press have made thugs into heroes and these acts are now apparently regarded as deeds of daring rather than common or garden theft and hooliganism.

How many watchmen are employed depends on the size of the ground and whether or not it is adequately enclosed or, on the other hand, open to all. Whoever is employed should be able-bodied; they may need to be. They should also be mobile.

237

Toilets

On grounds where there are no permanent flush lavatories toilet arrangements can cause a problem. This is the main reason for seeking a showground where permanent facilities are installed.

On these grounds where permanent flush lavatories and wash basins are already installed, it is usual and very necessary to employ attendants to keep them clean and tidy. Here, both exhibitors and the public are in default and co-operation from them would eliminate many of the more unsavoury aspects for which, with good flush lavatories, there is no excuse.

Where permanent lavatories are not available, it is possible to hire 'Portaloos' which have separate compartments inside an adequate trailer.

Catering

Perhaps the biggest decision of all for a show organiser is the catering department. This is less of a problem the bigger the show, because then there is a better chance of the contractors making a profit, when they are obviously going to be more co-operative, while organisers of small shows may have difficulty in getting a caterer to take on the job at all.

What with high wages, overtime and VAT, staff puts paid to any chance of profit unless the catering is on a very large scale, and self-service is the only solution. Provided this is well done it works, and at least one does not have to wait until a waitress comes to take your order. The layout is important. It requires a clearly defined queue, plates of food attractively arranged together with the necessary implements, kept constantly supplied, and with a competent cashier. Good, courteous, quick service, whether here or at the bar, are essential. So often staff are offhand or completely uninterested. The simpler, fresher, and more attractively the food is offered, the better. The everlasting salad must be crisp and not wilting. Cold roast beef, tongue and ham is surely preferable to broiler chickens or frozen turkeys which have no taste. Salmon must be kept fresh. Personally I am all for a good thick hot soup in the prevailing English weather, which can be changed to fruit juices should the weather ever be hot. Hot potatoes and peas or beans as a change from salad are appreciated, especially by stockmen. Good cheese and biscuits and butter are preferable to made-up sweets with synthetic cream. Rolls and butter are surely a necessity.

238

Exhibitors and members of the public who grumble about the food at shows should remember the difficulties the caterers are up against, and be reasonable in their demands. What there is should be good and plentiful, and of course the quality and quantity depends on the charge. For a sit-down lunch, a three-course meal should be possible with an alternative main item and coffee extra, or cheese can be included as well as a sweet. Stockmen and stockwomen, lorrydrivers, and exhibitors who do their own animals obviously require more substantial fare, and at two- and three-day shows it is essential to provide breakfast not later than 7.30 a.m. and suppers up to 10 o'clock at night for these hardworking people. On the whole, charges for these meals are remarkably low, when one considers what one would have to pay to get meals at these hours anywhere else, if indeed one got them at all.

The president should, of course, have a tent or compartment to himself, as should the members and the exhibitors and stockmen. Judges, stewards, and other officials must either have tables reserved for them in the members' tent or else have a separate compartment with quick service. Prompt service for judges and stewards is a must at a well-run show, and something should always be kept back for those who have classes over the lunch hour and who come in late.

Except at very small local shows or gymkhanas where a buffet or snack bar suffices, it is necessary to have a sit-down lunch marquee, especially for the judges, stewards, and other hardworking officials. The size of the president's lunch should depend on how important it is to entertain certain people (and it often is very important and only courteous) but must also depend on the financial state of the show.

I have known exhibitors arrive in the evening of a two-day show to find there is nothing at all to eat, while others who have got up at 4 a.m. to get there on time have had to wait until lunch-time to get anything, even a cup of coffee. When children are involved food of some kind is even more necessary, even if it is only biscuits and milk or Coca-Cola. The majority of parents bring their own picnic lunches, but it should be possible at a well-run show to get a cup of coffee by 9.30 a.m. for which exhibitors should be prepared to pay but which should be sent out free to the judges, stewards, and commentator.

Caterers should be given every possible facility: namely, a decent size marquee in which to work and which does not leak, divided by partitions as directed and a smaller tent in the rear to act either as a kitchen or a store. A sump must be already dug for them for liquid refuse, and litter-bags, which are obtainable from the local authority, free of charge, supplied. Water, is, of course, an essential and must be available near at hand. Electricity, not only for lighting in the evening, but for powering cutting machines and refrigerators is absolutely essential, at large shows and in hot weather, and especially where food has to be kept overnight.

Caterers expect to have all tents and furniture supplied. It is, however, sometimes possible to obtain a large marquee free of charge from the local brewery by arrangement with the caterer, who then stocks their products.

While large shows may give separate contracts for ice-cream, soft-drinks, and hot-dogs, at small shows it is only fair to allow the caterer to arrange these contracts.

Undoubtedly large shows, and especially the large agricultural and county ones, are well advised to divide their catering between more than one firm, that is, one to cater for the VIPs and members; another to be responsible for exhibitors and stockmen and a third to cater for the public. At small local shows and gymkhanas local people frequently help and may even undertake the whole of the catering, but this can only be on a very small scale.

Some caterers give a donation or commission to the show, but at small shows their profit is so small that this may not be possible unless the charges are out of all proportion to the standard of the food.

I have yet to attend a show where someone or other has not grumbled about this department, sometimes justifiably, sometimes unreasonably. I feel we should all remember that food at shows is simply supplied to keep body and soul together and too much should not be expected. So long as what is presented is fresh and good, and the service quick and courteous, a certain amount of give and take should be exercised.

Trade Stands

These are a paying proposition and, provided there is sufficient space, are to be encouraged. However, there must be a sufficient gate to attract them, although some firms will attend specialist shows which happen to be in their line of business. The large agricultural and county shows of course depend for a large part of their revenue on this trade support. Moreover, the public like them.

Naturally, the price depends upon the site and the footage necessary. Small shows with small gates must perforce use their discretion when deciding what to charge.

Allocation needs very careful planning and measurement if peace is to reign. The trade stands should be sited well away from the stock lines.

Advertisements

Obviously, the more advertisements obtained for both the schedule and the programme, the better, and every effort should be made to obtain these. The price per page must depend firstly on the cost of printing and secondly on the circulation and importance of the show. Breed catalogues can ask more as they constitute a reference book, which can usefully be retained.

A close watch should be kept on the number of words which an advertiser uses in his copy. Some are so wordy that the amount of typesetting involved incurs a loss to the show.

Members of committee and others can often help in obtaining advertisements, but it is of course up to the Secretary and his staff to get the copy in good time, which he does either from the advertiser direct or, in the case of national advertisers, from his agent.

Forms should be made out stating the name and date of the show, publication concerned, the type area, the screen for blocks, and the latest date for copy. Proofs will have to be sent to the advertiser for any corrections, so that plenty of time should be given for this operation.

A voucher copy will have to be sent both to the client and to his advertising agent together with the invoice. Agents will claim ten per cent commission unless they can be persuaded to waive this, which is not often the case even if the show is a charity.

If the show or society is a registered charity, national advertisers are often very generous and helpful.

If clients send in photographs from which blocks have to be made, the cost of the block must be paid by the advertiser.

Publicity and Press Relations

This department is of vital importance. Very large shows are well advised to employ a public relations officer, provided he knows his subject and can write. But in small organisations this onerous, very specialised job falls on the secretary or a member of his staff.

Good press relations can save an organisation hundreds, if not thousands, of pounds a year, by obtaining free editorial notices. It all depends if the person concerned knows how to put news – however thin – across to the newspapers. Unfortunately, few trained journalists have knowledge of equestrian matters and terminology, and their fees are often beyond most societies' pockets, but if they can write this can often be got over. In the main, however, press relations in the equestrian world are largely in the hands of aspiring amateurs who may know about horses but cannot write, or professionals who can write but who know nothing about horses.

All the same, a competent secretary should be able to keep his society or show constantly in front of the public, by sending editors news dished up in palatable fashion. It is a job that can be learnt and meanwhile it is a good idea to keep on good terms with the press, especially locally. Gradually, the secretary will develop the art of finding a peg upon which to hang a coat so that any excuse is used to keep his society or show in the public eye. But this takes time, which is not always available.

Press releases should be available before a show and marked copies of the programme at the end of it. Someone with the necessary knowledge should be detailed off to answer the innumerable questions invariably asked by reporters. It is in the interests of every show to give all possible information and to treat the press with courtesy.

Within reason, free meal tickets are a good investment, while editors and other local potentates appreciate being sent guest tickets. After all, every free editorial is worth something.

Parades

As parades come at the end of the day, I have left these until the last. They are staged at nearly all the main shows, especially the big agricultural and county ones, generally towards the end of the afternoon of the last day. They are very difficult to organise effectively, are not popular even with successful exhibitors, and most unpopular with unsuccessful ones. Indeed, I feel that it is hardly fair, especially in these days of high costs, to expect exhibitors *who are not in the money* to stay an extra day or even to stay until the afternoon, having been beaten in the morning. This particularly applies to those who have hired transport, or who have a long journey ahead, or who may even have to remain another night, when at least free stabling should be granted.

While purely equine parades are fairly simple, mixing cattle and horses, etc., is not easy owing to their varying gait.

If, however, a parade is to be informative and act as a true spectacle, it must be properly organised. The commentary should synchronise as far as possible with the exhibits, or it will simply be a muddle. The commentary should apply to the animal(s) it is describing and not some other breed or type altogether. How can the public be expected to remember the numbers, open their programmes and find, not only the class, but the animal's number, before the commentator passes on to the next item? Therefore, not just the number but the owner's name must be given. In fact, I consider that it is essential that the commentator be supplied with the name and owner of at least the first three in each class, and that there be a focal point where he describes each animal as it passes this point.

If the parade is worth staging at all, time should be given to the commentator to make sense of it. At least the equine classes can be sent in in programme order (not timetable order) and the native ponies in alphabetical order (with banners with the breed names on them carried by boy scouts, or what have you), then the broodmares followed by youngstock, and then the ridden classes.

Index

Page numbers in *italic* indicate illustrations